To sweep the Augean Stable.

———

FOR PRESIDENT,

Andrew Jackson.

FOR VICE-PRESIDENT,

JOHN C. CALHOUN.

———

ETHAN ALLEN BROWN, of Hamilton
ROBERT HARPER, Ashtabula.
WILLIAM PIATT, Hamilton.
JAMES SHIELDS, Butler.
HENRY BARRINGTON, Miami.
THOMAS GILLESPIE. Green.
THOMAS L. HAMER, Brown,
VALENTINE KEFFER, Pickaway.
ROBERT LUCAS, Pike.
JOHN M'ELVAIN, Franklin.
SAMUEL HERRICK, Muskingum.
GEORGE SHARP, Belmont.
WALTER M. BLAKE, Tuscarawas.
BENJAMIN JONES, Wayne.
WILLIAM RAYEN, Trumbull.
HUGH M' FALL, Richland.

THE BIRTH OF
MODERN
POLITICS

PIVOTAL MOMENTS
IN AMERICAN HISTORY

Series Editors

David Hackett Fischer
James M. McPherson

James T. Patterson
Brown v. Board of Education: A Civil Rights Milestone and Its Troubled Legacy

Maury Klein
Rainbow's End: The Crash of 1929

James M. McPherson
Crossroads of Freedom: The Battle of Antietam

Glenn C. Altschuler
All Shook Up: How Rock 'n' Roll Changed America

David Hackett Fischer
Washington's Crossing

John Ferling
Adams vs. Jefferson: The Tumultuous Election of 1800

Joel H. Silbey
Storm over Texas: The Annexation Controversy and the Road to Civil War

Raymond Arsenault
Freedom Riders: 1961 and the Struggle for Racial Justice

Colin G. Calloway
The Scratch of a Pen: 1763 and the Transformation of North America

Richard Labunski
James Madison and the Struggle for the Bill of Rights

Sally McMillen
Seneca Falls and the Origins of the Women's Rights Movement

Howard Jones
The Bay of Pigs

Elliott West
The Last Indian War: The Nez Perce Story

THE BIRTH OF
MODERN
POLITICS

Andrew Jackson, John Quincy Adams,
and the Election of 1828

LYNN HUDSON PARSONS

OXFORD
UNIVERSITY PRESS

2009

OXFORD
UNIVERSITY PRESS

Oxford University Press, Inc., publishes works that further
Oxford University's objective of excellence
in research, scholarship, and education.

Oxford   New York
Auckland   Cape Town   Dar es Salaam   Hong Kong   Karachi
Kuala Lumpur   Madrid   Melbourne   Mexico City   Nairobi
New Delhi   Shanghai   Taipei   Toronto

With offices in
Argentina   Austria   Brazil   Chile   Czech Republic   France   Greece
Guatemala   Hungary   Italy   Japan   Poland   Portugal   Singapore
South Korea   Switzerland   Thailand   Turkey   Ukraine   Vietnam

Copyright © 2009 by Lynn Hudson Parsons

Published by Oxford University Press, Inc.
198 Madison Avenue, New York, New York 10016

www.oup.com

Oxford is a registered trademark of Oxford University Press

Library of Congress Cataloging-in-Publication Data
Parsons, Lynn H.
The birth of modern politics : Andrew Jackson, John Quincy Adams,
and the election of 1828 / by Lynn Hudson Parsons.
p.   cm. — (Pivotal moments in American history)
Includes bibliographical references and index.
ISBN 978-0-19-531287-4
1. Presidents—United States—Election—1828.
2. Political campaigns—United States—History—19th century.
3. Jackson, Andrew, 1767–1845.   4. Adams, John Quincy, 1767–1848.
5. Political culture—United States—History—19th century.
6. Political parties—United States—History—19th century.
7. United States—Politics and government—19th century.
8. Presidents—United States—Biography.   I. Title.
E380.P37 2009
324.70973—dc22   2008037359

1 3 5 7 9 8 6 4 2

Printed in the United States of America
on acid-free paper

For Anne

Contents

Editor's Note

The Founding Fathers of the United States feared the potential of political parties to undermine the stability of the republic. The evils of "faction," as they termed parties, would eat away the foundation of selfless "virtue" necessary to uphold the public interest until the nation degenerated into tyranny or collapsed from the weight of corruption. "There is nothing I dread so much as the division of the republic into two great parties...concerting measures in opposition to each other," wrote John Adams in 1780. "This, in my opinion, is to be dreaded as the greatest evil under our Constitution." James Madison defended the division of powers under the Constitution of 1787 for "its tendency to break and control the violence of faction."

Despite these sentiments, political parties evolved in the 1790s—and both Adams and Madison played prominent parts in that process. The Founding generation nevertheless continued to deplore parties as factions that endangered the polity. They were "the curse of the country," wrote President James Monroe in the 1820s. By then, however, parties were on course to becoming a permanent fixture on the political landscape. The presidential election of 1824, in which none of the four candidates received a majority of electoral votes, temporarily masked this trajectory. In the next few years, however, the New York politico Martin Van Buren placed himself at the head of a new party that in 1828 called itself the Democratic Republicans and nominated Andrew Jackson for president. Van Buren essentially invented the modern national two-party system, which he considered the bedrock of the American republic and guarantor of its stability. "We must always have party distinctions," wrote Van Buren. They "are inseparable from a free government" because they "rouse the sluggish to exertion, give increased energy to the most active intellect, excite a salutary vigilance of the public functionaries, and prevent that apathy which has proved the ruin of Republics."

The presidential election of 1828 generated unprecedented excitement among the electorate. The percentage of eligible voters who cast their ballots jumped from 27 percent in 1824 to 57 percent in 1828. "The era of mass political parties began with the election of 1828," writes Lynn Hudson Parsons in this absorbing narrative of the contest between Andrew Jackson and John Quincy Adams. Many features of modern presidential campaigns first appeared in 1828: large organized rallies, coordinated media efforts, fund raising, opposition research, negative advertisements, opinion polling, slogans and buttons and other campaign paraphernalia, and the creation of a cult of personality to promote Jackson's candidacy.

Other presidential elections have also proved to be pivotal moments in American history: 1800, when the losing incumbent peacefully yielded power to the winner; 1860, when the losers refused to yield and precipitated a war that ended by giving America a new lease on life and a new birth of freedom; 1932, when the relationship between government and the socioeconomic order was forever altered; and perhaps 2008, when the barrier of race that has divided Americans for centuries was breached. As *The Birth of Modern Politics* demonstrates, however, the election of 1828 belongs near the top of this list, for it marked the death of the elitist political culture of the early republic and the birth of true democracy. That is the story that Lynn Hudson Parsons tells with extraordinary clarity and verve in the following pages.

James M. McPherson

Prologue

It was late February 1829, and Mrs. Samuel Harrison Smith, a longtime Washington resident who knew most of the capital city's important people, was not happy. "Our streets are now deep in slush—snow, mud, mire!" she complained. The winter had indeed been unusually cold and wet. But on March 4 a brilliant sunrise promised a warm and early spring day. It was, declared the *New York Post*, "as if nature was willing to lend her aid towards contributing to the happiness of the thousands that crowded to behold the great ceremony." The "great ceremony" was, of course, the inauguration of Major General Andrew Jackson as the seventh president of the United States.[1]

It was not to be a solemn event. Previous presidential inaugurals were generally attended only by members of Congress and other dignitaries. This one would be held outside, on the east front of the Capitol building, and would be open to the public. The city had never seen anything like it, and entrepreneurs were quick to take advantage. Room rents tripled, as did the price of food and firewood. One observer saw "great numbers of *young* men, some of whom look as if they had footed it all the way from Tennessee...walking arm in arm, and gazing on all around them with the vacant stare of undisguised curiosity and wonder." Some slept "on the floors in tap rooms, and many in less choice places," according to another.[2]

"With what anxiety and impatience have thousands looked forward to the present period, and crowded from all parts of the union, to our metropolis to witness the splendour of Genl. J.'s reception and his inauguration," Mrs. Smith reported. On the day before the ceremony, the streets were so crowded that passage was nearly impossible. By ten o'clock on the fourth, Pennsylvania Avenue was jammed with a variety of carriages, from the most opulent to the most humble. By noon, several thousand had gathered in front of the Capitol building (a much smaller version of the one we know today), "with their eyes fixed on the front of that edifice, waiting the appearance of the President in the portico."[3]

Tragedy had darkened Jackson's victory. His beloved wife, Rachel, had died only a few weeks following his election, and many, including the general himself, blamed her death on the attacks leveled at her by elements of the opposition. As he made plans to travel to Washington from his plantation outside of Nashville, the grieving president-elect sent word ahead that he wanted no celebratory parade when he arrived. Traveling up the Ohio River, he had been met at Cincinnati by a quiet and respectful crowd. Mrs. Frances Trollope, an English traveler who didn't think much of Americans in general, was nonetheless impressed. "He wore his grey hair, carelessly, but not ungracefully arranged, and, in spite of his harsh gaunt features, he looks like a gentleman and a soldier." By the time his boat reached Wheeling, in Virginia, there were more crowds. And in Pittsburgh, the pressure from onlookers had become so intense that a member of the reception committee feared that Jackson and his friends might wind up in "the muddy waters of the Monongalia [sic]." He slipped into Washington, virtually unnoticed, on February 11.[4]

In 1800 Thomas Jefferson had defeated the incumbent John Adams of Massachusetts for the presidency. Now, with a cruel twist of irony for the Adamses at least, Jackson was about to replace John Adams's son, John Quincy Adams.

When Jefferson took the oath of office in 1801, he was about to preside over a nation of fewer than four million people. Andrew Jackson's America had more than tripled that number, to nearly thirteen million. Then Jefferson faced a Congress of 106 representatives and 32 senators from 16 states. Jackson was about to face a Congress of 213 representatives and 48 senators from 24 states. Washington, too, had changed. Government buildings that in 1801 had existed either in rudimentary form or only in the minds of architects now graced Pennsylvania Avenue and its adjoining streets. Hotels, shops, taverns, and bordellos were all within walking distance of one another. The city's population grew from barely three thousand to nearly nineteen thousand. And there were plans for future growth. "They have already rooted up trees for ten miles around," wrote the young French aristocrat Alexis de Tocqueville, "lest they should get in the way of the future citizens of this imagined capital."[5]

Yet in other respects, neither the nation nor the city had changed. In 1829 Washington was still, and would remain for many years, a southern city. Nearly all of the manual labor in the capital was performed by enslaved African Americans. The slave-trader's auctioneering chant could easily be heard from the Capitol itself. The president-elect, like all but two of his predecessors (the Adamses), was a slaveholder. As for the nation, both the slave and free populations had grown with it, with most of the free population still engaged, as they were in 1801, in some form of agricultural endeavor or in work directly connected to it. The minority of Americans who were involved in commerce or manufacturing still resided in a handful of cities or in small towns, most within fifty miles of the seaboard.

The thousands who turned out to see Andrew Jackson inaugurated were convinced that an immense change was about to take place. Most welcomed it. Senator Robert Y. Hayne of South Carolina told Jackson that his election was "a triumph of principle over intrigue, of truth over falsehood; in one word, of the *people* over corruption."[6] In an age in which classical mythology was part of the popular culture, Jackson had become a modern Hercules, charged with the task of cleaning out the Augean stables left behind by previous administrations. The steamboat that carried him up the Ohio River had brooms attached to its bow, symbolizing the "cleansing" that his proponents claimed was about to take place. "People have come five hundred miles to see General Jackson, and they really seem to think that the country has been rescued from some dreadful danger," mused Senator Daniel Webster of Massachusetts, who had worked hard to prevent Jackson's election.[7]

Others were appalled. A frontier brawler and duelist, a man with next to no experience, next to no education, and with a hot temper that on more than one occasion had erupted into fistfights, stabbings, and death, had been elevated to the office once held by Washington, Adams, and Jefferson. "A great revolution has taken place," wrote one observer. It was, said another, "the howl of raving Democracy."[8] The election had been "the most anxious and ardent, as well as the most rude and ruthless political contest that ever took place in the United States," declared Hezekiah Niles, the editor of *Niles' Weekly Register*, the nation's foremost weekly newspaper. And Mrs. Smith mourned "so many changes in society—so many families broken up, and those of the first distinction....Oh! 'tis melancholy."[9]

On the morning of the fourth, following a thirteen-gun salute, Jackson was escorted to the Capitol by an elderly group of officers from the Revolutionary army. "Thousands and thousands of people," recalled

Mrs. Smith (who attended, accompanied by Francis Scott Key), "without distinction of rank, collected in an immense mass round the Capitol, orderly, and tranquil, with their eyes fixed on the front of that edifice, waiting an appearance of the President in the portico."¹⁰ Still dressed in mourning, the general was easily visible, owing to his six-foot-one-inch height and his shock of white hair. After witnessing the swearing in of his vice president, John C. Calhoun, he emerged at high noon to read his inaugural address and take the oath of office from Chief Justice John Marshall, who had administered the same oath to Thomas Jefferson twenty-eight years before.

Then came a sequence of events, never to be forgotten by those who were there. Hundreds of well-wishers surged forward to congratulate the new president, so much so that he was forced back into the Capitol and out the other side, where he mounted a horse and rode back to the White House. There a reception had been planned, but it was disrupted by yet another crowd, who invaded the mansion, trampled the rugs, stepped on the furniture, and smashed the dishes, all in an attempt to greet the new president. Jackson, recalled one witness, was "*literally* nearly pressed to death and almost suffocated and torn to pieces" by the mob. People of all classes and races could be seen mingling and jostling one another. "I never saw such a mixture," sniffed Supreme Court Justice Joseph Story. "The reign of KING MOB seemed triumphant. I was glad to escape from the scene as soon as possible." Others were pleased, in spite of the mayhem. "Notwithstanding the row the Demos kicked up," one senator reported to New York's Governor Martin Van Buren, soon to be named Jackson's secretary of state, "the whole matter went off very well." The editor of the Washington *National Intelligencer*, who had supported Adams, conceded that "the Sovereign People were a little uproarious, indeed, but it was in anything but a malicious spirit."¹¹

While the new president's enthusiasts were storming the White House, ex-president John Quincy Adams rode by himself to the outskirts of the city and back. On the advice of all but one of his outgoing cabinet, he had not remained to witness the inauguration of the man who had defeated him. (There was precedent for this. His father, John Adams, had not stayed to witness Jefferson's inaugural either.) Once an admirer of Jackson who had more than once defended him against his political enemies, Adams felt betrayed.

No one, before or since, had come to the presidency with a more impressive résumé than John Quincy Adams. As a teenager he had walked the streets of Paris with Thomas Jefferson and dined with Lafayette. George Washington had appointed him the American Minister to the Netherlands and later to Portugal. His own father, while president himself, had sent him to Prussia. He had served five years in the United States Senate. President James Madison had sent him to St. Petersburg as the first American Minister there, where he had met and conversed with Czar Alexander I. He helped negotiate an end to the War of 1812 while Andrew Jackson was facing the British at New Orleans. President James Monroe had appointed him secretary of state, where he had negotiated an extension of American claims to the Pacific, acquired Florida for the United States, and had helped to formulate the policies that later became known as the Monroe Doctrine.

Adams brought not only experience but also education: fluent in half a dozen languages; well versed in classical studies; familiar with art, music, and literature—he was in many ways a virtual walking encyclopedia. Yet only a few months earlier he had been soundly defeated for reelection. "The sun of my political life sets in deepest gloom," he had admitted to his ever-present diary, which he had begun in 1779 when he was barely a teenager, "but that of my country shines unclouded." On his way home, "I was overtaken by a man named Dulaney, who first inquired of me whether I could inform him how he could see John Quincy Adams."[12]

There have been more than fifty presidential elections since the creation of the American Republic. In almost every one, presidential hopefuls have claimed that the American people stood on the verge of making a historic choice that would make that particular election one of the most crucial in the nation's history. Only in retrospect can we see that some were more crucial—or pivotal—than others, and some not particularly crucial at all. Few would deny, for example, that the election of 1860, which propelled for the first time an openly antislavery candidate to the presidency and precipitated secession and civil war, was an important turning point. Likewise, that of 1932, marking the beginning of a dramatic change in the relationship of the federal government to the states and the citizens, has come to be seen as standing apart from most presidential elections in the first half of the twentieth century. Some might include the election of 1800, as much for what did *not* happen as for what did: an incumbent executive was denied reelection, and unlike in many unhappy republics before and after, relinquished power quietly if not enthusiastically.[13]

Andrew Jackson's 1828 victory over John Quincy Adams (son of the aforementioned incumbent executive) did not bring on a civil war, nor did it mark a radical change in the structure of American government, or a dramatic reinterpretation of the Constitution. Nonetheless, historians and others have long hailed the presidential election of 1828 as a "watershed" event in American political history, although not always for the same reasons. For some, the election was the first truly "democratic" election, in that eligible voters participated to a degree not seen before. As a result, it marked the beginning of "mass" political parties, as opposed to those controlled by upper-class elites. But skeptics have argued that the increase came later, and have questioned whether the emergence of "mass" political parties in reality meant the disappearance of elite control.[14]

Many political historians have also suggested that Jackson's election marks the beginning of a pattern of tightly contested contests in which two nationally organized political parties would compete for power in virtually every state.[15] They have further argued that, in contrast to the beliefs of the Founders of the Republic, people's attitudes toward political parties and partisanship changed after 1828, and that organized competition for public office came to be seen as contributing to the Republic's vitality, rather than weakening it. Others have argued that whatever the Founders may have believed, political parties had already come to be accepted by many before 1828, and that the election merely confirmed an established trend.

The two parties whose outlines began to form around Adams and Jackson in 1828 began a dialogue that in many respects continues today. Those whose cultural, social, and economic values reflect community-based decisions, in which democracy is converted into power on behalf of the common good, were arrayed against those whose democratic values relied less on the community and more on the individual. In the latter view, the common good is best promoted by leaving individuals as much freedom as possible to promote their own interests, from which the common good will emerge. From that day to this, the names of the parties might change, old issues would die and new ones be born, the parties might even change positions, but as with Hamlet and Laertes, the duel would continue.

And last, no account of the election of 1828 would be complete without focusing on the two men who confronted each other in that year. John Quincy Adams's résumé may indeed have been impressive, but his defeat in 1828 was a signal that in the future such résumés might not be sufficient and indeed might be handicaps. In the same way, his powers of intellect, conceded by friend and foe alike, and which had served him so well as a diplomat, were dismissed as irrelevant to the presidency. Although many of his ideas were ahead of his time, and while his public career by no means was ended by his defeat, he came to represent, and in many ways still represents, a lost era.

In contrast, it was the man who defeated him who would come to represent the future. "Jacksonianism" meant for many Americans the lifting of the political, social, and economic restraints that had stifled previous generations, as well as extending the American "Empire of Liberty" to the West and South. To others it meant the trampling of the Constitution in the name of Manifest Destiny and an abandonment of the standards of brilliance in public life established by the Founders of the Republic. The derision heaped on John Quincy Adams by the Jacksonians in 1828 established a pattern in American politics, warning aspiring politicians to conceal their intellect rather than proclaim it.

Finally, there can be no denying Jackson's impact on the presidency. He was the first president not to be from the state of Virginia or named Adams. He was the first (Washington excepted here, as in so many things) to have lacked a college education, and not to have previously served as secretary of state or vice president. Once elected, he would be the first president to proclaim himself the choice of the people, the first openly to head a political party, the first to use the power of the veto to block measures with which he disagreed, and, most important, the first president to sense what the Founders missed—that the office of president of the United States carried with it the potential to offset the powers of the other two branches of government. When Jackson left office in 1837, the presidency had been permanently altered.

This book will contend that very little of this was planned. Jackson and Adams came from different parts of the country, yet they started out not only sharing many of the same values, but were allies in a number of common causes. Born in the same year, Jackson and Adams, more than any other public figures of their day, shared an aversion to organized political parties and "electioneering." They both were staunch nationalists. Yet the principle of unintended consequences would affect both men. They were maneuvered as much by events as by individual ambition into virulent opposition, and in the end found themselves not only arrayed against one another personally but as political foes representing competing ideologies.

Little of this was foreseen in the years before the election of 1828. But for more than a decade, there had been a slow but steady shifting in the tectonic plates that underlay the bedrock of nation's social, economic, and political landscape. While the surface appeared to be the same, the substructure was moving. In 1828 the result would be, if not an earthquake, at least a re-arranging of the old landscape and the configuration of a new one. What historians and others call "political culture" would be transformed in ways that are still with us today. The behavior and assumptions inherited from the Founders that had guided men—and they were almost always men in the Early Republic—regarding politics and public life would disappear, to be replaced by new ones closer to those of our own day.[16]

THE BIRTH OF
MODERN
POLITICS

★ Chapter One ★

His statue still stands in the city of New Orleans, untouched by the hurricane disaster of 2005. In the town square named after him, he sits astride a horse that has risen to an anatomically impossible position and waves his hat in triumph over something or someone—perhaps the British, or the Indians. A replica of the statue faces the White House in Washington, and another may be seen at the state capitol in Nashville, Tennessee.[1] "Jackson" and "Jacksonville" rival "Washington" as place-names for cities and counties in the United States.[2]

Andrew Jackson was a fixture in the American consciousness even before his election in 1828. Often simply referred to as "the Hero" (no other explanation needed), and later "Old Hickory," he was the first president to be given a nickname. The conqueror of Indian "savages," the chastiser of the wily Spaniard, and, above all, the defender of the nation's honor against the British at New Orleans, he is one of the few Americans to have an entire era named after him.[3]

No one speaks of an "Age of Adams." Towns, counties, and even mountains are named "Adams," but they usually honor the father, John, signer of the Declaration of Independence, not the son, John Quincy, the brilliant diplomat and secretary of state. Americans have always been a bit wary of diplomats and diplomacy, tending to value action more than words. And Andrew Jackson was nothing if not a man of action. As the Tennessee legislature declared the first time it nominated him for president, "He deliberates, he decides, and he acts." Long after he was gone, one who knew both Jackson and Adams agreed: "Jackson made law. Adams quoted it."[4]

Yet Jackson has been denied entry into the very front rank of American presidents. In spite of his presence on the twenty-dollar bill, he falls short of the Washingtons, Jeffersons, Lincolns, and Roosevelts that came before and after him. In 1962 a group of historians ranked him in sixth place among presidents, one spot behind Jefferson and one step ahead of Theodore Roosevelt.[5] He was a slaveholder, but so were Washington and Jefferson. He was hated when in office, but so were Lincoln and the Roosevelts. He plays a prominent part in our history not so much for what he achieved as for what he came to represent. He was, as one historian famously put it, a symbol *for* an age, not *of* an age.[6]

Historians have never been sure what to make of Andrew Jackson. By the standards of his day he was the least qualified man ever to run for the presidency. He is the only president—thus far at least—to have deliberately killed a man as a civilian. His first serious biographer, writing when many of Old Hickory's friends and enemies were still living, described him as both "a patriot and a traitor." He was a bundle of contradictions, wrote James Parton in 1860, "a writer brilliant, elegant, eloquent, without being able to compose a correct sentence, or spell words of four syllables.... A most law-defying, law-obeying citizen. A stickler for discipline, he never hesitated to disobey a superior. A democratic autocrat. An urbane savage. An atrocious saint."[7] For years after his death Jackson remained a partisan figure, generally dismissed by scholars and others whose attachments were to the Republican Party, which had evolved from the old Whig Party that had been organized specifically to oppose Jackson and all he came to represent.

Not until the end of the nineteenth century did Jackson come to be seen as representing a progressive force in American politics. Then the great historian from Wisconsin, Frederick Jackson Turner (whose father, Andrew Jackson Turner, was born in 1837, the year Old Hickory left office), began to influence the writing of American history. Turner described Jackson as "that fierce Tennessee spirit, who broke the traditions of conservative rule, swept away the privacies and privileges of officialdom, and, like a Gothic leader, opened the temple of the nation to the populace."[8] Or so Turner believed. So did most historians and biographers until the 1960s, when a more inclusive view of the American past, embracing the stories not only of the traditional leaders and elites but of the dispossessed as well, brought about a reevaluation of the entire American experience. The result for Andrew Jackson was not good. The violent side of his character, his duels, his role in the dispossessing of Native Americans from their ancestral lands, his status as an aristocratic slaveholder who pronounced democratic platitudes, may have made him the "symbol for an age," but the age he symbolized came to be seen as far more complex than ever before: violent, racist, and characterized by a widening gap between haves and have-nots.[9] He became a subject for psychoanalytic historians, who pondered the effects of his early orphaned status, the origins of his legendary temper, and his childless marriage.[10] Even his military reputation, which had served him so well in his political career, became a target for critics of the post-Vietnam era, one of whom went so far as to dismiss him as a "Caudillo," a Latin American–style dictator.[11]

In more recent times his defenders have reemerged.[12] Derided or defended, Jackson still remains the dominant figure of his age, perhaps forever linked to the image of a young America bursting the bonds of restraint imposed on it by the bewigged gentlemen of an earlier era. The phrase "Jacksonian democracy" shapes much of our understanding of the second quarter of the nineteenth century.[13] Well over two centuries after his birth, members of the Democratic Party he helped to create still hold fund-raising dinners in his name.

No politicians hold fund-raising dinners honoring John Quincy Adams. Among historians he invariably ranks lower than Jackson as a president. When the New Englander is honored at all, it is either for his prepresidential career as a diplomat or his postpresidential career as an antislavery congressman. In recent times the Adamses, including not only John and John Quincy, but Abigail Adams, wife of the first and mother of the second, have enjoyed something of a revival in their fortunes. But in most instances this is due more to their reputations for fierce personal integrity and political sacrifice than for inspiring or commanding the affections of others.[14]

Andrew Jackson was born in South Carolina, in the Waxhaws, a district close to the North Carolina border. His father, also named Andrew, was part of a migration of a quarter of a million Scots Irish who came to colonial America in the mid-eighteenth century. Most of them settled in the colonial southwestern interior, on lands not already occupied by the English, whom they distrusted in varying degrees ranging from mild suspicion to outright hatred. This contentiousness was based partly on religion, partly on economics, but mostly on ethnicity. Their fervent Presbyterianism clashed with the upper-class, easygoing Anglicanism of the English. All too often they left Britain to escape deteriorating economic conditions exacerbated by rack-renting English landlords who looked down on them with ill-disguised contempt. They were, in the words of one historian, "a stern and dour people, long accustomed to thinking that they were surrounded by enemies who must be battled continually." They settled, not in nucleated villages, but on isolated homesteads, often on unsurveyed land, where they grimly defied any attempts at outside control. In the absence of a court system, violence was often the means for settling disputes. Most adult males carried a pistol, sometimes more than one. Their first loyalties were not to the community but to clan and family. Outsiders saw them as a violent, whiskey-drinking crowd of barbarians, characterized, according to one Anglican minister, by a "low, lazy, sluttish, heathenish, hellish life."[15]

We do not know a great deal about Jackson's father, though he does not seem to have shared the more boisterous traits of his countrymen. A landholding son of a prosperous merchant, the elder Jackson left Northern Ireland in 1765 with his wife, Elizabeth, and their two children. Andrew, their third son, would be born in March 1767. His father would not be there to see him, having been the victim of a tree-cutting accident a few months before. We also know little about the young Jackson's earliest years. His biographers have depended on oral accounts, some of them collected years after the general's death and not all of them reliable. No letters exist from either of Jackson's parents, nor from Jackson himself until he was in his twenties.[16]

Jackson's first years can be contrasted with those of the man he defeated in 1828. John Quincy Adams was born in Braintree, Massachusetts, four months after Jackson, in July 1767.[17] John and Abigail Adams were both destined to play significant roles in the establishment of the new nation. They were descendants of the English Puritans who emigrated to Massachusetts in the 1630s as part of their design to create a "Zion in the wilderness." By 1767, however, much of the earlier religious zeal had dissipated, and the Puritan was displaced by the Yankee.

The townships of Adams's New England differed greatly from the sparsely populated Carolina frontier. Houses were usually nestled close together. The crime rate was low. Villages such as Braintree were characterized by "meetinghouses and schools, stocks and pillories, animal pounds and training fields, town commons and enclosed fields, nucleated centers and rural neighborhoods."[18] And although the days of the expulsion of heretics and the hanging of witches had, thankfully, receded into the past, Yankees were still governed to a large extent by their covenant theology, which held that they were bound together as a community to promote and improve the commonwealth, resisting the centrifugal effects of individual ambition and passion.

Both Jackson and Adams were nine years old in 1776, the year of Independence. The Revolutionary War began in Adams's New England (he had watched from a distance the Battle of Bunker Hill alongside his mother, Abigail), but by 1780 it had moved to Jackson's Carolinas. Here in the South the Patriot cause initially met disaster. The city of Charleston fell easily to the Redcoats in May 1780. For the next six months the Waxhaws and neighboring districts were overrun by marauding bands of British soldiers, leaving countless dead and wounded in their wake. Elizabeth Jackson, assisted by the teenage Andrew and his older brother Robert, did what she could to care for the wounded. Eager to join the fight, Andrew attended the musters and drills of the local militia. According to a later source, he and his brother became acquainted with "the manual exercise, and had some idea of the different evolutions of the field." This was the beginning of Jackson's military education. He was a probable witness to the Battle of Hanging Rock in August 1780—another Patriot defeat—and later took refuge with relatives while enemy soldiers and their Loyalist allies continued to dominate the countryside.[19]

To make matters worse, civil war broke out as the local population turned against one another, Loyalists and Patriots looting, burning, killing, massacring. After one such incident, Jackson found himself in the company of a distant cousin, Lieutenant Thomas Crawford, while the enemy was ransacking his house. In the midst of the mayhem, the commanding officer ordered the fourteen-year-old Jackson to clean his boots. Jackson refused. The enraged officer swung his sword at Jackson's head, slashing the side of his face and leaving a scar that the future general and president would carry for the rest of his life—along with a hatred of Great Britain.[20]

Jackson's brother Robert was wounded as well, and the two were carted off to Camden as prisoners of war, along with some twenty others. Conditions in the prison were such that Robert's wounds grew worse and Andrew contracted smallpox. Eventually their mother arranged for an exchange of prisoners, including her two sons, but by that time it was too late to save Robert. Andrew's older brother, Hugh, had died the previous summer.

After nursing her surviving son back to health, Elizabeth Jackson, along with two other women, volunteered to go to Charleston to nurse American prisoners of war on the prison ships in the harbor. It was the summer of 1781. Although she and her friends could not know it, the war was drawing to a close. George Washington, with the help of the French, had successfully bottled up British General Cornwallis on the Yorktown peninsula, forcing his surrender. The war's end did not come soon enough for Elizabeth Jackson. She contracted cholera as a result of her ministrations and died soon after the surrender. Andrew was left an orphan without siblings. His short life up to then had known little but death and violence.[21]

While Jackson's scar was healing in the Carolinas, the teenage Adams was in Europe. His father, along with Benjamin Franklin and others, had been entrusted with securing at the negotiating table in Paris the victory that Washington had won on the battlefield in Virginia. Young Adams divided his time between his studies, which included Latin, Greek, French, German, and Dutch, and his travels, which in 1781 took him as far as St. Petersburg in Russia, where he acted briefly as an interpreter for the American representative. After returning from Russia he resumed his studies in Amsterdam and Paris, returning to Massachusetts in 1785. He entered Harvard College the following year.[22]

A college education was not in the cards for Jackson. His mother had hoped that her surviving son would choose the ministry for a career, and what limited education he had acquired was fashioned with that in mind. In 1781, after his mother's death, Jackson lived with a succession of her relatives and friends. It was not a happy time. Still recovering both physically and psychologically from his prison experience, young Jackson proved more than a handful to control. In his old age Jackson conceded this, offering examples of his explosive temperament, which in those days were often accompanied by a stream of obscenities and threats of violence.[23] His prospects were not improved by the arrival of a number of young male refugees from Charleston with whom he fell in, accompanying them on escapades of drinking, gambling, cockfighting, and other forms of recreation on the southern frontier. When his new friends returned to Charleston in the wake of the British exit, Jackson went with them and proceeded to squander what was left of a small inheritance from his grandfather in Ireland. When his only possession left was his horse, he staked it against two hundred dollars in a dice game. He won, paid off his creditors, and returned to the Waxhaws. After a few months of study in a private academy—there were no public schools in the South—Jackson abruptly left the Waxhaws, never to return. At age seventeen he moved north to Salisbury, North Carolina, where, despite his youth and lack of formal education, he persuaded a local attorney to accept him as a student.

In the absence of professional law schools, an aspiring lawyer in the late eighteenth century would, after paying a fee, study and work as an intern with an established attorney. After a year or two the mentor could certify his student as qualified to practice law, after which he would be admitted to the bar. For the next two years Jackson applied himself to his studies by day and caroused with his friends at night. According to one source, relocating outhouses was one of their major nocturnal occupations. "Andrew Jackson was the most roaring, rollicking, game-cocking, horse-racing, card-playing, mischievous fellow that ever lived in Salisbury," another recalled. But in 1787, at age twenty, Jackson presented himself before two judges of the Superior Court of Law and Equity of North Carolina. There he was found to be a man of "unblemished moral character" and was licensed to practice law within the state. Notwithstanding the findings regarding his "unblemished" character, he and a number of friends managed to get themselves arrested a month later on a charge of trespassing. Not much is known about the incident, except that it was apparently settled without jail time. It may have had a sobering effect on the high-spirited, tightly wound Jackson. Not long afterward he left Salisbury and headed for Guilford County, where he began his legal career.[24]

He met with little success. In 1788 he learned that John McNairy, a fellow carouser from the Salisbury days, had been elected a superior court judge for the Western District of North Carolina, the region beyond the mountains that is now the state of Tennessee. With the job went the right to appoint the public prosecutor for the district, and McNairy offered it to his old friend, Andrew Jackson. With his career stalled and his immediate family dead, Jackson, like so many others in that part of the world, opted for a fresh start. That spring he, McNairy, and a few friends crossed over the mountains to begin new lives. There they set up their practice in the town of Jonesborough. Henceforth Jackson would be forever associated with Tennessee and the southwestern frontier.

One of the earliest letters we have of John Quincy Adams was written at the age of nine to his father, asking for advice and a notebook.[25] The earliest letter we have of Andrew Jackson, written at the age of twenty-one, challenges a man to a duel. It seems that in arguing a court case he became incensed by a Jonesborough attorney, Waightstill Avery, whose sarcasm apparently struck a nerve. "My character you have injured," wrote the agitated young lawyer, "and further you have Insulted me in the presence of a court and large audianc [sic]."[26] The letter is instructive, not so much for its spelling—which in an age prior to standardized spelling was not unusual—but because it reflects the masculine concept of honor, the potential for violence that lay beneath the surface of southern frontier culture generally and of Andrew Jackson in particular. Reputation, especially in a newly forming community like that of Tennessee, was essential to one's standing.[27] Probably owing to the intercession of the seconds, this particular duel ended harmlessly, with both participants firing into the air. There would be others in the future, and the results would often be anything but harmless.

Not long afterward, perhaps resulting from this altercation with Avery, Jackson and McNairy moved on to a more central part of Tennessee and the newly established town of Nashville, population two hundred. Seeking comfortable accommodations, Jackson settled in at the boarding-house of the widowed Rachel Donelson. Here he met John Overton, destined to become one of his closest friends and political allies. Here, too, he met and fell in love with Widow Donelson's daughter, also named Rachel.

The problem was that Rachel Donelson Robards was married, though estranged from her abusive husband, Lewis. According to Jackson's subsequent defenders (both in his lifetime and later), the lovers were under the impression that Rachel's husband had divorced her, and accordingly, in 1790 or so, they either were married or proceeded to live together as common-law husband and wife hundreds of miles away, in Natchez, on the Mississippi River. Such casual arrangements were not unusual on the southern frontier. Indeed, the custom of "bridal abduction" seems to have been an import from parts of Ireland and Scotland.[28] In any event, if there was an abduction it was voluntary and does not seem to have raised much controversy at the time. It would be another two years before Lewis Robards was granted his divorce. In 1794 Andrew and Rachel were formally wed, either for the first time or the second. The record remains unclear, but Jackson's enemies (and most of his more recent biographers) maintained that the two knew all along that Rachel was still married, and lived together nonetheless. This would make Rachel guilty of adultery, a charge supported by Robards's petition for divorce, in which he stated that his wife had deserted him and had "lived in adultery with another man since desertion."[29] The matter remained a sensitive one for both Rachel and the volatile Jackson for years to come. It would explode in the presidential election of 1828.

In 1794 Jackson was appointed attorney general for the Mero District of the Tennessee Territory and a year later was named judge advocate of the Davidson County militia. It was his first military appointment, and it was one of the more important keys to economic and social success in that part of the country. Most of the political power in Tennessee lay in the hands of its appointed territorial governor, William Blount, a wheeler-dealer who eventually would be elected to, and expelled from, the U.S. Senate. Jackson owed his appointment to Blount. After his marriage he took it upon himself to enlarge his fortune. He became part of Governor Blount's inner circle and formed partnerships with land speculators, including Overton and William B. Lewis, another future confidante. Land was still cheap in Tennessee and available to those with the right connections. Between 1793 and 1797 Jackson invested twenty thousand dollars in land in sixteen different transactions. And with land went slaves, of whom the twenty-seven-year-old Jackson owned at least sixteen by 1794.[30]

At this point there were two obstacles to land speculation in Tennessee. One was the Indian tribes—Creeks, Choctaws, and Cherokees—who inconveniently occupied large portions of the territory. As an attorney general, and therefore a law enforcement officer, it was Jackson's responsibility to enforce the existing treaties with the various tribes and prosecute violators, no matter what their race. His heart was not in it. As with most frontiersmen, indeed as with most white Americans, Jackson had little or no patience with the Indians' claims to their ancestral lands. Indians, he thought, were primitive children, violent savages whose word was unreliable and whose capacity for barbarous torture and cruelty knew no bounds. Similar behavior on the part of whites was merely retaliation or self-defense. Whites could occasionally live with them, trade with them, even marry them, but they could never defer to them. Andrew Jackson was no anthropologist. "I fear that their Peace Talks are only Delusions," he declared in 1794. "Does not Experience teach us that Treaties answer No other Purpose than opening an Easy door for the Indians to pass through to Butcher our Citizens?"[31] In the 1790s Jackson would emerge as one of the leaders in the cause of rapid Indian removal. It was a position from which he would never waver and would do no harm to his standing among the people of Tennessee and the southwestern frontier.

The other obstacle to land speculation was the presence of the Spanish Empire just across the Mississippi River. The Louisiana Territory, although named after a French king, had passed into the hands of the Spanish following the French defeat in the French and Indian War of 1756–63. The Spanish thus controlled the city of New Orleans, vital to the passage of American wheat, corn, lumber, and other raw material down the Ohio and Mississippi Rivers. Their relatively liberal Indian policies made the Louisiana Territory a potential haven for hostile tribes beyond the reach of the Americans. So long as Louisiana lay in foreign hands the security of the Tennessee region was in doubt. War with the Spanish was out of the question, but an independent Tennessee, capable of allying itself with Spain for the mutual interest of both, was not. Congress must help, wrote Jackson to a friend. "Unless Congress lends us a more ample protection this Country [i.e., Tennessee] will have at length to break or seek a protection from some other Source than the present."[32] Patriotism, it would seem, was still negotiable among Tennesseans.

In the mid-1790s Governor Blount decided to press for Tennessee's admission to the Union as its sixteenth state. According to the existing federal law, a convention in the proposed state had to be held and a constitution adopted before a new state could be admitted. This was accordingly done, and the governor saw to it that his young friend and protégé Andrew Jackson was among the delegates elected to the convention. Thus it was that in early 1796 Jackson found himself in Knoxville, along with several dozen other delegates, entrusted with the drafting of a constitution that would be submitted for congressional approval. To no one's surprise Governor Blount was elected to preside over the convention.

No record of the convention debates exists, but it is possible to determine Jackson's role through an examination of motions made, seconded, and approved. Both his critics and allies in 1828 would examine the record carefully. He emerges as an opponent of those who wished to attach public service to religious conviction, opposing a requirement for a "profession of faith" by officeholders. He also opposed, less successfully, a ban on clergymen serving in public office, but supported such a ban for members of the state legislature. He supported the trend toward universal male suffrage (apparently including free blacks), yet favored a property requirement for membership in the two-house legislature and for governor.[33]

With its mixture of liberal suffrage and more conservative office-holding requirements, the Tennessee constitution was typical for the frontier states of that era. Jackson became its enthusiastic advocate. His reliability in its defense, as well as his growing popularity, made him a valued member of the Blount clique. To put it in modern terms, Jackson had both connections and charisma. When the statewide election for Tennessee's sole congressman was held after its admission to the Union in 1796, Jackson was easily chosen for the remaining few months of the two-year term. Late in the year, at age twenty-nine, he traveled to Philadelphia, the nation's temporary capital. George Washington was preparing to leave the presidency, and John Quincy Adams's father was preparing to assume it.[34]

The presidential election of 1796 was the first to be contested by competing candidates and competing political parties. John Adams of Massachusetts and the Federalist Party narrowly triumphed over Thomas Jefferson of Virginia and the Republicans. The names of the two parties are significant. By calling themselves Federalists, Adams, Alexander Hamilton, and their allies hoped to convince Americans that they were the true defenders of the Constitution of 1787 and that their opponents were irresponsible antifederalist malcontents seeking to undo the work of the Founding Fathers. In response Jefferson, James Madison, and others began calling themselves Republicans, claiming that they were the true heirs to the American Revolution and that their Federalist opponents were undermining the Constitution with the intention of creating an aristocracy in republican America.[35]

Just what "republicanism" meant, and what it implied, would be the defining political issue for Americans for the next half-century, including the generation of Andrew Jackson and John Quincy Adams. Originally the term meant little more than support for American independence and rejection of the British monarchy, along with its corrupt and privileged aristocracy. In the course of the Revolution it expanded to include rejection of all monarchies and all aristocracies, embracing instead the simple, frugal, uncorrupted, and more open society that Americans liked to think themselves as enjoying. It became the watchword and controlling ideology of the Founders and the generation that followed them.[36] As a Harvard undergraduate in the 1780s Adams had proudly written to his mother that he was "the best republican [there]."[37] A few years later, influenced by the French Revolution, there was a renewed emphasis on simplicity and lack of pretension on the part of the upper classes. Some, though not all, ceased to wear the wigs and waistcoats that had once distinguished them from the lower orders.

There was more to it than a change in clothing. Politically their revolution had taught American republicans the dangers of consolidated power in the hands of a few. *Power,* they came to believe, posed a constant, malignant threat to *liberty.*[38] The more there was of the first, the less there would be of the latter, and vice versa. Good government, therefore, consisted in restraining and, in the case of the American Constitution, distributing power so that it could not threaten liberty. Good republicans needed to be constantly on guard lest their leaders, like those in the former mother country, become corrupted by the temptations of power. By "corruption," American republicans did not necessarily mean outright theft or embezzlement, but rather submitting to the temptations offered by office holding and the manipulation and intrigue that went with it. Corruption could be fought only by cultivating a sense of virtue among the citizenry. In those days virtue had less to do with private conduct and more to do with public responsibility; it meant unceasing devotion to the public welfare—the commonwealth—as opposed to private interest and ambition. A republic, said the Virginia Constitution of 1776, required "a firm adherence to justice, moderation, temperance, frugality, and virtue."[39] Republicanism represented, in short, not merely a set of political opinions but a complex arrangement of social, political, and moral values as well.

For many, the very idea of an organized political party ran counter to true republicanism. Certainly the Framers of the Constitution of 1787 thought so. They were in unanimous agreement as to the danger posed to any future republic by organized parties, or "factions," as they tended to call them. Loyalty to a party threatened loyalty to the community. Political parties encouraged the very private ambition and corruption that republicans were supposed to be on guard against. They were "engines of corruption" that put the interests of selfish minorities ahead of the common good. They set the part against the whole, the particular against the general. "There is nothing which I dread so much," John

Adams wrote in 1780, "as a division of the republic into two great parties, each arranged under its leader, and concerting measures in opposition to each other. This, in my opinion, is to be dreaded as the greatest evil under our Constitution." In his Farewell Address, Washington warned against "the baneful effects of the spirit of party," insisting that it "serves always to distract the public councils and enfeeble the public administration." Washington spoke for most members of the revolutionary generation, who hoped the new Constitution and the republic it was creating would inspire its citizens to rise above partisanship. Writing as "Publius" in the *Federalist* essays in 1788, James Madison sought to convince his readers that one of the Constitution's main advantages was "its tendency to break and control the violence of faction."[40]

Nonetheless within five years political parties had developed, and none other than Madison himself would be one of their organizers. Patriots such as Hamilton, Madison, Adams, and Jefferson, who united in their resistance to British oppression in the 1770s and united again to support the Constitution in the 1780s, found themselves quarreling with one another in the 1790s, sometimes violently. Secretary of the Treasury Hamilton charged that Secretary of State Jefferson and his allies were covertly opposed to the Constitution and were trying to undermine and destroy it. Jefferson and Madison accused Hamilton and the Federalists of trying to use the Constitution to remake the nation into little more than a pale imitation of Great Britain. Exhibit A in the Republican indictment was Hamilton's proposal for financing the national debt through consolidating both federal and state debts into one colossal debt, to be financed by a new national bank, whose constitutionality, in the Republicans' view, was extremely doubtful. Exhibit B was Federalist opposition to the revolution in France, which Jefferson insisted for many years was merely the French version of the American struggle against monarchy and aristocracy. True republicans, the Jeffersonians maintained, could not support the revolution of 1776 in America and oppose that of 1789 in France.[41]

The bitterness was such that, as Jefferson famously remarked at the time, men who had once been friends would cross the street to avoid meeting one another.[42] Madison and Hamilton, close collaborators in the *Federalist* essays in 1788, regularly denounced each other in the newspapers after 1794. Jefferson and John Adams, fast friends in the 1780s, opposed each other in the presidential election of 1796 and again in 1800. Jefferson became permanently alienated from Washington over incautious remarks he made about the first president in a private letter that found its way into print. Thomas

Paine, whose *Common Sense* praised Washington in 1776, attacked him twenty years later, declaring that history would only ask whether Washington had betrayed his original principles or simply did not have any in the first place. And in 1804 the vice president of the United States, Aaron Burr, would shoot and kill Alexander Hamilton in a duel. No wonder that at least one historian has called the 1790s the Age of Passion.[43]

In retrospect, it is now clear that in adopting the name Republican for their party, the Jeffersonians scored a semantic victory, in spite of the fact that the existence of any political party ran counter to older republican assumptions. The term, if not its original meaning, has become a permanent part of the American political vocabulary and accepted as part of the political culture. It would be adopted by Abraham Lincoln's antislavery coalition in the 1850s and lives into the twenty-first century. The name Federalist, on the other hand, would in time become for many a "synonym for privilege and political depravity."[44]

When Andrew Jackson walked into the chamber of the House of Representatives in late 1796, Republicans in Congress were still seething in the aftermath not only of their recent narrow defeat but of the adoption of the allegedly pro-British Jay's Treaty. Chief Justice John Jay had been sent to London two years before by the president in hopes of resolving the remaining differences between the United States and Britain. These included the continued occupation by the British of forts on American soil, the British claim of the right to search private American vessels on the high seas for alleged deserters and to impress them back into the Royal Navy, and the right to intercept neutral shipping headed for France or any of its allies with whom they were at war.

Jay's Treaty was a disappointment. The British agreed to give up the forts, but they had already agreed to that in 1783. There was little or no progress made on matters of impressment or the rights of neutral trade in wartime. Republicans claimed that the Treaty in effect endorsed Britannia's rule of the waves. What was worse, the French now claimed the same rights of search and seizure and threatened retaliation if the U.S. Senate approved the Treaty, which it did by the narrowest possible margin.

The new state of Tennessee was not particularly concerned with neutral rights, impressment, or the Anglo-French war, but Congressman Jackson had no use for the Federalists or their foreign policy. Jay's Treaty only exacerbated his Anglophobia, cut into the side of his face by the

British officer's sword fifteen years earlier. Even before he took his seat he had erupted in a vituperative and not entirely coherent attack on the Treaty and on the men he thought responsible for it. "What an alarming Situation," he angrily told a North Carolina congressman, "has the late Negociation of Mr. Jay with Lord Greenvill, and that Negociation (for a Treaty of Commerce it cannot properly be Called, as it wants reciprocity) being ratified by the Two third of the senate & president has plunged our country in." He called for the impeachment and removal of those responsible for the Treaty, denouncing it as "that Child of aristocratic Secracy" that should be "removed Erased and obliterated from the archives of the Grand republick of the united States." He held George Washington personally responsible for the Treaty, and when the time came for the House of Representatives to vote on a resolution of thanks to the Great Man for his many services to the republic, Jackson was one of a handful who voted nay. His vote would not be forgotten in 1828.[45]

Jackson and his Tennessee friends objected not only to Jay's Treaty, but even more to the unwillingness of either the Washington or the new Adams administration to lend full support to the removal of Native American Indians from the southern frontier. Ironically, in view of his own future presidency, he also complained of excess partisanship, that under the Adams administration "the talents, virtues, or abilities of men, are no recommendation to bring them into office, if they do not think exactly with the Executive."[46]

Jackson's term was up in March 1797. Upon returning to Tennessee he barely avoided a political scandal that resulted in the expulsion of his mentor and benefactor, William Blount, from the U.S. Senate. Blount had been caught in an attempt to entice the British into financing American and Indian military operations against the French and Spanish in and around Florida and New Orleans. Ever faithful to his friends and supporters—a characteristic that would remain with Jackson throughout his career—Jackson stuck by Blount, as did most Tennesseans. As a reward he was elected by the Blount-dominated state legislature to a six-year term in the U.S. Senate. That autumn Senator Andrew Jackson was back in Philadelphia.

Like his congressional term, Jackson's senatorial term was to be brief. More than one of his biographers has suggested that Jackson was unfit at this time for the relatively sophisticated decorum of the Senate, with its extended oratory and parliamentary maneuverings.[47] Albert Gallatin, then a Republican congressman and later Jefferson's treasury secretary, remembered Jackson's entry into Congress, describing him as "a tall, lank, uncouth-looking personage, with long locks of hair hanging over his face, and a queue down his back tied in an eel skin, his dress singular, his manners and deportment those of a rough frontiersman." Jefferson himself, who as vice president presided over the Senate, recalled as an old man that the young Jackson was temperamentally unfit for the post. "When I was President of the Senate," he allegedly told Daniel Webster in 1824, "he was Senator, and he could never speak on account of the rashness of his feelings. I have seen him attempt it repeatedly, and as often choke with rage." Webster was a critic of Jackson, and the account has been challenged by others.[48] But it is true that Jackson's election to the Senate erupted into a dangerous confrontation with John Cocke, the man whom he replaced. Jackson loudly claimed that Cocke had injured his standing by publishing one of his private letters. His note to Cocke bristled with the standard vocabulary of the early nineteenth-century cult of southern honor: "Sir the baseness of your heart in violating a confidenc reposed in you in an hour of intimate friendship, should...bring down the indignation of the thinking part of mankind against you." He demanded justice "which I will obtain at the risque of my blood."[49] Again, a duel was averted only by intermediaries.

Jackson was less than comfortable in Philadelphia. As a senator he had little to say, and he resigned the position after barely six months, returning once more to Tennessee. Before he left he did vote against the appointment of John Quincy Adams as American commissioner to negotiate a treaty of amity and commerce with the government of Sweden.[50] The vote had nothing to do with animosity toward Adams, whom he had yet to meet and of whom he had little or no knowledge, but was in line with the Republican Party's thinking of the day, which held that foreign relations need be established only with those powers with whom Americans had immediate concerns, namely, Great Britain, France, and Spain. Any other diplomatic missions, Republicans thought, were a waste of taxpayers' money.

After graduating from Harvard in 1787 John Quincy Adams, like Jackson, studied law with an established attorney. He was admitted to the bar in 1790. Unlike Jackson, however, Adams hated the law, or at least the practice of it. In the early 1790s he spent much of his spare time in his Boston office writing newspaper essays defending the Washington administration and its attempt to steer between the competing claims of Great Britain and France for American sympathy and support in the ongoing Anglo-French war. He attracted considerable notice in 1791 when he published a series of letters signed "Publicola" in which he criticized Thomas Paine (whom he slightingly called "the Islam of democracy") for his complete and unreserved endorsement of the French Revolution. This and other writings attracted the attention of President Washington—no doubt with some assistance from his vice president—and in 1794 he appointed the younger Adams American minister to the Netherlands. It was the beginning of a long and distinguished diplomatic career. When the father took the oath of office in 1797 the son was in Berlin, as American minister to Prussia.[51]

John Adams would serve only one term as president. His impulsive temperament created difficulties within his own cabinet and among many of his fellow Federalists, including the equally impulsive Alexander Hamilton, to whom many Federalists continued to look for leadership. Adams eventually fired two members of his cabinet, including Timothy Pickering, his secretary of state. Pickering would live a long time and never forgot the humiliation. Although he successfully resolved matters with the French through negotiations with its new leader, Napoleon Bonaparte, news of the settlement arrived too late to help Adams in his contest with Jefferson for reelection.

In 1800 the Republicans benefited from a divided Federalist Party, fears raised by the standing army created to deal with a nonexistent French menace, and, most of all, from the reaction against the notorious Alien and Sedition Acts of 1798, offspring of anti-French hysteria. A standing army in peacetime revived republican memories of the menace posed to civilian life. The Acts provoked angry resolutions by the state legislatures of Virginia and Kentucky, declaring them to be flagrant abuses of the limited federal powers granted to Congress. It was a clear case of power threatening liberty. Although no other state followed their lead, the Virginia and Kentucky Resolutions of 1798 became the foundation for the strict construction, states' rights ideology held by many Americans for the next several decades. The Alien and Sedition Acts and their repercussions would affect the career of Adams's son thirty years later. In March 1801 an embittered Adams left Washington for good, not bothering to attend his opponent's inauguration, but not before recalling his diplomat son from Berlin. John Quincy Adams returned to Boston in 1801.[52]

At about that time Jackson received an appointment in Tennessee that was far more to his liking than his seat in the Senate. His friends among the still powerful Blount faction arranged for the state legislature to elect him, without opposition, to the state superior court. There he served for the next six years. The position meant travel to all parts of Tennessee, where he acquired a reputation for both integrity and swift decision making. According to an early biographer, tradition had it that Judge Jackson "maintained the dignity and authority of the bench, while he was *on* the bench; and that his decisions were short, untechnical, unlearned, sometimes ungrammatical, and generally right."[53] His temperament and character were suited to the rough-and-tumble southern frontier society in which he lived.

Service on the judicial bench carried great weight in Tennessee, but service in the state's militia carried even more. Command and leadership there were rewarded with prestige and power that outranked both political and judicial status. In a state like Tennessee, which saw itself continually under siege from both hostile natives and crafty foreign powers just across the Mississippi, men and women looked to the militia for protection. Even before serving in Congress Jackson had angled for the post of major general, but without success. The office was elective, chosen by the leading officers of the militia's three branches. Jackson lost, largely due to behind-the-scenes manipulations by the popular governor of the state, John Sevier, an Indian fighter and hero of the Revolutionary War. Upset at what he believed to be Sevier's improper role in his defeat, Jackson bided his time until 1802, when the post again became vacant. This time it was sought by Sevier himself, who had been forced to step down as governor by a state law forbidding more than three consecutive terms. But Jackson's friends were better organized than they had been before. The election resulted in a tie, broken only by the new governor in favor of Jackson.

Now it was Sevier who was angry, and relations between Jackson, the new major general, and Sevier, the ex-governor, soon deteriorated. Following his failed quest for the militia position, Sevier again declared his candidacy for the governorship in 1803. His opponent released damaging information about some of Sevier's earlier real estate dealings, suggesting that the former governor had manipulated the law to line his own pockets. Apparently, the source of the information was General Andrew Jackson. A series of exchanges followed, including a dangerous remark by Sevier about Jackson's "taking a trip to Natchez with another man's wife." Jackson issued the inevitable challenge, followed by a series of insulting letters by both men debating where the duel was to take place. It culminated in an opéra bouffe encounter outside of Knoxville, in which Sevier drew his sword, frightening his horse, who ran away with his pistols. This forced Sevier to hide behind a tree to avoid Jackson's fire. The seconds finally prevailed, and everyone calmed down. No blood was shed, and Sevier won his reelection. Jackson and Sevier never reconciled. The Sevier duel was Jackson's third, and he was beginning to acquire the reputation of a hothead, even in Tennessee. Moreover, he was developing a tendency to regard setbacks as evidence of conspiracies against him by personal enemies who would need to be exposed if justice were to prevail.[54]

In 1804 Jackson resigned his judgeship and, after paying off most of his debts, retired to a 420-acre plot of land that he had acquired outside of Nashville in the 1790s named the Hermitage. It was worked by perhaps two dozen slaves. Like most gentlemen on the southwestern frontier, Jackson aspired to a lifestyle that included slaveholding, real estate speculation, cockfighting, and horse racing, especially the last. Racing was not only a form of entertainment; it offered gentlemen a chance to display their wealth and power.[55] On a trip to Virginia Jackson purchased a stallion named Truxton, which he proposed to race back in Tennessee. In late 1805 Truxton was set to race Ploughboy, a stallion owned by a neighbor, Joseph Erwin. But Ploughboy pulled up lame shortly before the race, and, in keeping with prior arrangements, Erwin paid a forfeit. What happened afterward is hard to follow, but the end result was a duel between Jackson and Erwin's son-in-law, Charles Dickinson. Dickinson had previously made snide comments about Rachel Jackson, admittedly while drunk, for which he later apologized to her husband. Then he became involved in a quarrel centering on the validity of the promissory notes that his father-in-law had given to Jackson as the forfeit on the canceled race. The dispute lasted nearly a year and a half, climaxing with a publication in the *Nashville Review* in which Dickinson, known throughout western Tennessee as an expert pistol shot, called Jackson a "worthless scoundrel, a poltroon, and a coward." In the southern frontier culture of the day, Jackson had no choice but to challenge Dickinson, as Dickinson no doubt knew. To avoid legal complications, the duel was held across the Tennessee border in Kentucky, on May 30, 1806.

With full knowledge of Dickinson's prowess, Jackson and his second, John Overton's brother Thomas, determined to let Dickinson fire first, in hopes that either he would miss or that the wound would be superficial and allow the general to take his time before firing back. (Legend has it that Jackson wore a large overcoat to conceal his thin frame.) This is precisely what happened, with Dickinson hitting Jackson in the chest, next to his heart. The wound was not fatal. Jackson then took deliberate aim at the terrified Dickinson, but his pistol stuck at half-cock. Under the rules, Jackson was entitled to a second shot. This he took, and mortally wounded his opponent. Dickinson bled to death on the spot.[56]

What is significant about this tragedy is that Jackson, having excused Dickinson after his apology for the remarks about Rachel, was so infuriated over his later transgressions that he was determined to kill him. Duels, at least in the more sophisticated East, were not necessarily meant to end with the death of one of the participants.[57] Indeed, as Vice President Aaron Burr had learned two years before, the result could backfire; Burr remained vice president for eight months after killing Alexander Hamilton, but his political career was over. On the southern frontier the rules were different. A few years later, giving advice to a potential second in a duel in which he was not involved, Jackson urged him to advise his friend "to preserve his fire, until he shoots his antagonist through the *brain*." In 1806, although he had the opportunity to end matters by firing into the air or merely winging his opponent, Jackson chose to do neither. A number of Dickinson's friends proposed to run a memorial for their fallen comrade in one of the local papers, but when they learned that Jackson was particularly interested in learning their names, they hastily begged off. Andrew Jackson would carry the duel, its outcome, and Dickinson's bullet in his chest for the rest of his life. His standing in the community plummeted.[58]

In John Quincy Adams's New England the Yankee concept of honor rested more on what an individual thought of himself, rather than what the community may have believed. The tight-knit villages, as well as the law, forbade dueling and gunplay. Men seldom carried side arms of any sort, and community leaders were expected to settle their differences through debate and argument at town meetings, not through gunfire. The region had long ceased to be a frontier, and wild game was increasingly scarce. Rifles and muskets were still in abundance, usually as mementoes of the glory days of Lexington, Concord, and Bunker Hill. Adams, the former diplomat, made occasional reference to hunting forays in his diary, but the quarry was generally sparrows and squirrels.[59]

When he returned to Massachusetts Adams resolved to have nothing to do with partisan politics, roundly criticizing both Federalists and

Republicans. He had seen the result of partisan warfare both at home and in Europe, he said, and denounced it with standard republican vigor. Like his father, he was convinced that the Republicans under Jefferson and Madison were so blinded by their support for revolutionary France that they forgot the interests of their own country, and he blamed Federalist Francophobia for undermining his father's diplomacy, which led to his defeat in 1800. His reaction against both parties was visceral. "I will sooner turn scavenger and earn my living by clearing away the filth of the streets," he told his mother, than engage in partisan warfare. He later told his brother Thomas Boylston Adams, "There is not a political party in this country with which an honest man can act without blushing." To his diary he remarked, "A politician in this country must be a man of a party. I would fain be the man of my whole country."⁶⁰

This high-minded vow of political celibacy steadily weakened as Adams confronted a future in the hated legal profession. But the price of admission to politics in Massachusetts, especially for an Adams, was to enroll in the still dominant Federalist Party. So in 1802 he reluctantly became a Federalist candidate for election to the Massachusetts State Senate. He won. Then he ran for U.S. Congress, again as a Federalist. He lost. In 1803 his name was put forth in the Massachusetts legislature as a Federalist candidate for a vacancy in the U.S. Senate, along with that of former secretary of state Timothy Pickering, whose disloyalty to Adams's father had led to his dismissal. Pickering failed to get the needed majority in the legislature, and John Quincy Adams was elected instead. Then the other incumbent senator unexpectedly resigned, which led to Pickering's selection to fill the unexpired term. For the next few years Massachusetts would be represented by two senators who deeply distrusted one another.

The most important matter facing the Senate in 1804 was a vote on President Jefferson's purchase of the Louisiana Territory. Although Adams arrived too late to vote, he announced his support. He was the only Federalist in Congress to do so. He then turned around and opposed Jefferson's hasty takeover of the territory, arguing that it deprived the Louisianans of their rights as new American citizens to self-government. "Hitherto my conduct has given satisfaction to neither side," he proudly told his mother after only two months on the scene.⁶¹

Adams's nationalism and expansionism were predictable. The year before his election he had spoken at Plymouth, Massachusetts, on the annual occasion commemorating the landing of the Pilgrim fathers. Some day, he said, there would be more Americans than Europeans. "The destinies of this empire disdain the powers of human calculation," he declared, going on to quote the sentiments, if not the exact words, of England's Bishop William Berkeley: "Westward the Star of Empire takes its way."[62] Down in Tennessee Andrew Jackson also hailed the Louisiana Purchase. "All the Western Hemisphere rejoices at the Joyfull news of the cession of Louisiana, an event which places the peace happiness and liberty of our country on a lasting basis," he told President Jefferson.[63] Federalists and others might oppose the expansion of the United States, but in 1803 neither Senator John Quincy Adams of Massachusetts nor Major General Andrew Jackson of Tennessee would be among them.

When France and Britain resumed their war in 1803 the old divisions over foreign policy between Federalists and Republicans emerged once more. Soon the Royal Navy was capturing and confiscating cargoes on American ships headed for France, its colonies, and its allies and snatching men from American vessels, claiming they were deserters from His Majesty's ships. Federalists in New England had to choose between their concern for the mounting losses to their mercantile interests and their traditional support for Britain in its battle against revolutionary (now Napoleonic) France. Senator Adams did not hesitate. In 1806 he submitted two resolutions. The first condemned Britain's "unprovoked aggression upon the property of the citizens of these United States" and its "wanton violation of their neutral rights and a direct encroachment upon their national independence." The second requested that the president "demand and insist upon" reparations for lost American property. Both resolutions passed easily. Then, before Congress adjourned, it enacted a partial boycott of British manufactured goods. Again Adams was the only Federalist in either house to support the action. Federalists in both Washington and Massachusetts shook their heads in dismay. "Like a Kite without a Tail," one of them said, "he will be violent in his attempts to rise...and will pitch on one side and the other, as the popular Currents may happen to strike."[64]

On June 22, 1807, the British warship *Leopard* fired point-blank on the American frigate *Chesapeake* after the American captain refused a demand to search the vessel for alleged deserters. The incident touched off protests up and down the East Coast, including Boston. When Pickering and other Massachusetts Federalists failed to act, Adams joined with Republicans and helped draw up the resolutions denouncing the British. It was the beginning of the end of his relationship with the Federalist

Party. Looking back on it many years later, he told himself that the incident marked the beginning of "the really important part of my life."[65]

Facing renewed British hostility, President Jefferson had limited options. Republican cost-cutting had reduced the U.S. Navy to a handful of vessels, most of which were fighting pirates off the coast of North Africa. Most of the army was on the frontier, dealing with hostile Indians. A declaration of war against the most powerful naval force in the world made no sense. Believing American trade with the European powers was vital to their economic survival, Jefferson persuaded a reluctant Congress to adopt an embargo on all American trade with Europe until such time as the Great Powers should come around to the American position. Predictably, New England merchants were scathing in their denunciation of the Embargo Act, and the Federalists enjoyed a brief renaissance.

Again Adams supported Jefferson. Although skeptical—accurately, as it turned out—of the effectiveness of the embargo, he believed that the only alternative was to submit to continued British harassment of American shipping. The Massachusetts legislature showed what they thought of John Quincy Adams by choosing his successor a full year and a half before his term was up. Adams promptly resigned his seat, and with it his connection with the Federalists. It was a decision that would set him on the road to the presidency.[66]

While Adams was testing the patience of both political parties in Washington, Jackson was trying to avoid the backlash that followed the Dickinson duel. Then, in 1806, he suddenly issued an odd proclamation to the other generals in the Tennessee militia. Warning of a threat posed by the Spanish Empire and "the hostile appearance and menacing attitude of their armed forces already encamped within the limits of our government," he called on his officers to be ready to fill their quotas at the "shortest notice" for action.[67] Spain was not at war with the United States. The background to this bizarre and abrupt proclamation was the plot by former vice president Aaron Burr either to launch a filibustering attack against the Spanish in hopes of leading an independence move in Mexico, or to separate the trans-Mississippi West from the United States. The first was merely illegal; the second was treason. Jackson, along with others on the frontier, including the young Kentuckian Henry Clay, eagerly became involved.[68]

How much, and when, Jackson knew of Burr's real intentions is not clear. What is clear is his initial enthusiasm for the military honor and glory he might obtain by cooperating with Burr, a fellow duelist who had also killed his man, in an attack on the Spanish, driving them once and for all from the American Southwest. He took thirty-five hundred dollars from the former vice president for the purpose of collecting supplies and building boats. Jackson and dozens of others attended a banquet in Burr's honor in Nashville, where "many appropriate toasts were drunk, and a few of the most suitable songs were given."[69]

A few days later Jackson learned that Burr's real object might not be Mexico at all, but the city of New Orleans, now part of the United States. Burr insisted that the rumors were fantasies, and Jackson continued to meet with him and provide supplies. Then he learned that President Jefferson had issued a warrant for Burr's arrest on charges of conspiracy to commit treason. Jefferson called on Jackson to be ready to use his troops, not in support of Burr, but against him. Yet Jackson remained ambivalent. Years later some witnesses recalled that when he was summoned to Richmond, Virginia, to testify at Burr's trial Jackson loudly defended Burr and was critical of Jefferson.[70] Burr was acquitted for lack of evidence and faded into relative obscurity. Once again, Jackson's opportunity for glory had evaporated, and he never entirely escaped the suspicion that he had been part of the conspiracy from the beginning, bailing out only when it became too risky. The suspicion would reappear in the election of 1828.

In the meantime, faced with Napoleon's success on the European battlefield, Great Britain had no choice but to strengthen its hold on the ocean, which in turn meant heightened friction with the Americans. Whereas Jefferson, who stepped down from the presidency in 1809, was able to avoid a second war with Britain, Madison, his successor, was not so fortunate. In June 1812 President Madison asked for and received a congressional declaration of war.

The causes of the War of 1812 never were clear, even while it was being fought. Officially at issue were the British edicts known as the Orders in Council, which underscored Britain's determination to disrupt trade with France and its allies in ways particularly disadvantageous to the Americans. There was also the continued practice of impressment and the British refusal to apologize for the *Chesapeake-Leopard* affair in a satisfactory manner. In the South and West, far removed as they were from the commercial centers most affected by the British actions, so-called war hawks in Congress and elsewhere were among the most vocal in demanding action. Some have suggested that their eyes were focused more on opportunities for expansion south to Florida and north to Canada than on redressing commercial grievances. Critics of the war, then and since, pointed out that the Orders in Council were rescinded before war was declared, the news only arriving after the declaration. With the alleged cause removed, the same critics contend that the war, with one exception, was a military disaster, and that the one exception, the Battle of New Orleans, took place after the war was officially over. In retrospect the cause of the War of 1812 seems to have been American frustration at the refusal of the major powers to take the new nation seriously, and its need to justify its honor and independence, rather than any specific British act.[71]

Andrew Jackson was a war hawk. His military ambition had been stymied following the Dickinson duel and the collapse of the Burr plot. He had retired once again to the Hermitage, expanding it from its original 420 acres to 640, adding more slaves as he went along. He still was offering to raise troops against anyone: Spanish, British, French, Native American Indian, or any combination thereof. Until 1812 his offers were ignored. Then, anticipating a declaration of war, Congress authorized the enlistment of fifty thousand volunteers. Jackson moved swiftly. He was never more eloquent than when issuing calls to arms. "The hour of national vengeance is now at hand," he proclaimed on March 7. He expected that Tennessee volunteers, "full of martial ardor, indignant at their countries wrongs, and burning with impatience to illustrate their names by some signal exploit," were ready to march. For what were they to fight? Jackson combined both the maritime grievances of the East with the expansion opportunities of the West. He listed the complaints against Britain and the objectives of the war: "the protection of our maritime citizens, impressed on board British ships of war and compelled to fight the battles of our enemies against ourselves; to vindicate our right to a free trade, and open a market for the productions of our soil, now perishing on our hands because the *mistress of the ocean* has forbid us to carry them to any foreign nation." But he hinted at other results of the war's outcome as well. It might be necessary, he concluded, to guard against future aggression by "the conquest of all the British dominions" in North America. In that case, "how pleasing the prospect that would open to the young volunteer ... to view the stupendous works of nature, exemplified in the falls of Niagara."[72] When news arrived in June that President Madison had at last received the declaration of war, Jackson was delighted.

However, his thirst for action went unfulfilled again. Instead of viewing Niagara Falls, Jackson was ordered to prepare a detachment of Tennessee militia to be sent to New Orleans, possibly with the intention of attacking Spanish-held Florida. He put together a contingent of about fourteen hundred troops and sent them by boat down the Mississippi to Natchez, where they would await orders to proceed to New Orleans. The orders never came. Instead, Jackson was dismissed with thanks, ordered to turn over his troops and equipment to another command, and return to Tennessee. Furious, Jackson typically blamed unnamed conspirators against him, either those who were still linking him to the Burr affair or weak-willed civilians in Washington. He had little confidence in Madison, to whom he complained, "The misfortunes of our Country and the loss of our military reputation [require] every nerve to support the contest in which we are engaged."[73]

He then defied his orders and marched with his troops back to Nashville. It was a painful trek, but his willingness to share the cold and privation with his men earned him a reputation for toughness and determination that offset his disregard of orders. It was here, on the march from Natchez to Nashville in the winter of 1813, that the soldiers first started calling Andrew Jackson "Old Hickory"—a testament to his toughness and reliability. "Long will their General live in the memory of his volunteers of West Tennessee," shouted the Nashville *Whig* after his return. Memories of the Dickinson affair and the Burr conspiracy evaporated.[74] Jackson was about to move from local standing in Tennessee to national status.

But not before he became involved in yet another brawl. Again the circumstances were complicated, though centered around a duel between a friend, William Carroll, and his hotheaded opponent, Jesse Benton. In the spring of 1813 Carroll enlisted Jackson as his second, following Benton's challenge. Reluctantly the forty-six-year-old Jackson agreed and proceeded to advise the younger Carroll on strategy and positioning. The duel ended with Benton firing from a squatting position—a violation of the rules—and being ignominiously shot by Carroll through both buttocks. Only slightly wounded, the triumphant Carroll walked off the field.[75]

It should have ended there, but word of Benton's humiliation and alleged cowardice reached his older brother, Thomas Hart Benton, up to then a friend of Jackson's in the Tennessee militia. Thomas criticized Jackson for involving himself in the duel in the first place and, though not formally challenging him, made it clear that their friendship was over. Then Jackson and two of his friends ran into the Benton brothers in the City Hotel in Nashville. Words flew. Pistols and swords were drawn. Jesse Benton shot Jackson twice, wounding him severely in the arm and shoulder. His brother tried to shoot him again, missing before fleeing into the hotel. Bystanders intervened and carried the heavily bleeding Jackson to a nearby inn. Rejecting the advice of physicians to have his arm amputated, Jackson remained bedridden for three weeks. He now carried Jesse Benton's bullets in his shoulder as well as Dickinson's in his chest.[76]

While recovering from his wounds, Jackson learned of a bloody attack by Creek Indians on Fort Mims that summer, near the present Florida-Alabama border. More than 250 men, women, and children were massacred. The attack was part of the plan of the great warrior chief Tecumseh to unite all the Indian tribes and drive the white man once and for all from North America. With the onset of the War of 1812, Tecumseh and his allies had help and encouragement from both the British and the Spanish. Panic swept through western Tennessee. Frontier communities lived in daily fear of an attack and looked to Jackson's militia for protection. Jackson, who already favored action against the Indians before they could be "supported by their allies the British and the Spaniards," was only too happy to oblige.

That September, still weak and with one arm useless after the brawl with the Bentons, Jackson issued another call to arms. The long-awaited opportunity both to obtain military glory and to rid the southwest frontier of the twin threat posed by Indians and Europeans had at last arrived. Calling for "retaliatory vengeance" against the Creeks, Jackson urged Tennesseans not to "await the slow and tardy orders" of the Madison administration, but to move immediately. He assured them his health was restored. He would lead them in person.[77]

With financial and logistical help from Tennessee's governor Willie Blount (the half-brother of his earlier patron), Jackson proposed to march his militia of five thousand volunteers south through Alabama Territory all the way to the Gulf Coast, destroying the Creeks as he went. He would be aided in this by two detachments from the U.S. Army, one from Georgia and the other from Mississippi Territory. He would be joined also by a small contingent of Creeks and Cherokees who prudently decided to align themselves with the whites. Supplies were late in coming, but Jackson was determined to march, even with winter approaching. He set out in October 1813. A month later his forces surrounded the Creek fortress of Tallushatchee and systematically slaughtered nearly all of its inhabitants. "We shot them like dogs," the young Davy Crockett later remembered. "We have retaliated for the destruction of Fort Mims," Jackson reported to Governor Blount.[78] He was not through, however.

A week later he came to the aid of a group of friendly Creeks and routed another Indian force, leaving three hundred warriors dead, losing only fifteen of his own soldiers.

At this point trouble broke out. Both the regulars and the militia, citing the victories over the Creeks, the shortness of supplies, and the end of what they believed to be their commitment, proposed to return home. Jackson would have none of it. There was still work to be done. The arrival of supplies temporarily defused the crisis, but when a detachment of militia started to march back to Tennessee anyway they were confronted by an angry Jackson, who loudly threatened to shoot the first man who contin- ued on. No one dared to test his determination; the men turned back.

Two more attempts at mutiny occurred before the year was out, each with the same result. In the latter case Jackson threatened the mutineers with artillery fire before they changed their minds. To further his point he arrested two generals who had questioned his disciplinary methods and sent them home. An eighteen-year-old militiaman, John Woods, engaged in a fight with an officer from another unit, in which Woods lost his temper and unwisely grabbed a rifle, threatening to shoot any- one who laid hands on him. Being informed that another "mutiny" was under way, Jackson had Woods arrested and court-martialed. Upon his conviction, and in spite of several pleas for clemency, Jackson was deter- mined to make an example of the unfortunate Woods. He had him shot by a firing squad in front of the entire army. At least six other militiamen were also put on trial for desertion. These confrontations strengthened Jackson's image as a determined and courageous leader on one hand, and a ruthless and violent one on the other. On the southern frontier these characteristics were seen neither as contradictory nor negative. Even among his occasionally rebellious troops, whom he characterized privately as "mere, wining, complaining, Sedioners [seditioners]," his reputation for single-minded determination against all opposition was steadily enhanced.[79]

And he still was not through with the Creeks. He struck again in March 1814, this time with fresh recruits, at the Creek fortress at Horse- shoe Bend. Located on the Coosa River, it housed over a thousand war- riors and about three hundred women. Led by the young ensign Sam Houston, Jackson's forces, which again included friendly Creeks and Cherokees, breached the well-built earthworks and poured into the stronghold. Nearly nine hundred Indians were killed, while Jackson lost only 47 killed and another 159 wounded. In a report to General Thomas

Pinckney, his commanding officer in the regular army, he announced that he was "determined to exterminate" the Creeks.[80]

The Battle of Horseshoe Bend remains one of the bloodiest single encounters between whites and Indians ever to take place on the North American continent. The Creek nation was finished as a military force, and the vast territory stretching from Tennessee south to the Gulf of Mexico lay open for white expansion. The ensuing Treaty of Fort Jackson forced the defeated Creeks to give up most of what is now the state of Alabama. It "cedes to US 20 million acres of the cream Creek Country, opening a communication from Georgia to Mobile," Jackson exulted to John Overton, his old friend from the Donelson boarding-house.[81] The Treaty made no distinction between those Creeks who had supported him and those who had not. They all were Indians, and as such had to make way for the white man. The Creeks began to call Jackson "Sharp Knife." That spring Jackson returned in triumph to Nashville.

Jackson's attitude toward Native Americans is more complex than it might seem. Undoubtedly he regarded them as culturally and probably racially inferior. He believed, along with many others, that they would be better off in isolation from whites. To argue that he despised the natives, however, would be an overstatement. In warfare he was ruthless, even cruel. In peacetime he quickly assumed the paternal stance of most white leaders, using the standard vocabulary when dealing with the "children" of the forest. Because Jackson had no children of his own, this has led to a certain amount of psychoanalytic speculation on the part of modern historians and biographers. Unlike any of his critics, Jackson and his wife adopted an infant Creek, orphaned in one of Jackson's military engagements. Lyncoya, as he came to be called, lived in the Jackson household until he was apprenticed to a saddler in Nashville. Jackson's letters to him are worded no differently from those he wrote to his white dependents. Lyncoya died in 1828, in the midst of the election of that year, age sixteen.[82]

In 1814 the Madison administration, which had been wary of Jackson, at last took notice of him. "Without the personal firmness, popularity, and exertions of that officer," wrote one of the regular army generals to his civilian superiors in Washington, "the Indian war, on the part of Tennessee, would have been abandoned, at least for a time."[83] In contrast to the failures elsewhere, Jackson alone had a record of success. In June the president appointed him to the regular U.S. Army with the rank of major general. His command now covered not only Tennessee but the

Mississippi Territory, the Creek Nation, Louisiana, and, with it, the city of New Orleans.

While Jackson was chalking up victories over the Creeks, John Quincy Adams was back in Europe. His defection from the Federalists had been rewarded with his appointment by President Madison as the first American minister to Russia. In the summer of 1809 he left Boston, bound for Russia and its capital, St. Petersburg. He would not return for another eight years.

When Adams arrived in Russia Czar Alexander I was allied with France and Napoleon Bonaparte against Great Britain. But in the course of the next few years Alexander and Napoleon became alienated from one another, culminating in the latter's spectacular but doomed invasion of Russia in 1812, just as Britain and the United States went to war. Alexander now hoped that his new ally, Britain, could be extricated from the war with its former colonies in order to be free for the main event against France.[84]

Unlike Jackson, Adams was not a war hawk. War with Britain made no sense, he said, because commerce, the source of the conflict, would be destroyed entirely if war broke out. Moreover, he told his brother Thomas, should Americans be sucked into the vortex of the Anglo-French conflict, no matter the side, Americans "could scarcely hope for a better fate than to be sacrificed as one of the victims at its close." He did not learn of the declaration of war until two months after it was made. When he did, however, he reversed himself and defended the war against all comers. "No nation," he told William Plumer, a fellow ex-Federalist, "can be independent which suffers its citizens to be stolen from her at the discretion of the naval and military officers of another."[85] Jackson could not have put it better. Word reached Adams of opposition to the war in his own Massachusetts and throughout New England, including among relatives and former friends. There was even talk of New England's secession from the Union. Wasn't the lesson of a quarreling and bleeding Europe plain enough? Adams asked his mother. Unless the forces that threatened to pull the nation apart were crushed, he fumed, the republican experiment created by the Founders was doomed. "Instead of a nation coextensive with the North American continent, destined by God and nature to be the most populous and most powerful people ever combined under one social compact, we shall have an endless multitude of little insignificant clans and tribes at eternal war with one another for a rock, or a fish pond, the sport and fable of European masters and oppressors."[86]

Jackson's victories over the Indians notwithstanding, the war was not going well. In the North the fort at Detroit surrendered almost as soon as hostilities began. New England sat on its hands. At sea, after a scattering of victories principally involving the USS *Constitution* ("Old Ironsides"), the tiny U.S. Navy had been manhandled by the much larger Royal Navy. President Madison, already sensing the futility of the war, took advantage of Czar Alexander's offer of mediation, and in 1813 appointed a high-level delegation to go to Europe and participate in negotiations. The British rejected Alexander's offer but substituted a proposal of their own: face-to-face negotiations between the two sides at a mutually agreeable neutral site. Madison accepted. The American delegation would be headed by his minister to Russia, John Quincy Adams. The site selected was the city of Ghent in what is now Belgium.

Adams was building a reputation for aggressiveness and determination in diplomacy that matched Jackson's on the battlefield. He did not fit the stereotype of the clever and manipulative diplomat. "Of all the men whom it was ever my lot to accost and waste civilities upon," wrote an Englishman who knew him at the time, Adams "was the most dogged and systemically repulsive. With a vinegar aspect [i.e., facial expression], cotton in his leathern ears, and hatred to England in his heart, he sat in the frivolous assemblies of St. Petersburg like a bull-dog among spaniels."[87] Adams's patriotism was as deep as Jackson's. So was his republicanism. "My duty to my country is in my mind the first and most imperious of all obligations," he told Louisa Johnson, his English-born fiancée, in 1796, "before which every interest and every feeling inconsistent with it must forever disappear."[88] In the spring of 1814, as Jackson prepared to negotiate with the defeated Creeks, Adams headed for Ghent to negotiate with Great Britain, the world's leading naval power.

"I owe to Britain a debt of retaliatory vengeance," wrote Jackson to his wife that summer. "Should our forces meet," he added, "I trust I shall pay the debt. She is in conjunction with Spain arming the hostile Indians to butcher our women and children."[89] Although Spain was technically a neutral power, it clearly was allowing the British to occupy and arm parts of Spanish Florida, including the fort at Pensacola. After warning the Spanish governor, Jackson marched his army first to the U.S. fort at Mobile, then east to Pensacola, forcing the British to withdraw. Only upon his return to Mobile in mid-November 1814 did he learn that a British fleet of sixty ships and seventeen thousand men had sailed from Jamaica and was headed for New Orleans. Capture of that city would mark a successful conclusion for the British in the War of 1812. In a hasty note to his wife, Jackson asked that she meet him in New Orleans. He arrived on December 1, 1814.[90]

On that very day, four thousand miles to the east, Adams was sitting down with four American colleagues, including Albert Gallatin, Thomas Jefferson's former treasury secretary, and Henry Clay, whose career would cross both Adams's and Jackson's in the years to come. They faced a three-man delegation from London, who earlier had sent them newspapers reporting that the British Army had ransacked the city of Washington, burned its public buildings, and chased President Madison and his wife to the safety of Virginia. On the continent, Napoleon had surrendered to the allied powers of Britain, Russia, Prussia, and Austria. Now, freed from their entanglement with Napoleon, the British were confident that the sacking of Washington, combined with the capture of New Orleans, would put an end to the annoying war with the Americans, up to then a mere sideshow to the larger conflict in Europe. "I do not think that the negotiation will be of long continuance," Adams wrote to his wife in Russia not long after his arrival.[91]

Adams and his colleagues were under instructions to sign no treaty that did not require the British to abandon the practice of impressment. The three British delegates were under instructions to demand an Indian buffer zone between the United States and Canada that would block western expansion by the Americans, extending roughly from a line drawn through the present state of Ohio, closing off all of the present states of Illinois, Wisconsin, and Minnesota. Adams was indignant. If Great Britain was intending to restrict the westward settlement of the American people, he pointedly remarked, "she must not think of doing it by a treaty. She must formally undertake, and accomplish, their utter extermination." Nothing else, he declared, could stop what a later generation would call "Manifest Destiny."[92]

Fortunately, both sides received later instructions to retreat from their initial positions. Although news of the sacking of Washington dispirited the Americans, they were encouraged by subsequent news that the British had failed to take Baltimore ("The flag was still there," as Francis Scott Key's poem would recall) and of an American victory at Plattsburgh, New York, which guaranteed them control of the Great Lakes. If they were aware as well of Jackson's victory over the Creeks there is no record of it. Gradually the two sides inched toward one another as they began to contemplate a final settlement based on the principle of *status quo ante bellum:* each side reverting to the boundaries established prior to the war. "For the first time I now entertain hope that the British government is inclined to conclude the peace," Adams could report to his wife.[93]

In the meantime Jackson was rallying the people of New Orleans.[94] It was not an easy task: morale was low, supplies were short, and the defense force consisted of only seven hundred men. It had been only eleven years since this heady mixture of twenty thousand French-speaking, Spanish-speaking, German-speaking, and English-speaking residents, not to mention a contingent of both slave and free African Americans, had become part of the United States. There were still many in 1814 who doubted that their absorption into the United States would last. In a brief address Jackson announced that he had come to save the city. He called on the citizens to lay aside whatever ethnic grievances or feuds they may have had in the past. His remarks were translated into French by an old colleague and fellow former congressman, Edward Livingston, formerly of New York, now of Louisiana. Although no one saw any need to mention it then, Livingston was among the handful of congressmen in 1796 who, along with Jackson, had voted against the resolution of thanks to the departing President Washington.

To defend the city successfully Jackson needed all the help he could get. This included the famed Baratarian pirates under Jean Lafitte and two battalions of free blacks. Jackson told Governor Claiborne of Louisiana, "The free men of colour...are inured to the Southern climate and would make excellent Soldiers. They will not remain quiet spectators of the interesting contest."[95] Jackson later personally reviewed both battalions and promised each man the regular bounty of 160 acres of land and $124 in cash. But his best hope lay in his fellow Tennesseans, two thousand of whom were slowly descending the Mississippi, with another two thousand waiting at Baton Rouge.

Upon inspecting the Mississippi River downstream, Jackson concluded, rightly enough, that a British invasion by the river route would be foolhardy because the fleet would be vulnerable to attack from both banks. A more logical approach would be via Lake Borgne just east of

New Orleans. The lake could be easily crossed, after which troops could be landed only a few miles from the city. This indeed proved to be the choice. The British squadron appeared offshore on December 13 and on the following day routed the small American force from Lake Borgne. The citizens of New Orleans panicked. Jackson declared martial law over the objections of the state legislature. He organized a review of the existing troops in front of the city cathedral, where Livingston read Jackson's call to arms, intended to reassure the citizenry of their eventual success:

> Fellow citizens of every description! remember for what and against whom you contend. For all that can render life desirable—for a country blessed with every gift of nature—for property, for life—for those dearer than either, your wives and children—and for liberty, dearer than all, without which country, life, property, are no longer worth possessing.... You are to contend for all this against an enemy whose continued effort is to deprive you of the last of these blessings—who avows a war of vengeance and desolation, proclaimed and marked by cruelty, lust, and horrours unknown to civilized nations.[96]

Whatever misgivings the citizens had about Jackson's leadership evaporated.

On December 22 the British crossed the swampland between Lake Borgne and the Mississippi. They were then ten miles south of the city, with dry land in front of them and the Mississippi to their left. Jackson defiantly advanced to a canal only five hundred yards from the British lines and proceeded to construct a formidable rampart five feet high and twenty feet deep. The British, now commanded by the Duke of Wellington's brother-in-law, Sir Edward Pakenham, chose to await more troops, believing, erroneously as it turned out, that Jackson had more men than he actually had. It was a fatal mistake, giving Jackson time to assemble fresh troops from Tennessee, Kentucky, and Louisiana. When the assault finally came Jackson had more than four thousand soldiers in his command, plus another thousand in reserve, about the same number as Pakenham.

On January 8, 1815, the British launched their frontal assault against Jackson's entrenched forces. When it was over, Pakenham was dead and the invaders had lost over two thousand men, killed, wounded, or captured, to the Americans' seventy-one. The city was saved, American pride was restored, and the nation had a new hero. "ALMOST INCREDIBLE

VICTORY!," "GLORIOUS NEWS," "GLORIOUS!!!," "UNPARAL-
LELED VICTORY," "RISING GLORY OF THE AMERICAN
REPUBLIC!"—these are only a few examples of the headlines in the
newspapers of early February 1815 once the news arrived from New
Orleans.[97]

Then came the news that John Quincy Adams and his colleagues had
successfully concluded their negotiations with the British on Christmas
Eve 1814, two weeks before the battle. The war ended on the basis of status
quo ante bellum. The issues that had allegedly caused it—impressment
and the rights of neutrals in wartime—were not mentioned. Adams
expressed his hope that it would be the last treaty of peace between Great
Britain and the United States.[98]

Thus it was that in 1815 Andrew Jackson and John Quincy Adams,
who would clash in a bitter presidential election thirteen years later, first
made their mark.

The story of Jackson's victory over the British at New Orleans would
become one of the great tales of the American saga. Americans were
vicariously purged of shame and frustration. At a moment of disillusion-
ment the outcome reaffirmed the young nation's self-belief, restoring a
sense of national prowess and destiny. Orations would be proclaimed,
songs would be sung, novels would be written, and even movies made,
all celebrating the great event.[99] It was not a mere military triumph. The
victory came to be symbolic of a young, vibrant America defeating an old,
effete Europe. "Never did a country occupy more lofty ground," rejoiced
a Supreme Court justice. "We have stood the contest, single-handed,
against the conqueror of Europe; and we are at peace, with all our blushing victories thick crowding on us."[100]

Americans were told that the invaders had more on their mind than
capturing the city. "Beauty and Booty," it was said, without much evidence, were the twin aims of the presumably sex-starved hordes. But
bold, unlettered, untrained frontiersmen, fresh from the countryside, had
beaten back the uniformed invaders from the sea and saved endangered
female virtue. Although most of the British casualties were the result
of murderous artillery fire, the legend nonetheless grew that volunteer
sharpshooters from the forest, with their trusty rifles, had carried the
day against the feckless conscripted offscourings from the Old World.
A popular folk song, "The Hunters of Kentucky," recounted the story

of the battle in countless music halls throughout the nation for the next thirty years. (Jackson in fact had been highly critical of the late arrival of the Kentucky militiamen, but no matter.) America versus Europe, the West versus the East, the Forest versus the City, Virtuous Innocence versus Sophisticated Depravity—all came to be wrapped up in the legends attached to the Battle of New Orleans. So too, in time, did they become wrapped up in the man who personified the triumph.[101]

Upon learning of the victory, but before learning of the Treaty of Ghent, Congress unanimously adopted a resolution of thanks "to Major General Jackson, and through him, to the officers and soldiers of the regular army, of the volunteers, and of the militia under his command...for their uniform gallantry and good conduct displayed against the enemy, from the time of his landing before New Orleans until his expulsion therefrom." The resolution further asked the president of the United States "to cause to be struck a gold medal, with devices emblematical of this splendid achievement, and presented to General Jackson as a testimony of the high sense entertained by Congress of his judicious and distinguished conduct on that memorable occasion."[102]

As had happened so often before, in the midst of a triumph Jackson managed to embroil himself in yet another dispute that threatened to undermine all he had achieved. In early January he refused to lift the martial law he had declared before the battle. For all he knew, the war was still on. He signed off on the order of execution for six Tennessee militiamen for alleged mutiny during the Creek campaign in Alabama months before. Even after rumors of the Ghent settlement arrived he refused to restore civilian rule. The Louisiana legislature responded by adopting a resolution in February thanking by name all the leading officers in the army except Jackson. When French-descended citizens of the city claimed French citizenship and therefore discharge from military service, Jackson ordered them out of the city. When an article appeared in the French-language newspaper *Le Courriere de la Louisiana* criticizing him, Jackson had the author, Louis Louailler, arrested. When a New Orleans judge, Dominick Hall, issued a writ of habeas corpus freeing Louailler, Jackson had Judge Hall arrested too, accusing him of "aiding abetting and exciting mutiny" in the city.[103] When a court-martial acquitted Louailler, Jackson set aside the verdict and hustled Judge Hall out of the city. Only when official word of the ratification of the Treaty of Ghent arrived in March did Jackson lift martial law in New Orleans.

But that was not the end of it. A week later the newly emancipated Judge Hall ordered Jackson to appear before him to show cause why he should not be held in contempt of court for refusal to obey his writ. Jackson appeared, now dressed in civilian attire and accompanied by his attorney, the faithful Edward Livingston. After overruling defense objections to the case itself and after listening to Jackson's dignified defense of his actions, Judge Hall fined him one thousand dollars—no small sum in those days—but declined to throw him in jail. Jackson paid the fine. With civilian rule restored, his heroic stature was also restored, although the acting secretary of war pointedly reminded Jackson, "The President of the United States instructs me to take this opportunity of requesting that a conciliatory deportment be observed towards the State authorities and citizens of New Orleans."[104]

Jackson's difficulties with the civilian authorities in New Orleans were forgotten. Like the Dickinson duel and the brawl with the Bentons, they would be resurrected a decade later, when he emerged as a presidential candidate. They were evidence of the reckless side of his character that in the past had limited his effectiveness in Congress, drawn him into brawls and duels, led him to insist on the execution of one of his own militiamen, and created at least the appearance of a man whose audacity could place him outside the law. Whether such recklessness and audacity would prove a liability in the nation at large remained to be seen.

That April, Jackson, accompanied by Rachel, began what turned out to be a triumphal tour, first to Nashville and then to Washington. On his way he passed through Virginia and the town of Lynchburg, whose residents turned out en masse to greet him. Among the throng was the seventy-two-year-old Thomas Jefferson, who made a rare descent from his mountaintop home to salute the victor of New Orleans; whatever reservations Jefferson may have had about Jackson were held in abeyance. Upon his arrival in the nation's capital, Jackson was met by President Madison, who had also harbored reservations about him but who nonetheless honored him at an elaborate reception at the Executive Mansion.

Already Jackson was being referred to as "the Hero." John Reid, one of his aides at New Orleans, had begun a biography of him, which after Reid's death was completed by Jackson's fellow Tennessean John Henry Eaton and published in 1817.[105] An admirer had written him in February, "The Immortal Honor which you have *Honistly & Gallantly* won was proof that you ought to fill the Chair of the Chief magestrate of this Union in march 1817." There could be "little doubt," another wrote in

October, that "with the proper management of your friends" he could be elected "to the highest Office in the American Government."[106] And Aaron Burr, back from exile in Europe, told his son-in-law, "If...there be a man in the United States of firmness and decision, and having standing enough to afford even a hope of success, it is your duty to hold him up to public view: that man is *Andrew Jackson*."[107]

John Quincy Adams's reward for his services at Ghent was to be promoted by President Madison in 1815 to the post of American minister to Great Britain, the highest ranking diplomatic position then available to an American and one his father had held in the 1780s. From London, Adams followed events at home in 1816, an election year. Two Republicans, Secretary of State James Monroe and Secretary of the Treasury William Crawford, were both candidates to succeed Madison, who, like Washington and Jefferson before him, declined to serve a third term. Consistent with earlier practice, the Republicans would choose between the two in a congressional caucus of all Republican congressmen and senators. Looking on from London, Adams could not help but favor Monroe because his vacating the post of secretary of state might open it up for Adams himself. His parents urged him to come home and be more visible, yet he resisted. "I have made it the general principle of my life," he told his father while awaiting the results of the election, "to take the situation assigned to me by the regular authority of my country."[108] He would not maneuver to seek any appointment. For true republicans civic office was not a prize to be connived at by the ambitious.

Early in 1817 Adams learned not only that Monroe had succeeded Madison as president but also that, with the Senate's approval, Monroe had indeed appointed him secretary of state. "I have thought it advisable to select a person for the Department of State from the eastern states," Monroe explained to Jefferson, "in consequence of which my attention has been turned to Mr. Adams, who by his age, long experience in our foreign affairs, and adoption into the republican party, seems to have superior qualifications to any there."[109]

"I have no hesitation in saying," Jackson told Monroe, "you have made the best selection, to fill the Department of State, that could be made. Mr Adams in the hour of dificulty will be an able helpmate, and I am convinced his appointment will afford general satisfaction."[110]

★ Chapter Two ★

In 1817 Andrew Jackson and John Quincy Adams each turned fifty. They belonged to what might be called the "second generation" of American political leaders, born in the eighteenth century but too young to have played any significant role in the outcome of either the American Revolution or the establishment of the Republic. (Jackson's teenage confrontation with the British officer would nonetheless be highlighted in his presidential campaigns.) Their contemporaries, all of whom emerged on the national scene in the years following the War of 1812, included Henry Clay of Kentucky, John C. Calhoun of South Carolina, and Martin Van Buren of New York, each of whom was destined to play a significant role in the lives of both Jackson and Adams. The new president, James Monroe, however, belonged to the "first generation," along with Washington, Jefferson, Madison, and John Adams. The "last of the cocked hats," Monroe took the oath of office in March 1817 wearing the knee breeches and shoe buckles of an earlier day.[1]

Jackson's health was not good. In addition to the pain caused by the bullets he carried from his duels with Dickinson and the Bentons, he was subject to continual attacks of dysentery. His lungs were weak, which frequently produced prolonged fits of coughing. His prematurely white hair and angular, even emaciated frame projected the image of a man whose days were numbered, as he himself believed. One who saw him at New Orleans described him as "a long haggard man, with limbs like a skeleton."[2] But this was offset by the effect of his piercing blue eyes, which, according to witnesses, transfixed those who engaged his attention. When Andrew Jackson walked into a room he was difficult to ignore.

One could not say the same about John Quincy Adams. An admittedly hostile American observer who knew him in Russia wrote, "[Adams] has no manners, is gauche, never was intended for a Foreign Minister, and is only fit to turn over musty law authorities. You would blush to see him in society ... walking about perfectly listless, speaking to no one, and absolutely looking as if he were in a dream." Adams was of modest height, balding, and plagued with watery eyes, brought on, some said, by his excessive nighttime reading. He would fight a continual battle against stoutness, which he tried to offset by rigorous exercise. In London, and later in Washington, he could be seen jogging about the streets in the early morning hours. In the Washington summers he would swim in the Potomac, sometimes wearing what passed for a swimming suit, sometimes nothing at all. Adams seemed to agree with his critics. "I am a man of reserved, cold, austere, and forbidding manners," he admitted to his diary, "my political adversaries say, a gloomy misanthropist, and my personal enemies, an unsocial savage." He admitted there wasn't much he could do about it.[3]

In 1817, with the end of the Anglo-French war, Americans were turning their attention away from Europe, with its constant threat of "foreign entanglement," and toward the West, with its potential for profit, renewal, and adventure. They swarmed over the Appalachian Mountains, down the Ohio River, and across the Mississippi. Six new states, all but one of them from beyond the Appalachians, entered the Union during Monroe's first term. The rise of the "new West" altered the political scenery, for now people thought in terms of three great sections instead of two. "Old America," wrote an English observer in 1817, "seems to be breaking up and moving westward."[4]

In that same year the state of New York, hoping both to encourage and to benefit from the westward migration, began work on the Erie Canal, which, when completed eight years later, would link the Great Lakes with New York City and the Atlantic Ocean.[5] The canal was part of what later would be called the Transportation Revolution, which made the movement of both commodities and individuals in the North easier, cheaper, and safer. It scattered Americans throughout the North in greater numbers than before and at the same time encouraged the growth of cities in the Northeast.[6] In the South, with the Indian presence in retreat, thousands of settlers were flocking to the rich soil the Indians had been forced to abandon and looked hungrily at what little the Indians still occupied. The availability of slave labor, combined with improved technology and access to cheap land, laid the groundwork for an immense cotton boom that would dominate the South's economy for most of the nineteenth century.

Not only was the geographic landscape changing; metaphorically, there were shifts in the tectonic plates that underlay the social, intellectual, and economic landscapes as well. The result would become evident in the emergence of a new political culture, one quite different from that of the Founders' generation.

In the summer of 1817 President Monroe made a goodwill tour of the northern states. Its high point was a six-day visit to the city of Boston, for most Republicans the capital of Federalist enemy territory. After a series of public appearances, the president journeyed out to Quincy, where he met and dined with a former political adversary, John Adams. With Monroe's recent appointment of the old man's son as secretary of state, a pleasant conversation no doubt followed. Abigail Adams presented the president with a white and a red rose intertwined: "York and Lancaster united," she reported happily to a friend. A Federalist newspaper editorial summed up the spirit of Monroe's visit when it declared that an "Era of Good Feelings" had arrived.[7] Though subsequent events would prove it to be misleading, the phrase has stuck ever since as a description of postwar America. At the time it appeared that partisan bickering between Federalists and Republicans was at an end.

Most Americans welcomed the end of party conflict. Former presidents John Adams and Thomas Jefferson had already restored their broken friendship in 1812 and had begun a famous exchange of letters and reminiscences that would continue for the rest of their lives. Mathew Carey, a Philadelphia pamphleteer and sometime economist, issued a treatise titled *The Olive Branch, or Faults on Both Sides, Federal and Democratic—A Serious Appeal on the Necessity of Mutual Forgiveness and Harmony, Dedicated to a Beloved but Bleeding Country, Torn in Pieces by Factious and Ruinous Contests for Power.* Carey argued that in general the Federalists had had the better case regarding domestic questions, but that the Republicans were closer to America's true interests in foreign affairs. *The Olive Branch* went through several editions.[8]

As for the new president, there was a time when Monroe had been one of the most partisan of Republicans. His states' rights, strict construction ideology was such that, unlike Jefferson and Madison, he had opposed the adoption of the Constitution in 1788. George Washington nonetheless appointed him American minister to France in the 1790s. His outspoken opposition to his own country's foreign policy, including Jay's Treaty, led to his recall. As a congressman his partisanship nearly provoked a duel with Alexander Hamilton. He once even contemplated challenging President John Adams himself. But in the intervening years Monroe had mellowed, as his visit to Boston suggested. The end of the War of 1812, he hoped, would be a turning point, an end to the partisanship that had divided Americans throughout his mature years, and a return to true republican virtue and simplicity.[9]

Some people think, he wrote, that "free government cannot exist without parties." He disagreed. "Discord," he declared in his Inaugural Address, "does not belong to our system."[10] Writing to the president-elect from Tennessee, Andrew Jackson supported nonpartisanship for choosing a cabinet: "Party feelings, ought to be laid out of view, for now is the time to put them down." From London, John Quincy Adams, too, agreed that the time had come for "the wise and honest men" of both parties to "discard their prejudices and turn the experience of the war to the benefit of their common country."[11] Nothing, perhaps, symbolized the spirit of the Era of Good Feelings more than Monroe's appointment of the younger Adams, a former Federalist, to the premier position in his cabinet, and one from which Monroe himself, as well as Madison and Jefferson before him, had eventually gone on to serve as president.

The Federalists helped Monroe by committing political suicide. In late 1814, as Jackson was rallying the citizens of New Orleans and Adams was signing the Treaty of Ghent, a group of New England Federalists met at Hartford, Connecticut. The Hartford Convention, as it came to be known, had been called by the Federalist-controlled Massachusetts legislature to discuss the means by which New England could more effectively challenge the War of 1812, or what they liked to call "Mr. Madison's War." A few of the more extremist delegates, urged on by former secretary of state Timothy Pickering, were even prepared to contemplate secession from the Union if the war did not end. Most were moderates, however, seeking ways to arrest what they correctly perceived to be the declining influence of their region and their party—which for them was pretty much the same thing.

No record of their day-to-day deliberations exists.[12] Their final report, though not mentioning or even hinting at secession, denounced the war and called for a number of constitutional amendments intended to preserve New England's status in the nation, including an end to the "three-fifths" clause that gave southern states representation for their slaves. The report was issued on January 5, 1815. Three days later Jackson and his men triumphed over the British at New Orleans. Six weeks later news of the Treaty of Ghent arrived.

The Federalists never recovered. The Hartford Convention remains one of the all-time leading examples of poor political timing. It was seen at best as an example of selfish sectionalism, and at worst as seditious treason. "As for our beloved native New England," Adams wrote from London to William Eustis, a fellow Yankee, "I blush to think of the part she has performed, for her shame is still the disgrace of the nation." Jackson was more blunt. "Had I commanded the military Department where the Hartford convention met," he later told Monroe, "if it had been the last act of my life, I should have hung up the principle leaders of the party.... These kind of men atho called Federalist, are really monarchrist, and traitors to the constituted government."[13] In opposing a war that most Americans believed had ended with a glorious victory, the Federalists placed themselves outside the pale of the consensus that emerged in the wake of the war. Although they remained a force to be reckoned with in a handful of states, including Massachusetts, Connecticut, and Delaware, their days as a national party were over. Those who still claimed the title were put on the defensive.

It is now clear to most historians that the American Revolution did more than sever the colonies' ties with the British Empire. It encouraged as well a newer version of republicanism that went beyond rejection of monarchy and aristocracy, beyond the alleged tension between liberty and power, and beyond the demand for simplicity in dress and manners. In the years following the adoption of the Constitution there emerged a growing and persistent demand for a broader voice in public affairs by those who in the past had been excluded by a lack of property. A younger generation of American republicans was prepared to argue that if the revolutionary mantra "No taxation without representation" was followed to its logical conclusion, those who are taxed should have a say in selecting who was to do the taxing.[14]

Not everyone was comfortable with this, including many of the revolutionary leaders themselves. John Adams, just before he signed the Declaration of Independence, was one. "Depend upon it, Sir," he lectured a fellow Massachusetts citizen, "it is dangerous to open so fruitful a source of controversy and altercation as would be opened by attempting to alter the qualifications of voters; there will be no end to it. New claims will arise; women will demand the vote; lads from twelve to twenty-one will think their rights not enough attended to; and every man who has not a farthing, will demand an equal voice with any other, in all acts of state."[15]

The elder Adams spoke for the eighteenth-century view of republicanism, common in both Britain and America. They believed that legitimate government rested on the consent of the governed, as Thomas Jefferson had famously stated, but they also believed that consent should be obtained only from those who had a "stake in society." In most cases this meant ownership of property, preferably real estate. Moreover, those without property—renters or employees, for example—inevitably would be intimidated or manipulated by those with property; consequently they had, as the phrase had it, "no will of their own." Eighteenth-century republicans, in other words, were not democrats. They were products of, and lived in, what has been frequently called a "deferential" society, one in which citizens were equal before the law, but which was still "leader-oriented."[16] Political power was in most cases reserved to "gentlemen of property and standing." Thus Founders such as John Adams, Alexander Hamilton, and James Madison had no difficulty connecting republican ideas of sturdy individual independence with a property qualification for voting. Even the young Andrew Jackson, as a member of the Tennessee Constitutional Convention, had favored a property qualification for officeholders, although not for voters.

Historians are not in agreement as to how limiting this qualification actually was, when land in America was more easily attained than in Europe. And while the older, property-oriented version of republicanism was in retreat in the years following the Revolution, there were limits to the new, revised version. With only a handful of exceptions, even the most radical of those who wished to expand the franchise in the Early Republic had no intention of expanding it beyond adult white males. With very few exceptions, females and black Americans, whether slave or free, would remain excluded from equal participation in the electorate for at least the next half-century.

Nonetheless, the tectonic plates were shifting, and the new republicanism was reflected in state constitutional changes. Maryland abolished the property requirement for voting as early as 1802, and New Jersey followed in 1807. Connecticut in 1818, Massachusetts in 1820, and New York in 1821 each held conventions whose main purpose was to lower the property requirement, if not abolish it entirely.[17] Newer states, such as Tennessee, Alabama, and Illinois, had few or no property requirements to begin with. Some replaced the property requirement with proof of taxpayer status or service in the militia, but these were not seen as major impediments. By 1824 only five states still required property ownership in order for an adult white male to cast a ballot. (Ironically, one of the five was Jefferson's Virginia.) As a result, in more and more cases candidates for public office had to appeal to a broader constituency than had those of the previous generation, and voter participation for state and local elections increased dramatically, even in those states that still restricted the franchise. Whereas only 31 percent of the adult white males in Massachusetts voted for governor in 1800, nearly twice as many showed up ten years later, and 68 percent voted in 1812. In that year adult white males in North Carolina voted for congressional candidates in spectacular fashion, ranging from 65 percent participation in one district to 90 percent in another.[18]

Another shift was the gradual divestiture by state legislatures of the power to choose presidential electors. The Constitution of 1787 left the method of selection up to the states. Few of the Founders expected rank-and-file voters to be involved in choosing a president, who, like the federal government itself, they expected to be "at a distance and out of sight," as Alexander Hamilton had put it in 1788. When Jefferson defeated Adams in 1800 the state legislatures in eleven of the sixteen states chose the presidential electors. By 1824 this was true of only six out of twenty-four, and by 1828 the number had dropped to two.

The combined results of these two shifts changed the nature of American political culture in general, and presidential elections in particular. In earlier years, when the voters were not directly involved in selecting a president, the largest voter turnout almost always occurred in contests for state office. Before 1824 the presidential popular vote topped the state popular vote in only two instances. By then the expansion of voter power had begun to have its effect. The number of voting districts increased while the size of the districts decreased, making it easier to get to the polls. Men whose perspective had never been broader than their personal concerns, or whose political involvement had hitherto been limited to state and local affairs, or who had been shut out entirely from voting now had the chance to participate in presidential elections as never before. Many grasped eagerly at the chance. How they would use it had yet to be determined.[19]

In 1816 the Federalists offered only token opposition to Monroe, carrying only three states. When Monroe stood for reelection four years later, the Republicans had the field to themselves. Indeed, one of the Monroe electors from Massachusetts was none other than John Adams. But while the end of national party competition resulted in a Republican monopoly, it did not mean the end of competition itself. John Quincy Adams had been in Washington for only a little over a year before he noted that affairs there were "assuming daily more and more a character of a cabal, and preparation, not for the next Presidential election, but for the one after."[20] Very few in 1818 would have predicted that Monroe's second term would be followed by an election pitting Jackson against Adams.

In retrospect it is easy to contrast the two, the northeastern Yankee and the southwestern frontiersman; the Man of Thought and the Man of Action. In time, John Quincy Adams of Massachusetts and Andrew Jackson of Tennessee would come to represent not only contrasting personalities but also opposing political values. In 1820, however, the differences had yet to emerge. Both were Republicans—Jackson from the very beginning and Adams a more recent convert. Both supported the War of 1812— again, Jackson from the very beginning and Adams from the moment he learned of Congress's declaration. Both were ardent expansionists. Jackson's military career had been focused on expelling any and all obstacles to that expansion, whether Spanish, British, or Native American Indian. Adams's diplomacy in Europe had similarly been grounded on the assumption that the United States was destined to be "a nation coextensive with the North American continent."[21]

Jackson's reputation was built not only on his victory at New Orleans, but on his determination to remove the American Indian from the path of white expansion, and nowhere was he more popular than on the southwestern frontier. Nonetheless the Yankee and the frontiersman were in remarkable accord. Like Jackson, Adams was no anthropologist. As early as 1802 he had derided "moralists" and "philanthropists" who claimed equal status for the European and the Indian.[22] Later, at Ghent, responding to the British proposal for an Indian buffer state, Adams trotted out the standard argument in favor of the white European: as mere hunters and gatherers, the natives used the land inefficiently when compared to the white man's agriculture. The British were fooling themselves, he told them, if they thought American expansion "could be long cramped or arrested by a treaty stipulation confining whole regions of territory to a few scattered hordes of savages, whose numbers to the end of ages would not amount to the population of one considerable city."[23] Although the British abandoned the proposal for a buffer state, they did insist on, and got, a clause in the Treaty of Ghent guaranteeing restoration of Indian lands taken as a result of the war. This in effect nullified portions of the Treaty of Fort Jackson, forced on the Creeks in 1814.

But in the months that followed the signing and ratification of the treaty Jackson proceeded to nullify the nullification. In 1815 President Madison made him military commander in charge of the U.S. Southern Department, with instructions from William H. Crawford, the new secretary of war, to "cooperate with all means in your power to conciliate the Indians, upon the principles of our agreement with Great Britain." Crawford then proceeded to negotiate a treaty with the Cherokees that restored some of the lands taken in the Treaty of Fort Jackson, plus about twenty-five thousand dollars for damages. Jackson was furious. The federal government should stop worrying about the rights of Indians, he thundered, and start worrying about the rights of its own citizens. Not wishing to challenge a popular war hero, Madison and Crawford backed off. In 1816 they set up a commission, with Jackson as a member, to renegotiate with the Choctaws, Chickasaws, and Cherokees, which resulted in their surrender of several million acres in addition to those already obtained from the Creeks. The British chose not to object to this obvious violation of the Treaty of Ghent. As a result, most of the Indians in the old Southwest were abandoned, and many of them fled to Spanish Florida.[24]

Not surprisingly, Jackson had the full support of the slaveholders and land speculators in Georgia and elsewhere who appreciated the value of the lands the Indians were being forced to abandon. From their perspective, the bigger threat was not so much the Indians in Georgia and Alabama as those Indians who had fled across the Spanish border to Florida.

Now calling themselves Seminoles, they were offering a haven for run-away slaves. Already in 1816 an American expedition crossed into Spanish territory and destroyed a "Negro Fort" on the Apalachicola River, killing some 270 Indians and escaped slaves. In November 1817 another expedition attacked an Indian settlement just north of the border. The Seminoles retaliated by ambushing and slaughtering an army convoy, including many women and children. Land speculators and slaveholders, including Jackson's friend John Henry Eaton, and John Donelson, Jackson's brother-in-law, demanded more action against the Seminoles, even if it meant an invasion of Spanish territory. The Spanish, for their part, professed to be unable to do anything about the Indians and their black allies.[25]

In December 1817 John C. Calhoun, the new secretary of war, directed General Edmund Gaines, then in command of the American troops in the region, to take whatever measures were necessary to "terminate" the conflict with the Seminoles. At the same time Gaines was ordered not to attack Spanish forts, even if they harbored Seminoles. Shortly thereafter Calhoun replaced Gaines with Jackson, although the orders and limitations presumably were the same.[26] Jackson chafed against the limitations. He believed that all of the Florida panhandle should be taken and "held as an indemnity for the outrages of Spain upon the property of our citizens," and said so in a letter addressed to President Monroe on January 6, 1818. Then he made an ominous suggestion: he was prepared not only to invade Florida but to seize it on behalf of the United States. "This can be done," he confidently told the president, without implicating the government. "Let it be signified to me through any channel (say Mr. J. Rhea [a congressman from Tennessee]) that the possession of the Floridas would be desirable to the United States, and in sixty days it will be accomplished."[27] In other words, to use a more modern expression, if Monroe wanted Florida, Jackson was offering him plausible deniability. All Monroe had to do was pass the word to Congressman Rhea, and Jackson would move.

In March Jackson crossed the Florida border, recapturing the old "Negro Fort" and fortifying it before turning east toward the Spanish settlement of St. Marks, which quickly surrendered. There he captured a Scotsman, Alexander Arbuthnot, whom the Americans had accused for several months of aiding and abetting the Seminoles. He held Arbuthnot for a future trial. Not so fortunate were two Seminole chieftains, Francis the Prophet and Himollemico. After being tricked by Jackson's crew flying the British Union Jack instead of the American Stars and Stripes, the two were captured and summarily hanged without a trial. So far as

Jackson was concerned, the rights normally extended to accused white men did not apply to Indians. "They will foment war no more," he grimly told his wife.[28]

Moving still further east toward Bowleg's Town, a haven for runaway slaves, Jackson captured seven runaways and another white, Robert Ambrister, who also stood charged with inciting the Seminoles. After torching the town, he returned to St. Marks. There he established a court-martial for Arbuthnot and Ambrister, on whom, he told Secretary Calhoun, they had found evidence "pointing out the Instigators of this savage war and in some measure involving the British Government in the Agency." Neither Arbuthnot nor Ambrister was afforded counsel, nor the opportunity to present witnesses. They were both tried, convicted, and sentenced within two days, Arbuthnot to be hanged and Ambrister to be whipped and put to hard labor for a year. Jackson overruled the Ambrister sentence and directed that both men be executed. The sentences were carried out the following day, thus avoiding any chance for an appeal. Jackson wrote confidently to Calhoun, "The execution of these Two unprincipled villains will prove an awfull example" to the British government and public. The facts later suggested that Arbuthnot was merely an idealist businessman who sympathized with the Indians but had tried to dissuade them from war-making. Ambrister was a soldier of fortune who indeed had encouraged the Seminoles to prepare for war— but against the Spanish, not the Americans.[29]

Then Jackson headed west with a force of twelve hundred men. This time the objective was the Spanish fort at Pensacola, on the Florida-Alabama border. It was weakly defended by the forces of the crumbling Spanish Empire, and after a token show of resistance it, too, fell to Jackson's army in late May. Jackson then announced the establishment of a provisional government for the territory. He told President Monroe that with some additional men he could capture St. Augustine on the Atlantic Coast; then he added that with some more help, "I will insure you Cuba in a few days."[30]

In little more than three months Jackson and his men had all but destroyed what was left of the Spanish Empire in Florida. He added to his reputation as an impulsive and hotheaded soldier, but also as a patriot who had the interests of the nation at heart—even if it meant breaking the law and disobeying orders. He also presented a major challenge to the new secretary of state, John Quincy Adams.

The implications of Jackson's Florida campaign were enormous. To invade the territory of one friendly nation was brazen enough, but to execute two citizens of another invited retaliation by either or both powers. Calls for Jackson's punishment echoed in London, Madrid, and Washington. The situation was further complicated by President Monroe's contention that he had not seen Jackson's letter of January 6, and that in fact no word had been passed to Congressman Rhea. Many years later Rhea claimed that he had indeed heard from Monroe, but his memory was fading by then, and it seems unlikely. In all probability Jackson acted on his own initiative.[31]

After waiting a full month for things to settle down Monroe consulted his cabinet. They were nearly united in the need to punish Jackson. Leading the charge was Jackson's embarrassed superior, Secretary Calhoun, who argued for censure and an official investigation. Although the restrictions regarding the Spanish forts had been sent to General Gaines and not to Jackson, Jackson had inherited Gaines's command and with it the limitations. Jackson had known this because he had remonstrated against them in his letter to the president. Supporting Calhoun was William H. Crawford, once Madison's secretary of war, now Monroe's treasury secretary. William Wirt, the attorney general, sided with the first two. The only dissent came from Adams, the secretary of state.

There had been no real violations of Jackson's instructions, Adams told the cabinet. Spain's inability to control the Seminoles was justification enough for Jackson's action, which under this interpretation was defensive in nature. As for the British, it was their responsibility to control their own citizens, and if they couldn't, others would. Adams presented the relevant texts on international law and usage that supported him. In any case, he said, "If the question is dubious, it is better to err on the side of vigor than of weakness—on the side of our own officer, who has rendered the most eminent services to our nation, than on the side of our bitterest enemies, and against him."[32]

Privately Adams was not so sure. When he first learned of Jackson's capture of the Spanish fort he noted that it was "contrary to his orders." Jackson's conduct in deceiving the Indian chiefs and executing them without a trial was "without due regard to humanity," and Adams was "not prepared for such a mode of warfare."[33] Publicly, however, he continued to defend Jackson in powerful diplomatic notes sent to both foreigners and American ministers abroad. "Contending with such enemies," he told the American minister to Spain, "although humanity revolts at entire retaliation upon them…mercy herself surrenders to retributive justice the lives of their leading warriors taken in arms." He quoted one of the recognized authorities on international law, Emerich Vattel: "When at war…with a ferocious nation which observes no rules, and grants no quarter, they may be chastised in the persons of those of them who may be taken…and by this rigor the attempt may be made of bringing them to a sense of the laws of humanity."[34]

Adams's defense was less than perfect in both law and logic. Jackson may have had orders from Calhoun to eliminate the hostile Indian presence in Florida, but he had no orders to attack Spanish forts or punish British citizens. On the contrary, the instructions to Gaines, and to Jackson as his successor, forbade such actions. Nonetheless, Adams thought so much of his letter that he saw to it that it was published far and wide, even before it reached Spain. Thomas Jefferson thought it was the best diplomatic note he had ever read. Jackson's defenders in his presidential campaigns in 1824 and 1828 would cite it over and over.

As it turned out, the Florida invasion had no effect on Anglo-American relations. War, British Prime Minister Liverpool told the American minister in London, could have been declared merely "by holding up a finger." But the finger was not held up, and the British and Americans instead signed an agreement establishing much of the present U.S.– Canadian border. That border was more important to the British than the doings of Andrew Jackson in Spanish Florida or the fate of the Seminoles. For the time being, Arbuthnot and Ambrister were forgotten.

The irony of Adams's defense of the very man who would eventually become his political nemesis has not been lost on later biographers of each man.[35] Yet there is even more irony. Jackson's most vocal critic in the cabinet, the man who most wanted him investigated and censured, was John C. Calhoun, who later helped Jackson defeat Adams in 1828. In later years, when the temptation must have been great, Adams never wavered from his defense of Jackson's invasion of Florida.[36]

Jackson had powerful critics in Congress, led by Kentucky's Henry Clay, speaker of the House of Representatives. He was joined by the allies of Treasury Secretary Crawford. Clay had been one of John Quincy Adams's colleagues at Ghent four years before and, along with Calhoun, one of the original war hawks. The Kentuckian had wanted to be secretary of state, and when Monroe turned instead to Adams, Clay emerged as one of the administration's most severe critics.

On January 12, 1819, the House Committee on Military Affairs brought out a report condemning the executions of Arbuthnot and Ambrister.

Amendments to the report were added by Crawford supporters critical of the seizures of St. Marks and Pensacola. Jackson's fear of conspiracies was easily aroused. "There's a combination in Congress to ruin me," he told a friend. The allies of Clay and Crawford, sensing in Jackson a possible political rival with both western and southern credentials, were determined to cut him down to size. Secretary Calhoun prudently stayed silent. Jackson hurried to Washington to meet with President Monroe. As he was leaving Monroe's office on January 23, 1819, Jackson met Adams. The two men shook hands for the first time.[37]

While Jackson was on his way to Washington, Clay launched his attack. Henry Clay was one of the great orators of his time. Virginia-born, like Jackson he had moved west from his native state, but to Kentucky, not Tennessee. Like Jackson he was a slaveholder with a hot temper. Unlike Jackson, however, he was usually able to keep his temper under control and preferred gambling to horse racing. He also rarely carried political disagreement beyond the floor of Congress and often went out of his way to mix socially with his political opponents. His assault on Jackson in January 1819 was memorable for both its rhetoric and its content, portraying him as a threat to American prestige abroad and a menace to civilian authority at home. So far as Clay was concerned, the origins of the war lay in the unjust Treaty of Fort Jackson, which had created a colony of refugees around the Florida border. The trickery associated with the capture of the two Indian leaders and the kangaroo court that condemned Arbuthnot and Ambrister were violations of both the law and humanity.

There were two indictments consistently lodged against the United States by its European enemies, Clay told a packed chamber. "The one is an inordinate spirit of aggrandizement—of coveting other people's goods. The other is the treatment we extend to the Indians." Jackson's invasion gave ammunition to both charges. "Beware how you give a fatal sanction, in this infant period of our republic, scarcely two score years old, to military insubordination." Recalling the record of other generals who had subverted civilian authority and later became dictators—Alexander the Great, Julius Caesar, Oliver Cromwell, Napoleon Bonaparte—Clay warned that not to condemn Jackson would be "a triumph of the principle of insubordination—a triumph of the military over the civil authority—a triumph over the powers of this house—a triumph over the constitution of the land."[38]

Jackson's defenders, including Congressman Rhea, dismissed Clay's arguments with those put forth by Adams in his letter to the American minister in Spain. Jackson was authorized, Rhea claimed, by "the supreme law of nature and nations, the law of self-defense…to enter the Spanish territory of Florida in pursuit of, and to destroy, hostile, murdering savages, not bound by any obligation, who were without the practice of any moral principle reciprocally obligatory on nations."[39]

Jackson could understand neither Clay's speech nor Clay himself. To attack someone politically one day and then to expect cordiality the next was not Jackson's way. "[Clay's] hypocracy & baseness," in pretending personal friendship while skewering him on the floor of the House "make me despise the Villain," he told a friend. He also sensed that Clay's rhetoric would not sit well on the frontier, and had copies of the speech sent to friends with instructions to have it published as widely as possible. "I hope the western people will appreciate his conduct appropriately," he wrote. He added that the support he had received from Secretary Adams deserved a "proper ulogium" as well.[40]

Jackson's instincts told him that Americans would be more sympathetic to the results of his Florida action than hostile to his methods. He was right. Clay's attack served only to enhance Jackson's standing and his image, not just in the West but throughout the nation. The Kentuckian became the first of many to miscalculate Jackson's appeal to ordinary Americans. Jackson's congressional supporters rallied, and on February 8, 1819, all of the anti-Jackson resolutions went down to defeat in the House of Representatives by nearly two-to-one margins. The last one, prohibiting American troops from entering foreign territory without prior congressional approval, lost by nearly three to one.[41] The victory in Congress and among the general public suggested that in a crisis, real or imagined, Americans will always rally behind boldness and direct action, especially if they are successful, regardless of legal or constitutional niceties.

Once again Jackson was the man of the hour, once again the guest of honor at a White House reception. Adams watched him carefully. "From the earnestness with which the company pressed round him, the eagerness with which multitudes pushed to obtain personal introductions to him, and the eye of respect and gratitude which from every quarter beamed upon him, it has as much the appearance of being his drawing-room as the President's," he wrote in his diary. Concealing his private reservations, Adams told Jackson he thought his conduct "had been correct and proper," and he invited Jackson to visit him. A month later the two men exchanged dinners at each other's homes.[42]

After the House vote Jackson departed on a tour of northern cities and was greeted by large crowds in New York, Philadelphia, and Baltimore.

Upon learning that the Senate had issued its own report, which was more devastating than Clay's rhetoric on the House floor, he rushed back to Washington. The Senate committee, which included Jefferson's son-in-law, John W. Eppes, had carefully reviewed the evidence and by a five-to-three vote condemned the executions of Arbuthnot and Ambrister and the seizure of Florida as well. The executions, they said, were "an unnecessary act of severity on the part of a commanding general and a departure from that mild and humane system...honorable to the national character."[43]

Fortunately for Jackson, the report was released just as Congress was about to adjourn; it was permanently tabled and never debated. Adams's wife, Louisa, was particularly struck by Jackson's demeanor following the release of the Senate's report. Observing him while a guest for dinner at their home, she remarked in her private journal, "Our hero looked depressed and dejected and appears to be...more severely wounded than one would suppose he could be after the public expression of the people which has been so proudly manifested on his recent journey."[44] Jackson was not depressed; he was livid. He was particularly enraged at Eppes, whom he intended to challenge to a duel until talked out of it by his friends. Months later Monroe and Adams were still worried that if Jackson and Eppes were to meet in Washington there would be fisticuffs, or worse.[45]

The Adams-Jackson alliance, if it may be called that, was based partly on genuine admiration and partly on a mutually shared goal. Each man desired to acquire Florida for the United States. Adams hoped to do it by diplomacy and cash, Jackson by force, if necessary. His invasion, regardless of its legitimacy, demonstrated that Spain's hold not only in Florida but on the entire North American continent was weak. Adams was able to press this advantage with the Spanish minister, Luis de Onis, and win from Spain not just Florida, but more. The Transcontinental Treaty of 1819, also called the Adams-Onis Treaty, not only acquired Florida in exchange for some five million dollars, but extended American claims to the Pacific Coast. The only concession Adams made in the negotiations with Onis was to back off from the American claim to Texas—dubious at best—as part of the Louisiana Purchase.[46]

Before agreeing to the Treaty Monroe instructed Adams to confer with Jackson. This Adams did on two occasions prior to the general's leaving on his northern tour. Jackson agreed with the Texas concession, noting, as Adams put it in his diary, "The enemies of the Administration would certainly make a handle of it to assail them; but the possession of the Floridas was of so great importance to the southern frontier of the United States, and so essential even to their safety, that the vast majority of the nation would be satisfied with the western boundary as we propose, if we obtain the Floridas." (Years later, when the two men were bitter enemies, Jackson would vigorously deny that he was consulted about the Treaty or the concession. But Adams kept a diary, and Jackson did not.)[47]

Diplomatic snags prevented the Transcontinental Treaty from being implemented for another two years. In February 1821 Florida at last became part of the United States. The president proposed to make Jackson Florida's first territorial governor; Adams agreed.[48] Jackson himself was dubious at first, partly because his wife objected to the move on the grounds of his health. But as he told a friend, "With a small fund and good recommendations a great spec [i.e., speculation] might be made at Pensacola and Ft St Augustine." On the frontier, territorial expansion, Indian removal, and land speculation were always closely linked.[49]

The Jacksons arrived at Pensacola by way of New Orleans and Mobile in July. No sooner had he taken up his residence at Pensacola, however, than Jackson again created difficulties for himself and the Monroe administration. Irritated by the procrastinating ways of the outgoing Spanish governor, Jose Callava, regarding the turnover of the territory, he had him arrested by a detachment of American soldiers and thrown in jail. Then he tossed Callava's immediate officers out of the territory. In a near-repeat of New Orleans, Governor Jackson was confronted by a writ of habeas corpus issued by a recently appointed judge, Eligius Fromentin, an ex-senator, albeit one of dubious background and qualifications.[50]

At issue was whether Jackson, who had resigned as general in charge of the Southern District, had authority as a civilian governor to issue military orders. Rather than throwing Fromentin in jail, his response to a similar situation in 1815, Jackson confronted the judge, who ultimately backed down, vowing to carry his dispute to Washington instead. Fromentin and Callava both regarded themselves as above the law, or at least the law as established by Andrew Jackson. In a lengthy letter to Secretary Adams, Jackson explained himself: He hoped what he called his "lecture" would "cause him to obey the spirit of his commission... instead of attempting to oppose me, under Spanish influence."[51]

The president was embarrassed. Once again Secretaries Calhoun and Crawford as well as Attorney General Wirt were ready to disown Jackson.

The general "knows no law except the law of force," Wirt told the president, "and his want of information, combined with his violence, is perpetually plunging him into difficulties."[52] Once again Secretary Adams was his only defender, placing the blame squarely on Fromentin. It was he who exceeded his authority, not Jackson, whose executive powers as governor included the right of issuing orders to the military. Otherwise "he had no means of executing his decrees, administrative or judicial."[53] Callava eventually turned up in Washington to protest his treatment to the authorities there. Secretary Adams listened politely but offered no help. The fault, he said, lay with the Spanish for their delaying the transfer, which was "a high and aggravated outrage upon [Jackson's] lawful authority."[54]

But Jackson was ill at ease with his responsibilities and returned to Tennessee later in the year. He remained grateful for Adams's continued support. At about that time he told a friend, in words that would sound odd a few years later, "You know my private opinion of Mr Adams Talents, virtue, and integrity, and I am free to declare that I have never changed this opinion of Mr Adams since it was first formed, I think him a man of the first rate mind of any in America as a civilian and scholar, and I have never doubted of his attachment to our republican Government." At about the same time Adams was confiding to his diary, "General Jackson has rendered such services to this Nation, that it is impossible for me to contemplate his character or conduct without veneration."[55]

Looking forward to the end of his second term, Monroe persisted in his belief that organized political parties were "the curse of the country." Yet, as he admitted to former president Madison, in spite of their disappearance the nation was still in a "restless and disturbed" state. The disappearance of two-party rancor had not brought about the harmony Monroe had expected. Animosity between Federalists and Republicans had been replaced by animosity among Republicans themselves, often over the same issues that had once separated them from the Federalists. The "restless and disturbed" state had two causes. The first was the Panic of 1819, which led to the nation's first serious economic depression; the second was the reverberations from the crisis that followed a year later over slavery and its future in the United States. Behind each lay profound constitutional, social, and economic issues that would not easily be resolved.

First, the Panic. The end of the War of 1812, and the century-long Anglo-French world war of which it was a part, brought about a reassessment of some traditional republican economic values that coincided with the shifting political values already mentioned. The arrival of peace and the reduction of the Indian presence opened up the prospect of opportunities in the West, especially those afforded by cheap land. Yet however cheap, the land was never free, and to take advantage of it usually meant turning to banks and borrowing money. In 1800 there were thirty banks in the entire nation. By 1820 there would be more than four hundred, most of them eager to loan money to speculators and would-be pioneers expecting to profit from the rise in the price of land.[56] In the meantime the Republican-controlled Congress in 1816 created a second Bank of the United States, with a twenty-year charter. Once upon a time, the constitutionality of the Bank was one of the defining issues between Republicans and Federalists. Advocated by Alexander Hamilton, it had been roundly attacked by both the young James Madison and the young James Monroe. By 1816, however, enough Republicans, including former war hawks Clay and Calhoun, had witnessed what they believed to be too much weakness on the part of the federal government in wartime and were persuaded that a national bank was needed. Such a bank could provide credit to the federal government should it be necessary in a crisis and could also exercise its power as the federal government's sole agent to curb inflation and control speculation by submitting the notes of smaller banks for payment in gold or silver (specie), should they become overzealous in extending credit themselves. The prospect of a Republican Congress enacting a second Bank of the United States and a Republican president, James Madison, signing it into law was troublesome to many orthodox Republicans.[57]

Equally troublesome was the about-face taken by many Republicans regarding strict construction of the Constitution. The Virginia and Kentucky Resolutions of 1798 were drafted by Madison and Jefferson as a protest against what they saw as an unwarranted extension of federal power in the form of the Alien and Sedition Acts. Since then Republicans had looked to the Resolutions as holy writ, the cornerstone of their opposition to the threat posed by federal power over republican liberty. Now, in the aftermath of the War of 1812, many Republicans, again led by Clay and Calhoun, were not only supporting a second Bank but were proposing federal funding for "internal improvements," what in later times would be called "infrastructure." They argued that the recent war had found the nation lacking in means of transportation and communication, and that nothing short of federal support for the dredging of harbors and the building of roads and canals would meet the need. They succeeded in passing an ambitious program of internal improvements in the last days of the Madison administration, only to have it vetoed by the outgoing president in March 1817.

Manufacturers, who had not done badly during the war when overseas commerce was limited, now looked on with dismay as ship after ship, mostly from Great Britain, arrived in American ports and disgorged clothing, furniture, shoes, books, and ironware produced by lower-paid workers and priced well below the American competition. In the absence of an income tax, revenue from import duties had been the principal source of income for the federal government, funding, for example, the armed forces. Representatives from manufacturing districts now insisted that duties be used to raise the price of cheaper imports to a level that would allow the more expensive domestic equivalents to compete with them—hence the term "protective tariff." This, too, had been proposed by Alexander Hamilton in the 1790s and opposed by most Republicans. In 1816 it drew the support of most Republicans, including President Madison, who signed it into law. Although he objected to federal subsidies for internal improvements, Madison evidently had less difficulty with the Bank and the protective tariff.[58]

Leading the opposition to the Tariff of 1816 was the young Federalist congressman from New Hampshire, Daniel Webster, who spoke for the commercial shipping magnates who had no interest in limiting or restricting overseas trade. Webster was joined by a vocal minority of fundamentalist-minded "Old Republicans," who continued to wage war against the Bank, federally subsidized internal improvements, and protective tariffs. Nowhere in the Constitution, they said, was there a provision for a federal bank, for the construction of internal improvements—other than those connected to the military or the Post Office—or for a tariff other than for raising revenue. Such proposals were nothing more than an increase of power and a decrease in liberty. The "New Republicans," led by Henry Clay, dubbed the three-part program the "American System," to distinguish it from the system of predatory Europeans looking to take advantage of American economic vulnerabilities. The goal was to create a stable economy through a centralized banking system, stimulated by an ever widening web of transportation and communication, through which domestic manufactures could eventually reach all parts of the Union.[59]

Most, if not all, of the American System would be enacted, if not in Clay's generation, then in the next, as the nation modernized and rationalized its economy. But its departure from eighteenth-century republicanism placed it on a politically fragile footing, one that might be threatened in the face of an economic collapse. The collapse came in 1819.

The return of peace in Europe, while offering opportunity for western expansion in America, also meant that land on that continent that had once been soaked with the blood of armies was now once again growing food and fiber, which in turn meant that the Old World was no longer as dependent on the New to supply its needs. Inevitably the prices for American corn, wheat, cotton, and tobacco dropped, and by 1819 they were dropping sharply. The price of cotton, for example, began a decade-long decline, from 30.8 cents a pound in 1818 to 8.3 cents in 1831. The overall price index (with the year 1825 = 100) went from 220 in 1813 to 145 in 1815 to 100 in 1820, and remained low thereafter. The drop in prices meant a corresponding decrease in the value of frontier land; by 1819 it had dropped by 50 percent to 75 percent. Four years earlier Americans had borrowed three million dollars, mostly from banks, to invest in Western lands; by 1819 the debt had increased more than sevenfold, to twenty-two million dollars. Investors who had borrowed money expecting a perpetual increase in the price of land now found themselves holding property that was losing value. They were no longer able to meet their obligations, and thousands went bankrupt, followed by many of the banks themselves. Merchants in the port cities of New York, Philadelphia, Boston, and elsewhere could not find profitable customers. Ships lay idle at their docks. Bank notes, with which workers were often paid, also steadily declined in value, and consequently were often not accepted as payment for groceries or services. In Philadelphia employment dropped from 9,672 in 1816 to 2,137 in 1819; in Pittsburgh from 1,960 to 672. One source estimated some fifty thousand unemployed in New York City, Philadelphia, and Baltimore. Americans looked for an explanation and zeroed in on the Second Bank of the United States.[60]

Between 1817 and 1819 the states of Maryland, Tennessee, Georgia, North Carolina, Kentucky, and Ohio attempted to tax the Bank in hopes of reducing its power. In 1819 the Supreme Court was provided the opportunity to settle once and for all—or so it believed—both the question of the Bank's constitutionality and the right of a state to tax it. The Bank's opponents were disappointed but not surprised when Chief Justice John Marshall, a Virginia Federalist, spoke for a unanimous Court and upheld the Bank. Repeating almost word for word Alexander Hamilton's reasoning in 1791, Marshall ruled in *McCulloch v. Maryland* that if Congress was given a specific power by the Constitution, such as levying taxes or borrowing money, it followed that any means for carrying out that power, such as a bank, was also constitutional, whether expressly stated or not. Moreover, states could not tax the Bank because, as Marshall put it, "the power to tax is the power to destroy."[61]

The timing of the *McCulloch* decision was unfortunate for the Bank's future. Under more conservative leadership, it was responding to the economic crisis by calling in its loans, which in turn forced state banks to do the same, which forced them to foreclose on loans made with little or no reserve. This only made the situation worse. "The Bank was saved," noted William Gouge, a leading critic, "and the people were ruined."[62] In the South and West, where land speculation and overborrowing had been most rampant, the Bank was a particularly convenient target. A growing number of critics supported the Old Republican position and blamed not only the Bank but the expansion of government in general, calling for "retrenchment" across the board. The New Republicans fought back, defending the Bank, internal improvements, and tariff protection.

Neither Jackson nor Adams took a public stance regarding these issues. Jackson was too busy defending himself against his critics, and Adams was too wrapped up in the duties of his office. Privately, however, their perspectives regarding both the causes of and the remedies for the economic shambles that lay strewn about them were significantly different, reflecting their contrasting backgrounds. Jackson followed the Old Republican line in blaming banks in general for the collapse. Most Tennesseans agreed with him. "Banking in all its forms, under every disguise, is a rank fraud upon the laboring and industrious part of society," declared a successful Tennessee congressional candidate. "It is in truth a scheme...to make idleness productive and filch from industry, the hard produce of its earnings."[63] Although as a land speculator he had used banks himself and often had profited from them, Jackson was among those who resisted attempts to establish a branch of the Bank in Nashville. "You know my op[in]ion as to the Banks, that is, that the constitution of our State, as well as the constitution of the united States prohibits the establishment of Banks in every State," he told a friend in 1820.[64] Given that a number of Jackson's close friends, including John Henry Eaton and William B. Lewis, were involved in Tennessee banking at the time, he confined his feelings to private correspondence. Only later, as president, would he emerge as a full-blown enemy, not only of the Bank but of banks in general. His critics, then and since, claimed that he was either ignorant of their function or was seeking revenge owing to some personal losses in the early days. His defenders, then and since, maintain that in taking on the banking community he was merely following good republican thinking.[65]

Adams, on the other hand, supported the Bank. The cause of the current crisis, he said, lay not with banks in general but with "the extravagant multiplication of banks and the unprincipled manner in which many of them have been managed." The crisis would continue, he told President Monroe, so long as "every State exercised an unlimited power of making paper money." A national bank was the only remedy, he said, under the auspices of the federal government and "substantially under its control, and always regulating the national currency."[66]

The problem for orthodox republicans was that all banks were a form of monopoly and therefore examples of unlimited power. A private corporation chartered by Congress, the Bank of the United States was the exclusive financial agent of the federal government, and unlike those of any other bank, its notes were legal tender. For those who saw it as a useful regulator of the currency, the Bank's power was a guard against inflation and rampant speculation. For others, the Bank was yet another symbol of the threat against American liberty.

The hostile reaction of many, like Jackson, to the Bank's alleged role in the Panic was a hint of a broader and deeper reaction that went beyond economics. The economy—and the social system—had never seen anything like it. To the extent that republicanism rested on independence, both of the individual and the nation, the Panic of 1819 posed a number of problems. Farmers in Ohio were losing their land because of bumper crops in France; workers in Boston were losing their jobs because of a labor surplus in Liverpool. What the next century would term "rugged individualism" was being challenged by the realities of a world market. For the first time in their history, U.S. citizens found themselves subject to sweeping economic forces over which they had no control. The republican ideal of the self-sufficient individual who would rise or fall in keeping with his own efforts had been undermined, or so it seemed. Looking for answers—and scapegoats—many focused not only on the Bank but on the neofederalism that had helped to create it. In one way or another, Henry Clay, John C. Calhoun, and John Quincy Adams had all been involved, but not Andrew Jackson.

It was slavery, its relationship to republicanism, and above all to its future, that would in time reveal the most profound difference between Jackson and Adams. In the midst of the Panic and its steadily spreading aftershocks, the citizens of the Missouri Territory petitioned to enter the Union as a slave state. By itself there was nothing unusual in this. Several slave states had been admitted since 1787 without controversy, although always balanced by a free state. Until then the North had acquiesced in accepting slavery in new states such as Mississippi and Alabama, where it had existed for some time and whose territory had been part of the original United States. The proposed state of Missouri would be the first to be carved entirely from the Louisiana Purchase, and its embrace of slavery carried with it the implication that all future states carved from the Purchase would carry slavery with them as well, perhaps all the way to the Canadian border. And this time no free state was proposed to balance it. Most northern congressmen were determined to block Missouri's admission as a slave state. Southerners were equally determined to bring it about, some going so far as to deny Congress's right to regulate the expansion of slavery in the first place.[67]

Not since the 1790s had Congress been forced to confront the issue of slavery and its future. Although no northern congressman even came close to advocating slavery's abolition, feelings ran high nonetheless. The entire issue, Jefferson wrote at the time, was like a "fire-bell in the night," perhaps even "the death-knell of the Union." Jefferson himself became the object of attention as northerners reminded their southern brethren that the author of the Declaration of Independence, though a slaveholder, had more than once expressed his wish that slavery eventually disappear. "You have kindled a fire which all the waters of the ocean cannot put out, which seas of blood can only extinguish," a Georgia congressman told James Tallmadge, the New York congressman who introduced the antislavery restriction in 1820. Tallmadge replied, "If a dissolution of the Union must take place, let it be so! If civil war, which gentlemen so much threaten, must come, I can only say, let it come!"[68]

The issue was constitutional and political as well as moral. Did the North have the right to stop the South's growth? Did Congress have the constitutional power to stop slavery at all? Eventually the Missouri Compromise, brokered through the efforts of Henry Clay, settled the question for the time being by drawing a geographic line through the Louisiana Territory below which slavery would be permitted, above which it would be denied. Missouri did enter as a slave state, balanced by the admission of the new state of Maine, formerly part of Massachusetts.

As a slaveholder Jackson's commitment to the "peculiar institution" could be taken for granted. His willingness to enlist free blacks in defense of New Orleans did not mean that he regarded blacks as equal to whites or that he in any way disputed the prevailing notion among slavery's advocates that servitude was their "natural" condition. In the years following the Battle of New Orleans Jackson expanded both his landholding and his slaveholding. His nephew and ward, Andrew Jackson Donelson, was his principal agent for slave purchases. In 1822 Jackson was in need of a young male slave for work at the Hermitage and was ready to buy, he told Donelson, "if the fellow is not more than 22 years old, [and] if he is not subject to runaway and is healthy and stout." Not only that, but "I want two or three girls about fifteen or Eighteen years old also." Such correspondence was typical of most wealthy slaveholders of that era. Like them, Jackson saw nothing but mischief in the attempt to stop slavery's growth. It was "the entering wedge to seperate the union," he said, and he feared that even the discussion of the question might incite the slaves themselves "to insurrection and masacre." Behind it was "the wicked design of demagogues, who talk about humanity, but whose sole object is self-agrandisement regardless of the happiness of the nation." It was, he declared, a power struggle between the South and West on one side, and "the Eastern interests" on the other. "They will find the southern and western states equally resolved to support their constitutional rights," he told Donelson.[69]

Adams, like most New Englanders, never owned a slave nor aspired to own one. Although Yankees had profited from the slave trade in the seventeenth and eighteenth centuries, slavery itself had never played an important part in Massachusetts's economy, and its abrupt end following the American Revolution was not seriously challenged. Early in his career Adams did not concern himself with slavery and its implications. Indeed, as a U.S. senator he opposed attempts to limit the importation of slaves into the new territory. "Slavery in a moral sense is an evil," he declared, but "as connected with commerce, it has its uses." In 1806 he opposed as well any acceleration of the abolition of slave importation before 1808, as permitted by the Constitution. And he had no problem arguing on behalf of slaveholders and their rights under the Treaty of Ghent while in London following the War of 1812. At the time, Adams's nationalism and expansionism outweighed whatever antislavery sentiments he may have had.[70]

By 1820 Adams had privately modified his position. As he followed the congressional debates he marveled at the unity of the slaveholding interest when compared to the frequent waffling of some northerners. "With the Declaration of Independence on their lips, and the merciless scourge of slavery in their hands, a more flagrant image of human inconsistency can scarcely be conceived than one of our Southern slave-holding republicans." Slavery, he confessed, was "the great and foul stain upon the North American Union." The issue of its future might indeed bring about a separation of the Union, he told a somewhat shocked Pennsylvania congressman, and that might indeed be followed by a slave insurrection and much bloodshed, but "so glorious would be its final issue, that, as God shall judge me, I dare not say it is not to be desired."[71]

Adams saw the Missouri crisis as one that pitted North against South. Jackson saw it as brought on by the "Eastern interests" against the South and West. Ever since his exposure to the culture of Philadelphia in the 1790s Jackson had been both suspicious of and uncomfortable among eastern urbanites. Following a notorious fight on the floor of the House of Representatives in 1798 between Matthew Lyon, a Republican who, after being insulted by Rufus Griswold, a Federalist, spat at him, Congressman Jackson noted the contrast between the sophisticated East and the frontier. "Sticks and Spittle," he reported contemptuously to his friend Willie Blount, "are substituted by the Eastern representatives, in Place of Pistols." To many on the southern frontier, including Jackson, easterners tended to be effete, patronizing, and, above all, unsympathetic, even hostile, to their needs. In 1805 Jackson offered this Fourth of July toast at a banquet of Nashville citizens: "To the rising greatness of the West—may it never be impeded by the jealousy of the East."[72] It had been "easterners"—Yankees from New England—who had dragged their feet in the War of 1812. Many in the West saw them as obstacles to expansion and Indian removal; in the South they were seen as threats to the preservation of slavery and therefore of southern society itself.

Jackson exempted Adams, his ally and chief supporter in Washington, from these suspicions, at least for the time being. Their differences on slavery and the limitations on federal power remained submerged. In the meantime, in the months and years following the twin crises of the Panic of 1819 and the controversy over slavery in Missouri, whatever feelings there might have been in Monroe's second administration were not good.

For Secretary of State Adams the Panic and the Missouri Crisis lay outside his official responsibilities. "I deeply lament that my time is so much absorbed by other and more immediate and indispensable duties," he wrote of the economy in general.[73] By "more immediate and indispensable duties" he meant his responsibilities in not only foreign affairs but domestic ones as well. As secretary of state he was responsible for organizing and conducting the decennial national census in 1820, which in the past had been less than well organized. And he had been directed by Congress to issue a *Report on Weights and Measures*, and more specifically to recommend whether the United States should adopt the French-inspired metric system of grams and kilometers that was increasingly prevalent in Europe or stick with the more familiar British system of ounces and miles. In a brilliant essay published in 1821 Adams traced the history of measurement from biblical times to the present, but basically ducked the question. The metric system had logic on its side, he argued, but custom and habit must be given their due as well.[74]

But diplomacy remained Adams's main concern. His success with the Treaty of 1819 did not mean immunity from criticism. Henry Clay, for example, in addition to being a thorn in Jackson's side, targeted Adams as well. He criticized the secretary of state and the Monroe administration for not doing enough to aid the colonial rebellions in Latin America. Simón Bolívar and his fellow revolutionaries were the George Washingtons of their day, said Clay, and were entitled to more than just rhetorical support from Americans. Adams disagreed. On July 4, 1821, when Jackson was on his way to Florida, Adams delivered an oration before the citizens of Washington that encapsulated his perspective. After indulging in the standard denunciations of bad King George and British tyranny, he went on to declare that the Latin American revolutionaries should not count on American assistance. "Wherever the standard of freedom and independence has been or shall be unfurled," he said of the United States, "there will her heart, her benedictions, and her prayers be. But she goes not abroad in search of monsters to destroy." Though supporting the freedom and independence of all nations, "she is the champion and vindicator only of her own."[75]

Having defined the U.S. role in Latin America, Adams took a more aggressive position closer to home. The rest of the world, he told Monroe's cabinet, "should be familiarized with the idea of considering our proper domain to be the continent of North America," so that it should become "a settled geographical element that the United States and North America are identical." He had a series of shouting matches with Stratford Canning, the British minister to the United States and a cousin of the prime minister. The Americans would not challenge the British presence in Canada, Adams said, but would not look kindly on any further expansion on their part. "Keep what is yours," he said, "but leave the rest of the continent to us."[76] Adams's expansionism in the early 1820s was, if anything, more robust than that of Jackson, who was mainly concerned with ridding the southwestern frontier of Spaniards and Indians.

In 1823 Adams's influence led to a set of pronouncements that would be linked with President Monroe. The issue was simple enough. While the Spanish and Portuguese colonies in Central and Latin America were throwing off European rule, the reactionary "Holy Alliance" of Russia, Prussia, Austria, and France—but not Great Britain—contemplated intervention on behalf of the mother countries. Faced with the possibility of a European invasion of South America, Monroe, most of the cabinet, and ex-presidents Jefferson and Madison all favored a joint declaration with Britain warning against such a move. The Royal Navy could be counted on to block European intervention. Such a declaration seemed to make sense, although it would be a significant departure from U.S. foreign policy since the days of Washington's Farewell Address. Adams objected. There was no need, he said, to ally with the old enemy. If there was to be any declaration it would be better for Americans to stand alone than to come in "like a cock-boat, in the wake of the British Man of War."[77] Monroe agreed, and his Annual Message of December 1823, warning against the extension of Old World power into the New, became known as the Monroe Doctrine.[78] Andrew Jackson also approved. The "holy alience" had to be stopped, and their presence in the New World "must be prevented," he told his friend Lewis, "or ... we will have a bloody contest with the combined despotism of europe."[79]

"Of the public history of Mr. Monroe's administration," Adams wrote immodestly to his wife in 1822, "all that will be worth telling to posterity hitherto has been transacted through the Department of State." This was an exaggeration, though Adams had the right to be pleased. The acquisition of Florida, establishing the line of demarcation with both Britain and Spain that extended U.S. claims to the Pacific, and the formulation of the Monroe Doctrine were no mean achievements. For these and other reasons many have claimed Adams was the nation's greatest secretary of state. Three men in a row—Jefferson, Madison, and Monroe—had held that position before advancing to the presidency. And although Adams was limited both by tradition and by his own nature from conniving at the office, he, unlike Jackson at the time, hungered for it. His parents had conditioned him to believe it was his destiny. "If you do not rise to the head not only of your Profession, but of your country," his father had lectured him while he was still in his twenties, "it will be owing to your own *Laziness, Slovenliness,* and Obstinacy."[80]

Adams was aware of the obstacles that lay ahead, including those posed by his stubborn and occasionally self-righteous personality, the region from which he came, and the tainted party to which he had once belonged. His diplomacy was clearly influenced by this. Realizing that his Federalist and New England background would leave him vulnerable to charges of being soft on Great Britain, he went out of his way to denounce British tyranny in his Fourth of July Address in 1821, so much so that he was rebuked by some in his own state.[81] His shouting matches with the British minister, though private, were further indications that he could not be accused of Anglophilia. Most of all, while southern Republicans such as Jefferson, Madison, Monroe, Calhoun, and Crawford were all in favor of a joint declaration with the British against the Holy Alliance, it was Adams, the ex-Federalist from Massachusetts, who counseled against coming in "like a cock-boat, in the wake of the British Man of War."[82] He wisely kept his views on other matters, such as slavery and the Constitution, to himself.

In the presidential election of 1820 James Monroe fell short of a unanimous vote from the Electoral College only because one New Hampshire elector, much to the secretary of state's embarrassment, jumped the gun and voted for John Quincy Adams.[83]

★ Chapter Three ★

In 1824, for the first time, most American adult white males had the opportunity to participate in a presidential election. That year's election is the first for which we have meaningful returns.[1] It also remains the only election thus far to be resolved by the House of Representatives in accordance with the Constitution's Twelfth Amendment. The House awarded the presidency to John Quincy Adams and denied it to Andrew Jackson, bringing about a permanent rupture between the two men. The outcome guaranteed that all future presidential elections would be conducted under rules not envisioned by the Founders of the Republic.[2]

At least one historian has maintained that the presidential election of 1824 may have been more important than the one that came four years later.[3] Some claim the absence of organized parties meant that the contest was merely about personalities and images and that there was no meaningful debate about political or economic issues. Others see sectionalism as the deciding factor. Still others insist that behind sectionalism and the personal attraction of the candidates lay unresolved questions that would appear over and over in the next generation.[4]

★ ★ ★

"As the old line of demarcation between parties has broken down," John Quincy Adams noted, "personal has taken the place of principled opposition."[5] The lack of any clear heir apparent to James Monroe meant an unprecedented free-for-all among several candidates, each of whom claimed to be a Republican. Private and public speculation in the early 1820s focused on three members of Monroe's cabinet—Adams, William H. Crawford, and John C. Calhoun—plus the speaker of the House of Representatives, Henry Clay.

Andrew Jackson was rarely mentioned at first, but this did not mean he was uninterested. As early as 1821 he told his close friend James Gadsden that he was "at liberty to say in my name both to my friends and enemies—that I will as far as my influence extends support Mr Adams unless Mr Calhoun should be brought forward."[6] The letter was evidence not only of Jackson's confidence in Adams and Calhoun, but of his opposition to Crawford and Clay. Rather than vote for Crawford, Jackson said, he would support "the Devil first."[7] It had been Crawford who, as Madison's secretary of war, had tried to revise the Treaty of Fort Jackson in terms favorable to the vanquished Creeks. It had been Crawford who had allied himself with Clay in the congressional attack following Jackson's invasion of Florida. Clay's denunciation of Jackson as a "military chieftain" in 1819 earned him a place on the general's personal enemies list, a place he never relinquished. When Jackson at last entered the fray it had less to do with personal ambition and more to do with denying the presidency to Clay and Crawford. In this he succeeded only too well.

Everyone in Washington knew that if the past practice of elevating the secretary of state to the presidency were followed in 1824, Adams would succeed Monroe. Still, Adams had obstacles to be overcome. Although it was true that three presidents in a row had been former secretaries of state, it was also true that all three had been Virginians. The prospect of another Adams in the White House, and a former Federalist at that, was not something that the Virginia Republicans could be expected to embrace with much enthusiasm. Even Monroe, who had appointed Adams as much to provide regional balance in his cabinet as for his undisputed talents, allegedly assured others that he could not possibly be elected.[8] Some New Englanders seemed to agree. "It is thought here that J. Q. Adams will not be a successful candidate," Supreme Court Justice Joseph Story of Massachusetts told a friend. "It seems that the great objection to him is, that he is retiring and unobtrusive, studious, cool, and reflecting; that he does nothing to excite attention, or to gain friendships."⁹ "Secretary Adams is a poor timid Yankee," wrote an anonymous "Friend" to Jackson, "who can make no head against a Man of Crawford's energy even if he would attempt it." Adams was the product of "the cool and Catching cunning of a Northern Climate," and consequently was unequipped to compete with Crawford's machinations. "It appears to be the general opinion here," Jackson's personal physician reported from Washington in late 1821, "that Mr. Adams cannot succeed in opposition to a southern man." The anonymous "Friend" was more specific. "So Crawford is the next Presidt.," he warned Jackson, still in Florida, "unless some other Man than Adams is taken up. You must go back to Tennessee, and rouse the Western Country." He did go back to Tennessee, and for the time being waited upon events. In the meantime the Philadelphia *Columbian Observer* came out for Jackson for president.¹⁰

Indeed, most in Washington looked on Crawford, not Adams, as Monroe's most likely successor. The treasury secretary had served under Madison as minister to France and as acting secretary of war. He had narrowly missed the Republican nomination in 1816, giving way at the last minute to Monroe. Although he hailed from Georgia, he was a native Virginian. He had the support of Thomas Ritchie, the influential editor of the Richmond *Enquirer*. His post as treasury secretary meant that he controlled the appointment of revenue collectors and customs agents throughout the country, and these could be counted on to support him when the time came. He had legions of supporters in Congress as well. Crawford and his followers assumed that logic, loyalty, and good politics would make him president in 1824.¹¹

Henry Clay, like Crawford, was a native Virginian. He had wanted to be Monroe's secretary of state in 1817, aware of that post's status as the understudy for the presidency itself. When Monroe offered him any position in his cabinet except the one he wanted, Clay chose to remain speaker of the House of Representatives instead and joined the opposition to the Monroe administration, which meant opposition to both Adams and Jackson.

Adams, not surprisingly, found fault with both Crawford and Clay. "Crawford has been a worm preying on the vitals of the Administration," he wrote in 1821. As for Clay, "like almost all the eminent men in this country," he stuffily noted in his diary, Clay was "only half educated." In addition he had a reputation as a gambler, a drinker, and a womanizer. But

Clay had "large and liberal views of public affairs," Adams admitted, and should he become president "his principles relative to internal improvements would produce results honorable and useful to the nation."[12] In fact, while in the Senate in 1807, long before anyone outside of Kentucky had heard of Henry Clay, Adams had introduced a resolution embracing federal support for internal improvement.[13] Eventually it would become the hallmark, some would say the downfall, of his presidency.

Forty years old in 1822, John C. Calhoun was the youngest of the candidates. Yale-educated, Calhoun was the one member of Monroe's cabinet for whom John Quincy Adams had any respect. A supporter of the Bank of the United States and the protective tariff, Calhoun was a far cry from the impassioned, determined, and uncompromising defender of strict construction, states' rights, and chattel slavery that he eventually would become. Jackson's support of Calhoun for the presidency stemmed from his admiration for the man's undeniable talents as secretary of war and as a fellow South Carolina native. It would be another seven years before Jackson would learn of Calhoun's denunciation of his Florida invasion.[14]

The Missouri Crisis, the aftermath of the Panic of 1819, and the maneuvering within his cabinet all threatened Monroe's vision of a postwar partisan cease-fire. There were some, newspaper editors especially, who hoped for the resurrection of political controversy, whether between parties, within parties, or among individuals. Thomas Ritchie declared, "Republics will always be divided into opposite parties." A Delaware paper, the *American Watchman,* agreed: "A spirit of honorable contention calls for the talents of the community." Besides, political conflict sold newspapers.[15]

In late 1821 a politician arrived in Washington who agreed with the editors and disagreed with Monroe. Thirty-nine-year-old Martin Van Buren had been chosen senator from New York by his state legislature the year before and was destined to play a major role in the careers of Jackson, Adams, Calhoun, Clay, and Crawford. The son of a tavern keeper, he had risen to power as the leader of a group of New York partisans who for nearly ten years had distinguished themselves for their relentless opposition within the Republican Party to the friends and allies of DeWitt Clinton, formerly mayor of New York City and more recently governor of New York.

Best remembered today as the chief motivator behind the construction of the Erie Canal, in 1821 Clinton was held in suspicion by many

Republicans for his flirtation with the Federalists in 1812, when he challenged Madison for the presidency.[16] Although Clinton was unsuccessful then, many, including Van Buren, were persuaded that his ambition for higher office had not been extinguished. With the construction of the canal under way, Clinton continued to attract national attention for his vision and energy. When Jackson visited New York City after his congressional vindication in 1819 he went out of his way to pay tribute to the governor, much to Van Buren's dismay.

There was more to Van Buren's opposition than personal rivalry. DeWitt Clinton was the nephew of former vice president George Clinton, and thus heir to a prominent name in New York politics. Although learned, he was also arrogant and snobbish, relying on his fame and fortune to impose his leadership.[17] Van Buren had no such background and relied solely on his wits and powers of persuasion. Under his leadership Van Buren's "Bucktails" (so called for their tradition of wearing a buck's tail in their hats at party meetings) had attained what power they had in New York through internal discipline and the caucus system. Bucktails would gather to debate and select their candidates by majority vote; all were then bound to support the result. The system was both democratic and military: democratic, in that the wishes and opinions of the lowest ranking members of the group were given equal consideration; military, in that once a decision was made all were expected to support it. So long as they were united they were effective, wrote a close ally of Van Buren. "But the first man we see *step to the rear, we cut down*."[18]

In 1820 the Bucktails succeeded in wresting control of the state legislature from the Clintonians, which led to Van Buren's election to the Senate. Their opponents began calling Van Buren's group the Albany Regency, and the name stuck. The Regency was also among the first political organizations to be compared to a machine. Through discipline and patronage, an order, once given, was executed by the Bucktails, "right down to the last officeholder in the smallest hamlet of New York."[19]

Small in stature but with seemingly great powers of persuasion, Van Buren eventually became known as "the Little Magician." When he came to Washington in 1821 he expected that the same caucus method and the party discipline that had been so successful in New York could work on the national level as well. Organized political parties made it possible for ordinary folk, like the sons of tavern keepers, to band together and topple aristocrats like DeWitt Clinton. Parties, he wrote years later, "rouse the sluggish to exertion, give increased energy to the most active intellect, excite a salutary vigilance over the public functionaries, and prevent that apathy which has proved the ruin of Republics."[20] Far from being a threat to republicanism, as Monroe and the Founders believed, parties were the means of ensuring it. Furthermore, Monroe's amalgamationist "fusion policy," as Van Buren called it, threatened to erase the real differences that had once separated Republicans from their Federalist enemies. A friend reported that later Van Buren told him he hoped to "revive the old contest between federals and anti-federals and build up a party for himself on that."[21]

Van Buren was not happy with what he found in Washington. He was convinced that the survival of true republicanism, and therefore the Republican Party, required party unity. Those claiming to be Republicans should stick to the Republican principles as laid down by Jefferson and Madison in the 1790s, especially in the Virginia and Kentucky Resolutions. To his friends back in New York Van Buren announced, "A *radical reform* in the political feelings of this place has become necessary" and that it was "the proper moment to commence the work of a *general resuscitation* of the *old democratic party*."[22]

Van Buren's reference to the "old democratic party" is important. There had been a time when the word "democrat" or "democratic" was an epithet to be hurled at opponents. For most of the Founders the word conjured up visions of anarchy and mob rule. At various times John Adams, Madison, Hamilton, Washington, and others had condemned anything approaching a "democratic spirit." For social conservatives, and most Federalists who survived into the postwar era, the term still carried the old connotations. Van Buren represented a younger generation, many of whom were pressing for "democratic" reforms like the broadening of the franchise and who proudly claimed to be "democrats." This alteration in the American political vocabulary was further evidence of the shifting of the electoral substrata, and the social and cultural change that went with it.[23]

In his determination to resurrect and strengthen the divisions between the old parties Van Buren had a powerful ally. "You are told that there are no longer parties among us," Thomas Jefferson told his former treasury secretary, Albert Gallatin. "That they are now all amalgamated. The lion and the lamb lie down together in peace. Do not believe a word of it. The same parties exist now as they ever did." Although the name may have been "extinguished in the Battle of [New] Orleans," he went on, some, calling themselves Republicans, were still "preaching the rankest doctrines of the old Federalists."[24] In his later years Jefferson was more and more in tune with a group of so-called Old Republicans, mostly from the South, who saw themselves as the keepers of the orthodox Republican conscience. The Old Republicans, Jefferson, and now Martin Van Buren shared a common viewpoint: Republican principles were in danger from "fusionists" and "amalgamationists." Van Buren began to look about for a presidential candidate who could revive the contest "between federals and anti-federals."[25]

Like most men outside Tennessee, Van Buren, who one day would become Jackson's vice president and then president himself, never considered Jackson for the presidency in 1824. If anything, he was wary, remembering the general's praise for DeWitt Clinton in 1819. Adams's earlier federalism and cold personality made him ineligible as well. Clay's support of the American System, which made him an apostate in the minds of the Old Republicans, eliminated him, as did Calhoun's earlier flirting with heresies like the Bank and the protective tariff. That left Crawford, whose attacks on government spending following the economic collapse of 1819 made him the favorite of the Old Republicans and of the leading Old Republican himself, Thomas Jefferson. In due time Van Buren passed the word to the Albany Regency that Crawford was their man.[26]

Andrew Jackson may not have been ready to "rouse the Western Country" against Crawford, but many of his friends were. Politics in Tennessee still centered on the rivalry between the old Blount faction, led by Jackson's friends John Henry Eaton (now a U.S. senator), John Overton, and William B. Lewis, and their rivals, now led by Tennessee's other senator, John Williams, and Governor William Carroll, the same man who had been involved in Jackson's fight with the Benton brothers several years before. What dismayed Jackson, and ultimately drew him into the presidential fray, was the fact that the Williams group was aligned with the hated Crawford and Carroll was supporting Clay.

Indeed, without Jackson's knowledge, a number of his friends were quietly promoting Clay as the only westerner who could head off the Crawfordites in Tennessee.[27] To block Crawford's progress in Tennessee they hit upon the idea of having the state legislature nominate Jackson for president in 1822 as a diversionary tactic. Tennessee Crawfordites would then be forced to choose between a native son and an outsider. The resolution passed unanimously. "The welfare of a country," it trumpeted in July, "may be safely entrusted to the hands of him who has experienced every privation, and encouraged every danger, to promote its safety, its honor, and its glory." The general himself was reluctant. To those who were urging him to run, he said, "I give the same answer, that I have never been a candidate for any office. I never will." However, he added, "the people have a right to choose whom they will to perform their constitutional duties, and when the people call, the Citizen is bound to render the service required."[28] He would not "bargain" nor "intrigue" for the office, but he would accept it as a republican duty. Significantly, however, from the day of his nomination by the Tennessee legislature, he made no further mention of supporting anyone else.

Adams shared Jackson's attitude almost word for word. If the presidency "was to be the prize of cabal and intrigue," he told a would-be supporter, "of purchasing newspapers, bribing by appointments, or bargaining for foreign missions, I had no ticket in that lottery."[29] One of his friends remonstrated with him, accusing him of following a "Macbeth policy," alluding to the Shakespearian king's claim, "If chance will have me king, why, chance may crown me, without my stir." His friend reminded him that in America "kings are made by politicians and newspapers, and the man who sits down waiting to be crowned...will go bareheaded all his life."[30]

For Adams the presidency was a reward for public service, not a prize to be won through competition. To seek or organize support was to tamper with the outcome. "If your watch has no main-spring," he maintained, "you will not keep time by turning round the minute-hand. If I cannot move the mass, I do not wish to trifle with the indicator." Adams very much wanted to be president, perhaps more than any of the others, but the office would have to come to him, not he to it. Like Jackson, he agreed that if some "should be disposed to hold me up as a candidate for the suffrages of my country, I shall not, as present advised, withhold my name, but I shall neither solicit the nomination nor take any part whatever in procuring or supporting it."[31]

Both men were playing the role of what a recent historian has called the "Mute Tribune." Like George Washington, the Tribune had to be willing to serve but unwilling to do or say anything that could be construed as seeking the office. In the days when the selection of a president was left in the hands of a relatively small number of men, the Mute Tribune approach fit the realities of the political culture. Perhaps because Adams and Jackson were older than the other candidates, they maintained the stance longer than the others. Yet the shifting of the political substrata and the opening up of the selection process to more and more Americans meant that the future belonged to a younger group of would-be statesmen. Adams's friend was right. Presidents were increasingly being made by newspapers and politicians; the days of the Mute Tribune were numbered. In time, both Adams and Jackson would abandon it.[32]

Precedent may have favored secretaries of state for the presidential succession, but precedent also meant that presidential nominees would be chosen by a congressional caucus. In the years when there had been competition between Federalists and Republicans, congressmen and senators from each party met separately in Washington and selected their candidate. In this way the Republicans renominated Jefferson in 1804, chose Madison over Vice President Clinton in 1808, renominated Madison in 1812, chose Monroe over Crawford in 1816, and renominated Monroe without opposition in 1820. Federalists chose their candidates in a similar manner.[33] Once presidential candidates were chosen, party members were expected to support them, much in the manner followed by Van Buren's Bucktails in New York. The caucus system was usually followed on the state and local levels when party leaders selected candidates for Congress and state legislatures.

Like those of the Mute Tribune, the days of the caucus system were also numbered. The idea of a relatively small number of men meeting privately to select candidates for the voters to choose from was acceptable in an era in which the franchise was relatively restricted, but given the steady erosion of the limits on who could vote and for what office, the caucus system was bound to come under attack. The caucus system became even more vulnerable on the presidential level as more and more rank-and-file voters attained the right to vote directly for presidential electors instead of its being done for them by state legislatures. Weakening the system even further was the probability that in 1824, with no incumbent candidate and no competition from the Federalists, the choice of the Republican caucus would be virtually certain to be the next president. There would be no real need for an election, a prospect hardly in keeping with the spirit of republicanism.

Among those leading the charge against the congressional caucus system was Hezekiah Niles, editor of the Baltimore-based national weekly *Niles' Register*. It was, he complained in 1820, "an unwarrantable method of attempting to impose a President and Vice-President on the people of the United States." He did not let up. "I would rather learn that the halls of Congress were converted into common brothels, than that caucuses...be held in them," he declared two years later. "A nomination by *Congress* would be an act of dictation to the people," he concluded in 1823. "Surely, it was never designed that Congress should make a President." William Plumer, the ex-Federalist friend of Adams who kept a close watch on the Washington scene, agreed that caucuses "have, in general...too much regard for *private*, and too little respect for the public interest."[34] Adams himself, after thinking it over (and perhaps assessing his own chances for a caucus nomination), concluded that caucuses were "adverse to the spirit of the Constitution, and tending toward corruption."[35]

"Intrigue," "corruption," "manipulation," and similar epithets were part of the standard vocabulary of republicanism, transmitted down from the Revolutionary generation that had accused the king's ministers of similar behavior. Now, just as that generation was passing from the scene, the words took on new meaning. In 1823 and 1824 the legislatures of Tennessee, Maryland, South Carolina, Alabama, Ohio, and Indiana all passed resolutions denouncing the congressional caucus as a violation of the doctrine of separation of powers and an unrepublican restriction of the people's will.

Others defended the caucus. The New York and Virginia legislatures heartily endorsed it. Pro-caucus forces warned Pennsylvanians that Federalists were behind the attacks on the caucus in an attempt "to acquire their former control over the destinies of the nation" and "unite those who are hostile to the genuine principles of republicanism." While the caucus defenders were careful to praise all the candidates, they insisted that "the *propriety* of a caucus nomination, remains now, what it ever has been, a question, not of principle but one of *expediency*...upon the broad basis of *the public good*."[36] All true Republican congressmen and senators were urged to assemble in Washington, debate the merits of the candidates, make their choice, and go before the nation as a united party to face the enemy. Their problem was that in 1824 there was no enemy to face.

The attack on the caucus created a particular problem for Van Buren. His support of Crawford had been primarily ideological, as he was convinced that the treasury secretary was the one most likely to "revive the contest between federals and anti-federals." But it was pragmatic, too, because Crawford had strong support among congressmen and senators, especially among the Old Republicans, who now were often referred to as "the Radicals." For Crawford to be nominated, the caucus had to be preserved. If Crawford stood to gain from its preservation, it followed that other candidates stood to lose. It was no coincidence that the strongest denunciations of the caucus came from the supporters of the other candidates. Although Speaker Clay, like Crawford, could count on at least some support in Congress, he nonetheless joined the critics, foreseeing "the transition from a Congressional caucus to a praetorian cohort or hereditary monarchy."[37]

By then the candidacies of Clay and the others were well under way. True to the Mute Tribune tradition, Adams and Jackson remained aloof, notwithstanding the latter's nomination by the Tennessee legislature. With Crawford's chances tied to the congressional caucus in the capital, the other candidates hoped to challenge it by promoting their cases in the hinterlands. Clay's friends in the Missouri legislature, led by his wife's cousin Thomas Hart Benton (the same man who, with his brother Jesse, had brawled with Jackson in Nashville in 1814), endorsed the Kentuckian in late 1822, followed by the legislatures of Clay's home state and those of Ohio and Louisiana in 1823. Their message was clear: "[Kentuckians] will not...deny that they think the time has arrived, when the people of the west may, with some confidence appeal to the magnanimity of the whole union, for a favorable consideration of their equal and just claim to a fair participation in the executive government of these states."[38] There was no mention of Clay's American System or of any other issue. In the coming election, sectional considerations trumped issues in Kentucky.

In January 1823 the legislatures of Maine and Massachusetts convened to consider the candidacy of Adams, the native son. In the absence of any encouragement, both legislatures waffled. The Mainers expressed confidence in Adams but declined to endorse him or anyone else. The Massachusetts legislature also professed reluctance to make an endorsement. They had abundant praise for Adams, but they undercut it by asserting that "no determination is expressed to support the individual in question, at all events and under all possible circumstances." They would be happy to await further information.[39] If Adams was disturbed by such half-hearted support, he did not show it.

Jackson's presidential nomination, on the other hand, unexpectedly caught fire. His candidacy appealed to all those who were suspicious of the closed nature of the congressional caucus, disheartened by the dislocations following the Panic of 1819, and convinced that the Monroe administration was too much mired in intrigue over the next election. The first state outside of Tennessee to show enthusiasm for Jackson was Pennsylvania, the second largest in the Union behind New York. The Philadelphia-based *Columbian Observer*, whose editor, Stephen Simpson, had been a volunteer at the Battle of New Orleans, was founded with the clear purpose of supporting a Jackson candidacy. The *Observer* was the successor to the old Philadelphia *Aurora*, which in the 1790s had carried the banner for the Jeffersonian Republican cause. In December 1822 a public meeting at Greensburg nominated Jackson for president.[40] Whatever other plans they might once have had, Jackson's Tennessee friends hastily abandoned Clay and loudly proclaimed themselves Jacksonians.

Now Jackson's supporters faced a new problem. The very legislature that had nominated him to the presidency purely as an anti-Crawford ploy in 1822 was about to reelect the Crawfordite Senator John Williams to another six-year term in 1823. This could not be allowed if Jackson's candidacy was to be taken seriously. In a bold political maneuver his allies put forth Jackson himself as a candidate for the Senate. Breaking with his professed reluctance, Jackson briefly abandoned the pose of the Mute Tribune and traveled to the state capital on the eve of the election. On October 1, 1823, by a vote of thirty-five to twenty-five, the legislature defeated Williams and elected Jackson.[41] Two months later Senators Andrew Jackson and John Henry Eaton were on their way to Washington.

Contrary to the opinion of Jackson's anonymous "Friend," John Quincy Adams was not a "poor timid Yankee." He knew that if he were to be properly rewarded for his public service, it would help if the other presidential candidates were somehow eliminated from the competition. As early as 1819 he suggested to Calhoun that a little diplomatic experience abroad might do him some good. Calhoun said he couldn't afford it. In 1821 Adams casually asked Henry Clay, then his most severe critic, if he might be interested in an appointment abroad. Clay smiled, then declined. Adams asked again a year later, with the same result. When it looked like the Tennessee legislature would nominate Jackson for president, Adams asked President Monroe if he had considered the general for a diplomatic appointment. "He said he had; but was afraid of his getting us into a quarrel."[42] Adams defended him: "I said that although the language of General Jackson was sometimes too impassioned and violent, his conduct had always appeared to me calm and deliberate." Although on further thought Adams feared another attempt might look as though he was trying to get

Jackson out of the way, Monroe himself nominated Jackson as American minister to Mexico in early 1823. It was his hope, Adams told Jackson, that the "Country may on this occasion have the benefit of your services." Jackson declined, citing the unstable situation in Mexico. Besides, Rachel Jackson was adamantly opposed to his leaving the country.[43]

When it came to his own reputation Adams was as fierce a defender with his pen as was Jackson with other weapons. In 1822 a Clay supporter hinted publicly that at Ghent in 1814 Adams had been willing to betray the West in favor of New England's fishing rights, offering what appeared to be supporting documents. Adams struck back with a book-length pamphlet proving the documents to be forgeries. Clay quickly distanced himself from his erstwhile friend.[44] Jackson read Adams's pamphlet and was delighted with it. "It has done Mr Adams much credit, and instead of destroying his popularity in the south & west has increased it," he told his ward and nephew, Andrew Jackson Donelson. The book had "turned the Tables upon clay and Crawford, and...has placed Mr Adams on high ground, extended his popularity, and forever damd...all concerned in the vilanous scheme."[45]

To some, Adams's lengthy rebuttal appeared to be a case of overkill. Even his wife had her doubts. Adams, however, insisted that it was "an affair of more than life and death."[46] A few months later he was attacked by a Crawfordite congressman from Virginia who accused him of a host of transgressions, including being a closet monarchist and opposing the Louisiana Purchase as a senator in 1803. Adams fired off yet another pamphlet, reasserting his republicanism and correcting the record regarding the Purchase. Though unwilling to engage in "intrigue," Adams was nonetheless vigilant in his defense of his career as a public servant. He wanted to make completely sure that when the people delivered their verdict on his record of service, it would be based on the facts.[47]

After Jackson's presidential nomination by the Tennessee legislature, Senator Eaton quietly assumed responsibility for pushing his reluctant friend into the race. He watched the secretary of state very carefully. "Adams surely, confides rather much in the seeming strength of his pen," he reported from Washington in early 1823. Eaton was one of those who thought Adams was overdoing it. "There is such a thing as a man's rendering himself cheap, & falling gradually and insensibly in the estimation of the people, by to[o] frequently appearing before them." Moreover, Adams's repeated defense of his republican principles as a young man only served to renew interest in his father's administration, and especially the Alien and Sedition Acts that had brought forth the Virginia and Kentucky Resolutions. For those who regarded the Resolutions as the defining texts of the Republican Party, this could not be in the interest of the ex-Federalist son of John Adams.[48]

Eaton never lost the opportunity to provoke Jackson's republican instincts, as well as his fear of a Crawford presidency. He specifically targeted the congressional caucus. "The people," he complained, "have nothing to do with the filling of this high office." The social functions in the capital had no purpose other than to promote the interests of one candidate or another. "Time was when the virtue of the people would have laughed to scorn such attempts...but times alas are altered," Eaton mourned, denouncing the "deplorable picture of four gentlemen [Adams, Calhoun, Clay, and Crawford?] intriguing managing and seeking by little pretences to worm themselves into the favour of the folks of Congress."[49] Jackson, back in Tennessee, was not one of the "four gentlemen." After October, 1, 1823, he was a U.S. senator, and his arrival in Washington that December upset the calculations of all of them.

Even before Jackson's arrival there were signs that his candidacy was eroding the efforts of at least one of the four. Pennsylvania had long been thought to be safely in the hands of Secretary Calhoun, notwithstanding the outburst of support Jackson received there. Calhoun's economic nationalism and his support of the second Bank of the United States made him a favorite among those Republicans who had modified their earlier opposition to banks and tariffs. The Pennsylvania Calhounites had originally planned for their man to be nominated at a statewide convention in 1823, but they were ambushed by a well-organized group of antibank Republicans led by editor Stephen Simpson. Disillusioned with the party and the direction in which they believed the nation was heading, suspicious of anyone associated with Monroe's administration, the group turned to Jackson. The convention's address was a classic statement of orthodox republicanism. It complained that presidents were being chosen by "the Official Gentry at Washington," not by the people. The "great Augean Stable at Washington wants cleansing," they said, "and we know of no other Hercules" but Jackson. Still inspired by Greek mythology, the address claimed that a "circean web" was threatening to poison and strangle the infant republic. Although a disgruntled Calhounite dismissed the Jacksonians as "grog shop politicians of the villages & the rabble of Philadelphia and Pittsburg," Jackson was delighted, seeing it not so much as a setback for Calhoun, whom he still admired, as for Clay and Crawford, whom he detested. "If the people of Alabama, Mississippi, & Louisiana, follow the example of Pensylvania, they will place Clay & Crawford where they ultimately will be; *Dehors the political combat.*"[50]

Then came word of a sudden downturn in the physical condition of Secretary Crawford. That summer the fifty-one-year-old Georgian suffered a serious cerebral stroke that left him temporarily speechless and blind. Its extent was still unclear in December, and hopes were held out for a complete recovery. Gambling on this, Van Buren and the Radicals persisted in pushing for a congressional caucus to be held in early 1824. Supporters of Jackson, Adams, Clay, and Calhoun urged a boycott. When it was finally held on February 14 only sixty-eight members showed up, sixty-four of whom dutifully voted for the ailing Crawford. But 193 were absent. Following the result Jackson fired off all the familiar "republican" ammunition against it. "Should the people suffer themselves to be dictated to by designing demagogues, who carry on everything by intrigue and management," he told his brother-in-law, "they cannot expect to see the present happy government perpetuated; it must sink under the scenes of corruption that will be practised under such a system."[51]

The debacle might have been expected to end Crawford's candidacy, but Van Buren and the Radicals persisted, hoping for his recovery and hoping as well to persuade others that the congressional caucus was the only legitimate means of choosing a nominee. For Van Buren, Crawford was the official Republican nominee; all others were interlopers. Although his chances of gaining the required majority of electoral votes were evaporating steadily, no one else appeared capable of doing it either. Should that occur, the Twelfth Amendment to the Constitution provides that the House of Representatives makes the choice. Not surprisingly, individual congressmen now found themselves subjected to unusual attention from the friends of all five candidates.

"There is nothing done here but vissitting and *carding* [i.e., leaving visiting cards] *each other*," complained Jackson to Rachel shortly after his arrival in Washington. "You know how much I was disgusted with Those scenes when you and I were here, it has increased instead of diminishing."[52] Behind the "vissitting and carding" were secretive negotiations with the object of maneuvering one or more of the five candidates out of the picture by an alliance between two others. Sectional considerations made an alliance between two men of the same region unlikely; hence the tensions were greatest between Jackson and Clay, the two westerners, and Calhoun and Crawford, the two southerners. (For a while it appeared that DeWitt Clinton might qualify as a northern candidate, but he was now ex-Governor Clinton, thanks to Van Buren's Bucktails.)

As the only remaining northerner John Quincy Adams was at an advantage: he could ally himself with anyone if he so chose. A rumor circulated that Adams would accept the vice presidency under Crawford, a rumor whose truth Adams indignantly denied. At another point Calhoun was reported to have proposed a combination of Adams as president, Jackson as vice president, Clay as secretary of state, and he himself as treasury secretary, pointedly excluding Crawford. Adams at one point suggested Jackson for the vice presidency, presumably with himself as president. He thought "the place suited to him and him suited to the place. The thing was fitting in itself, and perfectly well suited to the usual geographic distribution of the two offices." In the meantime the state legislatures in Maine and Rhode Island finally came out unequivocally for Adams.[53]

Adams's hope for an alliance with Jackson was the impetus behind what turned out to be the most dazzling social event of the season. "Mrs. Adams has invited me to a party who are to celebrate the 8th of January at her house," Jackson told Rachel. "To this party I will have to go, and it will be the only party I mean to attend this winter."[54] January 8 was of course the ninth anniversary of the Battle of New Orleans. More than a thousand people were said to have invaded the Adams household that evening. "It is the universal opinion that nothing has ever equaled this party here either in brilliance of preparation or elegance of the company," wrote one breathless observer. Louisa Adams escorted the general to the dining table, where he toasted both Adamses. Dining and dancing went on well after midnight. People were still reading about it half a century later.[55]

Jackson remained aloof but continued obdurate in his opposition to Crawford, whose choice, he told a friend, "would be a great curse to the nation."[56] Yet it was clear that his own candidacy was gaining support nearly everywhere. He was, reported Daniel Webster, "the people's candidate in a great part of the southern and western country."[57] William Plumer Jr., son of Adams's ex-Federalist admirer, reported to his father that Adams had a surprisingly high opinion of the general: "And what was more, he not only considered him as strong, but also as meritorious. He had, he said, no hesitation in saying that he preferred him decidedly to any of the other candidates....I objected to him his rashness & indiscretion. He said that Jackson's character was not understood in that respect....He might, perhaps, as President, be guilty of some trifling indiscretions; but they would not affect the course of public measures, nor prevent his administering the government with perfect integrity & disinterestedness, free from all bargains, compromises, coalitions, or corruption." The secretary went on to declare "with great emphasis" that he preferred Jackson to any of the other three candidates.[58] An Adams supporter in New York was warned, "The rapid march of Genl. Jackson's popularity has far exceeded the expectations of his warm, decided friends. He may now be called, emphatically, the idol of the people."[59]

The general was enjoying himself, in spite of his complaints about "vissitting and carding." His unusually tall and thin frame, his shock of white hair, and his frontier background made him an object of curiosity. He had been told, he said, that many "were prepared to see me with a Tomahawk in one hand, and a scalping knife in the other," but their minds were changing. Eaton was concerned that Jackson's legendary temper would get him into trouble; nonetheless he was happily able to report to Rachel that her husband was smoothing over past differences with a variety of old enemies. "General Jackson's manners are more presidential than those of any of the candidates," reported Webster to his brother. "He is grave, mild, and reserved. My wife is for him decidedly."[60] On March 15 Adams, Clay, and Calhoun all attended a birthday party at Jackson's quarters, arranged by Eaton and Richard Keith Call, another Tennessee ally. "When it becomes necessary to philosophise & be meek, no man can command his temper better than I," Jackson assured his nephew.[61]

As a senator Jackson now had to take positions on a number of contentious issues that he had been able to avoid up to then, including the divisive issues of federal funding of internal improvements and the ever-present protective tariff. The Crawfordite Radicals had already adopted a hard-line, strict constructionist position that denied federal powers in both of these areas. Presidents Madison and Monroe had vetoed internal improvements, with Jackson's approval. To do otherwise, Jackson had then argued, would "produce in the end a consolidation of the States, to the utter destruction of those checks and balances of power at present existing under our confederation." In 1824 he nonetheless voted for the appropriation of federal money for roads, canals, and forts as part of Congress's obligation to "provide for the common defense," always provided that the states in which they were built gave their permission.[62]

The tariff question generally pitted the manufacturing interests in the "middle states," especially Pennsylvania, against most of the agricultural South and commercial New England. Tariff protection also enjoyed support in Clay's Kentucky, where the hemp growers feared competition from Russia. Jackson had to pick his way carefully through this mine field, and in the end he voted for a rather modest tariff in 1824. In a carefully crafted letter obviously intended for publication, Jackson took a mildly protectionist position, advocating a "judicious examination and revision" of the existing tariff, and then linking it none too subtly to his nascent Anglophobia. The last war should have taught the American people the lesson, he told an inquirer, that "our liberty and republican form of government" needed to be protected, and that meant that American workers should be "placed on a fair competition with those of Europe" so that in wartime the nation would have the means for its own defense. "In short, sir, we have been too long subject to the policy of the British merchants. It is time we should become a little more *Americanized,* and instead of feeding the paupers and laborers of Europe, feed our own, or else in a short time, by continuing our present policy, we shall all be paupers ourselves."[63] (On hearing of Jackson's support of a "judicious" tariff, Henry Clay was reported to have sarcastically announced that he favored an "*in*judicious" tariff.)

Finally, just as Congress was adjourning in May, Jackson joined with southerners and northern Crawfordites such as Van Buren in torpedoing the treaty, negotiated the year before by Secretary Adams, that would have cracked down on the international slave trade by permitting searches of suspected slave traders in American coastal waters.[64]

John C. Calhoun was the first to concede to Andrew Jackson's national strength. When a Pennsylvania nominating convention in March defeated him again, he swallowed his disappointment, withdrew his candidacy, and announced his willingness to serve as vice president with either Adams or Jackson. As the youngest of the candidates he could afford to wait. Adams, too, now recognized Jackson's appeal. There was no one, he told a hesitant supporter, "who had so solid a mass of popularity." To ex-Federalists who were nervous following the publication of Jackson's letter declaring that he would have hanged the leaders of the Hartford Convention, Adams took an indulgent and somewhat patronizing view. "The Vice-Presidency was a station in which the general could hang no one," he declared, "and in which he would need to quarrel with no one. His name and character would serve to restore the forgotten dignity of the place, and would afford an easy and dignified retirement to his old age." (Adams and Jackson were, of course, the same age.)[65]

The idea of an Adams-Jackson (or Jackson-Adams) combination was in the air that winter. Former congressman James Tallmadge of New

York, best known for introducing the bill restricting slavery in Missouri in 1820, wrote to both Jackson and Adams urging a combination of the two—in either order. Tallmadge was a Clintonian opponent of Van Buren and eager to head off New York's support of Crawford. Combine the two either way, he told Jackson, and "the vote of this state may be counted upon." In a reply to Tallmadge drafted by Eaton, Jackson now reverted to the role of the Mute Tribune. A portion of the nation had put him forward without any solicitation from him, he said. "I am content for her to decide without any sort of interference on my part....Should the choice fall on any other, believe me, my Dear Sir, that not one moment of displeasure will be felt by me."[66]

In the meantime Jackson continued to enjoy himself. "The General is calm, dignified and makes as polished a *bow* as any man I have seen at Court," reported Sam Houston. "He is much courted by the Great as well as the sovereign folks." Jackson attended church every Sunday—a different congregation each time. "He is constantly in motion to some Dinner party or other," Eaton reported to Rachel at the Hermitage. Her husband seemed amenable to patching up old quarrels, even with his old adversary, Senator Thomas Hart Benton. Jackson still carried the bullets in his side from the tavern brawl with the two Benton brothers. When Jackson and Benton found themselves on the Committee on Military Affairs, after eyeing one another suspiciously they learned that they had much in common. Like Jackson, Benton had emigrated from North Carolina to Tennessee but had found it in his interest to move even farther, to the new state of Missouri. Although Benton was still supporting the hated Clay, soon he and Jackson were dining together. Jackson's friendship with Benton evolved into one of the most significant and enduring alliances in American politics.

Unlike Jackson, Adams had no close-knit group of advisors or allies. His many admirers, both inside and outside of Washington, were largely on their own. He admitted, "When I consider that to me alone, of all the candidates before the nation, failure of success would be equal to a vote of censure by the nation upon my past service, I cannot dissemble to myself that I have more at stake upon the result than any other individual in the Union."[67] Jackson had said on more than one occasion that as far as the presidency was concerned he could take it or leave it, so long as neither Clay nor Crawford was chosen. Adams never made such a statement, publicly or privately. His long career, stretching back to the 1790s, placed more of a burden on him than on the others. As his earlier metaphor suggested, he would not move the minute hand on the clock. At least, not yet.

With the adjournment of Congress in May Jackson returned to Tennessee and Clay to Kentucky. Adams stayed on through most of the torrid Washington summer, as did Crawford, still recovering from his stroke. Secretary Calhoun, now out of the running for president but very much a candidate for vice president with either Adams or Jackson, contented himself with a tour of Pennsylvania, where he inspected possible sites for future roads and canals. He sent President Monroe a most enthusiastic endorsement of a program of federally sponsored internal improvements.[68]

That summer the nation began the complicated process of choosing electors in the first seriously contested presidential election since 1812. Unlike in later years, the choices were not made on a single day. Not until 1845 did Congress establish a single day for the casting of presidential ballots. In the meantime presidential electors could be chosen at any point between October 27 and December 1. There was no single method for selection. Many states held more than one election in the year, with state offices often chosen in the spring, before the planting season, and national offices chosen in October or November, after the harvest. The candidates themselves made no speeches nor issued any statements, but their supporters distributed broadsides (one-page sheets extolling their man), pamphlets, and newspaper editorials.

In the absence of political parties confidence in candidates themselves, regardless of ideology or regional loyalty, might suffice. Thus Adams could be attractive to some in Louisiana, Clay to Yankees in Rhode Island, Jackson to New Yorkers. There is supporting evidence in each case. However, the evidence also suggests the greater power of regionalism. Western states were not the only ones to have felt left out of the presidential picture. Massachusetts Republicans pointedly noted that they had "with pleasure, given their undivided support to elevate to office those illustrious citizens of the south, who have, for the last twenty-two years, so ably conducted the destinies of the nation." Perhaps the time had come to look elsewhere. Amos Kendall's pro-Clay *Argus of Western America* admitted that men were concerned "whether this or that section of the Union has been more perfectly represented in the executive department of the government." Residence in the West, another Kentucky newspaper argued,

was "peculiarly calculated to enlarge and liberalize the mind of a statesman." A pro-Jackson paper in Alabama agreed, stating that its candidate
would be "the President of the whole people, the enlightened ruler of
an undivided empire, and not a sectional magistrate devoted to the 'universal Yankee nation' of the East, or the mixed, mingled and confused
population of the South."[69] The swipe at the "universal Yankee nation"
was prophetic, indicating not only a political but a cultural hostility to
New England. "The whole mass of the people of New England entertain notions very inadequate to our merits," concluded the Nashville
Whig. "They think meanly of our intellectual improvements—our moral
conditions—and of our state institutions."[70]

One of the "state institutions" the *Whig* had in mind was slavery. Ever
since the Missouri debates southern slaveholders had been suspicious of the
role of the North and East in attempting to cut off the expansion of "the
peculiar institution." In 1824 their attention focused on Adams, the only
nonslaveholding candidate. They may well have had cause for concern. The
pro-Adams New York *American* complained that the South always raised
the charge of sectionalism whenever they faced a united North, and went
on to urge support for Adams as the only means to stop slavery's growth.[71]
Adams was widely—and inaccurately—believed to have opposed the
Missouri Compromise. The editor of the Petersburg (Virginia) *Republican* summarily rejected his candidacy for what it called "obvious reasons."
The *Delaware Gazette* declared, "No man who will attempt to excite local
prejudices and sectional feeling…as Mr. Adams has done" should ever be
elected president. Ritchie's proslavery Richmond *Enquirer*, committed to
Crawford, joined in the attack on the "universal Yankee nation" as well,
but the rival (and pro-Adams) Richmond *Constitutional Whig* called for an
"Atlantic Party" that could "curb the ambition of the western states."[72]

At the same time, and in contrast to what was to come four years later,
most of the campaign literature in 1824 avoided serious personal attacks
on opposition candidates. The reason was simple enough: given the role
everyone expected the House of Representatives to play in the election
of the president, today's rival might prove to be tomorrow's ally. Those
who nominated Clay in 1823 did so "without disparaging, in the smallest
degree, the very great and acknowledged merits of the other illustrious
men, to whom public attention has lately been directed."[73] Jacksonians in
New Jersey went out of their way to praise Adams, whose "knowledge
as a diplomatist, and his abilities as a writer, have been often exercised
with honour to himself and benefit to his country."[74] A pro-Adams writer

from Rhode Island promised that he would not denigrate any of his man's opponents and would "treat them *all* with that high respect that is due to men, who are honoured by the people—with a respect which I sincerely feel for their characters and publick services."[75]

Nonetheless, the encomiums occasionally carried a sting. Yes indeed, declared the Rhode Islander, Andrew Jackson was a great patriot and a military hero, but "his disregard of the local civilian authorities, in every place where he has holden the military command, is a subject of deep regret." "[Although] we cannot doubt the purity of the General's intention...the same excuse may, if allowed as a precedent, be resorted to by a bad man, to further designs of the most dangerous nature."[76] True enough, the New Jersey Jacksonians told the public, Adams was a great man, but "is the President of the United States always to be taken from the cabinet? If not, it is high time he were chosen by the people....Is the President always to continue thus to nominate his own successor?"[77] Unless there is a change, "the time will come," warned Senator Benton, "when the American President, like the Roman Emperors, will select his successor, take him by the hand, exhibit him to the people, place him upon the heights and eminences in the Republic..., make him the channel of all favor, and draw the whole tribe of parasites and office hunters to the feet of the favorite."[78]

There was also the occasional sharp elbow, the sharpest coming from Jesse Benton, the senator's brother. His *Address on the Presidential Question* was published in Nashville in the summer of 1824 and attracted a good deal of attention. Jackson, Jesse Benton said, was in Washington "with hosts of sycophants, dancing attendance on his person and flattering his vanity." It prefigured much of the anti-Jackson rhetoric that would emerge in 1828. "Boisterous in ordinary conversation, he makes up in oaths what he lacks in argument." For Jesse Benton, Jackson was and always would remain a violent, dueling, cursing, gambling, cockfighting hothead, unfit for any office at all, let alone the presidency.[79]

By 1824 the changes that had taken place regarding the selection of presidential electors were being felt not only in the process but in the political culture as well. Voters, many of them newly enfranchised and with new opportunities to influence the selection of a president, had to be approached in a manner different from that of the earlier generation. The electorate had changed both in size and in composition.

The campaign literature in 1824 reflects this. The emerging egalitarian rhetoric of second-generation American republicanism suggests that voters were more comfortable with candidates who were closer to them in education and experience. No one in the earlier generation claimed that Washington, Jefferson, Adams, or Madison was an ordinary American. The letters that passed between John Adams and Thomas Jefferson in their old age were sprinkled with passages in French, in Latin, even in Greek. Most voters were unversed in those languages, and might even be suspicious of a candidate who was. It was more important in this, the second quarter of the nineteenth century, to be, or at least appear to be, closer to the electorate. Andrew Jackson was not the only candidate whose supporters saw him as the "idol of the people." Before he withdrew Calhoun was presented by Missouri supporters as "the candidate of the people— he has not been caucused into notice, but the people are rallying around his standard, determined to choose for themselves."[80] The congressional caucus, with its elitist overtones, was a casualty of the 1824 election. Crawford's debilitated condition certainly did not help, but even had he been healthy (and he lived for another nine years), the changes in political culture, and the expectations Americans had come to accept as part of the political process, doomed the caucus in any event. In 1824 presidential politics began to acquire a popular dimension that would be emphasized even more in 1828, and thereafter would never be lost.[81]

Yet, paradoxically, there was much nostalgia in the air in 1824. James Monroe may not have been the most popular of presidents, but it was recognized by friend and critic alike that he was the last of the Revolutionary generation. The fiftieth anniversary of the Declaration of Independence was only two years away, and although John Adams and Thomas Jefferson lived on, they were two of the only three surviving signers of that document. Everyone recognized that the next president would belong to a new era, a new generation.

As if to make the point, much of the nation was diverted from politics in the summer of 1824 by the Farewell Tour of the Marquis de Lafayette, who arrived in New York from France and managed to stay for more than a year. Compared to the octogenarians Jefferson and Adams, the marquis was a youthful sixty-seven, and he showed it by taking in a good part of the country, visiting Adams at Quincy and Jefferson at Monticello.[82] Wherever he went, the Frenchman was greeted by tottering veterans, some of whom fell upon him in tears as they recalled the glory days of their youth and sacrifice. Lafayette's visit served only to reinforce the trend toward a wistful look back at the Republic's first half-century.

In many cases the nostalgia was tinged with foreboding. Would the second generation match the achievements of the first? For that matter, had those achievements been preserved at all? The notion of declension, the haunting feeling that the present is betraying the past, has its roots in seventeenth-century Puritanism and the jeremiads preached in those days from a hundred pulpits. It was reinforced by the republican conviction that liberty was always threatened by power, and that too many republics in the past had been destroyed by corruption. In the 1820s the uncertainty and sense of drift created by the economic downturn that followed the Panic of 1819 stood in sharp contrast to the heroic confidence and proud accomplishments of the departing generation. The quiet simplicity of traditional republicanism linked, accurately or not, to the earlier age, seemed to be lost. Banks, caucuses, intrigue, corruption, and other unrepublican—and now undemocratic—developments were contrasted with the earlier age and, many came to believe, were slowly corroding its luster.

Throughout 1824 many Americans were reading the letters of "Wyoming," a pseudonymous Jacksonian. They had originally appeared the year before in Stephen Simpson's *Columbian Observer* in Philadelphia and were later republished, in whole or in part, in a variety of newspapers from Florida to New England.[83] It is difficult to assess the exact extent of their readership, though it can be safely said that no other piece of electoral propaganda exceeded them in their impact. Wyoming's message was simple enough: the nation had drifted from its republican moorings, and only Jackson could pull it back. "We are not as we once were," proclaimed the author. "The people are slumbering at their posts; virtue is on the wane; and the republican principles with which we set out, are fast declining."[84] How did this come about? In Wyoming's view too many of the "leading men of the country" had distorted republicanism to their own ends, beginning with the presidency itself. It had been passed down to members of a closed circle, either to former vice presidents or former cabinet members, who, even as he wrote, were "intriguing" for the office. By implication at least, they were part of a conspiracy. "There is a struggle, which though well concealed still exists, gradually to undermine the rights of the people." If it continued, then "away with the right secured by the Constitution; for an ARISTOCRACY is rising in our land."[85]

One man, however, stood apart. One man "rests in retirement at home, while others are fighting in their grand drama, and immodestly urging their own pretensions." One man "stands aloof from all the contemptible intrigue and management of the day." Only Andrew Jackson held the promise of restoring and reinvigorating the hallowed values of the republican past. Although Wyoming didn't hesitate to remind his readers of Jackson's achievements at the Battle of New Orleans, he was more interested in linking him to a military hero of an earlier age, George Washington. In the purer atmosphere of the early days of the Republic, "it was not an inquiry, who could write a paragraph with the greatest classical purity [a swipe at Adams?]; or who, the most finished veteran at intrigue [Crawford?]; the question was, who is he, that, fearless of the consequences, and regardless of the danger, has breasted the storm in the hour of peril, and risked himself for his country." "Venerable remnant of revolutionary patriots!" the New Jersey Address proclaimed, "Jackson is one of you."[86]

Wyoming confronted the doubts about Jackson's temperament and turned them to the general's advantage. Did he violate the Constitution in New Orleans? Most certainly. He had to lay aside constitutional forms so that the Constitution itself could be preserved. "WASHINGTON would have done the same." The nation needed the forthright, masculine leadership that Jackson offered. Three of his four rivals had spent time in Europe, Wyoming sneered, and "may know how the people eat and sleep in Paris, and at London," but contact with effeminate Old World decadence and frivolity was irrelevant and possibly dangerous. "To wiser heads," the author went on, "and to those who may be conversant in the sublime science of dancing, it is left for discussion, if in the choice of a Chief Magistrate, it be a material enquiry, whether he may bow with the right or left foot foremost....I want a man, my countrymen, at the head of this nation, who will throw such trifles off; one who shall give us to see something of republican plainness."[87]

The Wyoming essays were written before Crawford's stroke sidelined him, and consequently the Georgian was their main target. "Intrigue," "corruption," "management," as well as the predictable attacks on the caucus system, constituted the bulk of the anti-Crawford case.[88] Clay and Calhoun were dismissed as too young, and as such could wait their turn. Adams, however, presented a more difficult target, given his name, his career, and his past support of Jackson. Wyoming's solution was to damn with faint praise, mixed with more than a hint of anti-intellectualism. "Mr. Adams is indeed famed for his *belle lettres* and classical acquirements," he began, "and may be, and no doubt is, a man of superior erudition than any spoken of." He was "a gentleman of high literary attainments, a finished scholar," who "stands indeed further from intrigue than any Cabinet minister we have." But in contrast to Jackson, "he is a closet man, and from his books has acquired all that he has learned: but hence knows little of man as he is." "His politics, however, have been questioned, perhaps for the reason that he happens to be his *father's son*." Crawford, in other words, was dismissed because he intrigued too much, Adams because he, the former Federalist, was too aloof from his fellow citizens to know how to intrigue. No, it was not to experience but to innocence that the nation should look: It was "to the yeomanry of our happy country, the men of agriculture and industry; who are toiling in pursuit of an honest sustenance, that we must look for security;—men who are unconnected with the Government, and with that system of flattery, folly, and intrigue."[89]

The declension theme may be found in other examples of pro-Jackson propaganda, but seldom, if ever, in that of his competitors. Pennsylvania Jacksonians deplored the "degeneracy" of modern times and the corruption of the Big City. "The metropolist of the Union already vies in aristocratic pomp and empty formalities of a modern autocrat," they grumbled. Look beyond the inner circle in Washington, New Jerseyites were told: "So shall you restore the administration of our government to its primitive purity."[90] In Michigan, which would not even become a state for another thirteen years, a Detroiter worried that too much was being made of "dexterous political management" and not enough of honest virtue and unselfish talent. Jackson was "the best fac-simile of Washington now in existence," "the Washington of his age." "NO ONE," Wyoming capitalized, "HAS DONE MORE FOR HIS COUNTRY SINCE THE DAYS OF WASHINGTON."[91]

The Wyoming letters and their offshoots showed considerable amnesia as well as nostalgia. To portray the bewigged Framers of the Constitution as closet democrats envisioning common folk choosing a president (while at the same time creating the Electoral College) required imagination, at the very least. To present Jackson as a second Washington, given that he was one of the few congressmen to oppose the resolution of thanks for the Great Man's services in 1797, was also a bit of a stretch. Not surprisingly, Wyoming made no mention of Jackson's congressional career. He had instead put his finger on a growing perception that somehow the will of the American people was being shoved aside by the intrigues and manipulations of a few.

Exactly when the true identity of Wyoming became known is not clear. The author clearly had detailed knowledge of Jackson yet was close to events in Washington as well. It should have come as no surprise, then, when Wyoming turned out to be none other than Jackson's close friend, biographer, and fellow senator, John Henry Eaton. Jackson himself did not know who wrote the letters until April 1824. He immediately recognized their worth. "These pieces I intend having collected in due time and published in pamphlet form," he told his nephew. Like Adams, he was above intrigue, but this did not prevent him from setting the record straight.[92]

At the Hermitage in Nashville the general calmly awaited the election results. Adams, after spending a few weeks at the family home in Quincy, returned to Washington in early October. He rejected a public banquet in his honor at Boston's Faneuil Hall. "It might have the aspect," he explained, "of a political expedient to make an ostentatious and equivocal exhibition of popularity, and perhaps even be represented as gotten up at my own desire for that purpose."[93]

In 1824 six states—Delaware, Georgia, Louisiana, New York, South Carolina, and Vermont—still had their presidential electors chosen by their respective legislatures. These states' votes, therefore, were determined by the results of earlier legislative elections, usually held in the spring. The results for three states could have been predicted. Georgia stuck by Crawford, the favorite son. Vermont's legislature went for Adams, its fellow Yankee. South Carolina, with Calhoun out of the running, went for Jackson, a native son. It is extremely unlikely that in these cases the result would have been any different had the voters themselves chosen the electors. In the cases of the remaining three states, however, those who were alert to "intrigue," "manipulation," and "corruption" had a field day.

The tiny state of Delaware had only three electors to choose. Federalism was still strong in there, but not all former Federalists could be assumed to be for Adams. Those with long memories recalled his apostasy in 1808, when he supported Jefferson's embargo, and were now ready and willing to take revenge. Following the state elections in October the legislature chose two Crawford and one Adams elector.[94] In Louisiana, which might be assumed to be solid for the Hero of New Orleans, matters were likewise complex. Much of the French-speaking community in New Orleans still harbored resentment against Jackson's treatment

of them in the weeks following the battle and offered vigorous opposition in the Louisiana legislature. Henry Clay had high hopes of success
there based on both political and family connections, but in the end the
Crawford, Adams, and Jackson forces combined against him and split the
state's five electoral votes: three for Jackson, two for Adams, and none for
either Clay or Crawford. Clay's shutout in Louisiana would prove to be
more significant than anyone thought at the time.[95]

But it was in Martin Van Buren's New York that the opportunity for
skullduggery and intrigue was displayed in its finest attire. To begin with,
the Albany Regency had committed a rare political blunder earlier in the
year by arbitrarily removing former governor Clinton from the largely
honorary position of president of the Board of Canal Commissioners. The
backlash that followed revived Clinton's statewide fortunes and renewed
his presidential ambitions, making him a possible northern rival to John
Quincy Adams. The Regency was also caught on the wrong side of a popular issue when it opposed the efforts of the Clintonians and others to
revise the state's laws to permit the voters to choose New York's presidential electors. With the legislature apparently committed to Crawford, Van
Buren and his allies could not afford to lose control, and thus opposed the
reform. Running on a People's Party ticket, Clinton rode triumphantly
back into the governorship in November, supported by a coalition of
Adams, Jackson, and Clay backers. Van Buren's Crawfordites still had a
plurality in the legislature, but they needed an absolute majority to capture
the state's thirty-six electoral votes. Here they were outfoxed by the same
Adams-Jackson-Clay coalition, this time put together by the young Thurlow Weed, a newspaper editor from Rochester. When the ballots were
finally counted the result was twenty-six electors for Adams, four for Clay,
one for Jackson, and only five for Crawford. It was a crushing defeat for
the Regency and for Van Buren, one that he never forgot. He returned
to Washington that fall, he recalled in his old age, "as completely broken
down a politician as my bitterest enemies could desire." In the years to
come Thurlow Weed would become one of those "bitterest enemies."[96]

The six states that chose their electors without direct popular participation thus produced thirty-six votes for Adams, sixteen for Crawford,
fifteen for Jackson, and only four for Clay.

It was several weeks before a pattern became clear. Because most states
had yet to establish the mechanisms for collecting and verifying the popular vote for electors, candidates and their supporters had to rely on newspaper accounts, which were often incomplete and inaccurate. When the

dust had settled the result showed the weakness of Clay, Crawford, and Adams beyond their own turf. Only Jackson showed strength beyond his section, although he ran poorly in New England and in parts of the South. In Virginia the Crawfordite Radicals continued to hold him in suspicion, seeing in him a man whose arbitrary actions as a military figure were hardly reassuring to those who clung to the republican assumptions about liberty's eternal conflict with power. Here he ran third, behind Crawford, who carried the state and all of its twenty-four votes, and Adams.

There was a spirited three-way race in Ohio, a frontier state in which there was sustained interest in economic development through internal improvements. Clay, who had built his career as both a Westerner and a promoter of the American System, expected to do well there, given Kentucky's proximity across the Ohio River. Indeed he did carry the state, but only slightly ahead of Jackson, who drew votes from Cincinnati and those counties along the Ohio River who were less interested in internal improvements. Clay and Adams split the pro–internal improvements vote, doing best in the more northerly counties that stood to benefit from the construction of new roads and canals. Adams also did well in the counties of the Western Reserve that had been settled by New Englanders, but he ran a poor third nonetheless. The result there suggested that at least in the Buckeye State issues were as much a determinant as personalities.[97]

Elsewhere, with one or two exceptions, the results could have been foreseen, with Jackson carrying most of the western states except Missouri, which Clay's friend Benton held for him, and with Clay carrying Kentucky, although Jackson ominously did quite well there. The exceptions, and ones that foretold the future, were in the middle states of Pennsylvania and New Jersey. Although he had pushed Calhoun out of the running in Pennsylvania earlier, it did not necessarily follow that Jackson would carry the Keystone State, with its ethnic, social, economic, and religiously mixed population. This he did, however, against a field clearly demoralized and outmaneuvered. Although fewer than 20 percent of the eligible voters turned out, they turned out in overwhelming numbers for Jackson, giving him all of Pennsylvania's twenty-eight votes. In a similar but less spectacular manner he carried New Jersey, with its eight votes.[98] Without the votes from these two states Jackson would have lagged behind Adams in the electoral vote. As it was, his strength there and elsewhere proved that if there was any truly national candidate, it was Jackson.

State	Jackson	Adams	Crawford	Clay
Maine	0	10,289	2,336	0
New Hampshire	0	9,389	643	0
Vermont*				
Massachusetts	0	30,687	6,616	0
Rhode Island	0	2,145	200	0
Connecticut	0	7,587	1,978	0
New York*				
New Jersey	10,985	9,110	1,196	0
Pennsylvania	36,100	5,441	4,206	1,690
Delaware*				
Maryland	14,523	14,632	3,364	695
Virginia	2,861	3,189	8,489	416
North Carolina	20,415	0	15,621	0
South Carolina*				
Georgia*				
Alabama	9,443	2,416	1,680	67
Mississippi	3,234	1,694	119	0
Louisiana*				
Kentucky	6,455	0	0	17,331
Tennessee	20,197	216	312	0
Missouri	987	311	0	1,401
Ohio	18,457	12,280	0	19,255
Indiana	7,343	3,095	0	5,315
Illinois	1,901	1,542	219	1,047
Total	**152,901**	**114,023**	**46,979**	**47,217**

Chosen by state legislature.

When Congress reassembled in December the results were fairly complete (see table above).[99]

In the electoral count, although everyone knew that no candidate would receive the required majority, the result was another triumph for Jackson nonetheless (see table on page 99).

To the surprise of many, the convalescing Crawford edged out the healthy Clay for third place, owing to the latter's forces being outmaneuvered in Louisiana. (Indeed, had it not been for the maneuverings of Weed and others in New York, Crawford might have placed second

State	Jackson	Adams	Crawford	Clay
Maine		9		
New Hampshire		8		
Vermont		7		
Massachusetts		15		
Rhode Island		4		
Connecticut		8		
New York	1	26	5	4
New Jersey	8			
Pennsylvania	28			
Delaware		1	2	
Maryland	7	3	1	
Virginia			24	
North Carolina	15			
South Carolina	11			
Georgia			9	
Alabama	5			
Mississippi	3			
Louisiana	3	2		
Kentucky				14
Tennessee	11			
Missouri				3
Ohio				16
Indiana	5			
Illinois	2	1		
Total Electoral Count	**99**	**84**	**41**	**37**

in the electoral count.) As it turned out, with Crawford still out of the picture, the final choice would be between Jackson and Adams, the two candidates that had done the least to advance their own cause. It also meant that Clay, although no longer a candidate himself, held the balance of power between two. As speaker, he had many allies in the House of Representatives, which would now choose the sixth president of the United States.

The new interest in the presidency among the expanded electorate did not yet mean that the office commanded more attention than contests at the state level. It still took second place in many states where there had been elections for governor in the same year. In Kentucky, for example, more than sixty-five thousand votes were cast in the gubernatorial election in August, but only about twenty-three thousand turned out in November. In Ohio, even with a tightly contested three-way presidential race, only 35 percent of those eligible voted for president, whereas 53 percent had voted for governor just two weeks before. In New England participation was surprisingly low, given the area's town meeting tradition and its high literacy rate. In no state was there a larger presidential turnout than for previous state elections.[100]

In some cases the low turnout for the presidential contest can be explained by the nature of the contest itself. In states where the favorite was strong and with little organized opposition, there was little incentive. Adams was the clear favorite in New England, where Jackson did not even appear on the ballot. Adams was on the ballot in Jackson's Tennessee and was defeated handily, but the overall turnout was less than 27 percent. In spite of the populist rhetoric in the campaign literature, participation in a presidential election was a new experience for many voters. Local and state governments still collected most of their taxes and made most of the decisions that affected their daily lives. It would take more than one election to coax them to the polls. In the opinion of one student of this era, "In strictly political terms, at least, the presidency was not yet the dramatic object of contention that it was soon to become."[101]

Jackson returned to Washington in December, accompanied this time by Rachel and Andrew Jackson Donelson. He had spent the summer enjoying the trickle of election results and sticking to his resolution not to "combine," "bargain," or "intrigue" for the presidency. When some Adams supporters attacked him for his stand on the tariff, even spreading the rumor that he had withdrawn from the race, he still insisted, "I have good feelings toward Mr Adams & there is no conduct of Hypocritical friends that can alter that feeling." Two months later he hardened a bit. Not only were the rumors about his withdrawal false, he said; they were "an unpardonable outrage, hardly to have been looked for by Mr. A's friends, nor indeed from any who love the freedom & sovereignty of the people; or who profess to do so."[102]

A week or so later Adams conceded, "[Jackson] will stand the highest on the list of candidates for the Presidency." Calhoun, with little or no opposition outside of a few disgruntled Crawfordites, was easily assured of the vice presidency. To many in the North this was disturbing. Were Jackson to become president and Calhoun vice president, it would mean that for the first time in the history of the Republic both the presidency and the vice presidency would be in the hands of southern slaveholders, resulting in, according to Adams, the "absolute proscription of New England." When the North had its candidate, he complained, "We did not even think of a Vice President from among ourselves—but voted for a Southern or a Western man." In 1824 the other sections were not returning the favor.[103]

The Twelfth Amendment to the Constitution was attached in 1804 following an embarrassing tie in the electoral count that had occurred four years earlier. Aaron Burr had matched the electoral vote for Thomas Jefferson, although Burr was intended only as a vice presidential candidate. The outcome was a result of the original Constitution, under which each presidential elector would cast two votes, but without distinguishing between president and vice president. In the absence of organized political parties the Framers assumed that the Electoral College would quietly and rationally choose a president purely on the basis of qualifications and experience, with the second highest recipient becoming vice president. Organized parties, or "factions," were not anticipated. But in 1800 Federalists and Republicans each put forth two candidates, with Republican electors voting for Jefferson and Burr in exactly equal numbers. The result nearly led to Burr being chosen over Jefferson for president by a lame-duck Federalist congressional majority in 1801. The Twelfth Amendment now requires that electors vote separately for president and vice president, recognizing that, whatever the Framers may have wished, political parties had become a fact of life.

Interestingly, in 1804, as a senator from Massachusetts, Adams had opposed the Twelfth Amendment, denouncing it as the "electioneering" amendment. He also was disturbed that the Amendment reduced from five to three the number of finalists from which the House could choose should no candidate receive a majority of the electoral votes. Had the original number been kept, Henry Clay, the speaker of the House of Representatives, would have joined Jackson, Crawford, and Adams as a finalist in 1824, and the end result could have been quite different.

When the House chooses from among the three finalists, each state has one vote, regardless of its size. The state's vote is determined by its representatives voting among themselves. In the case of a tie, the vote is lost. Thus Louis McLane, the single congressman from Delaware, had the same influence as all thirty-four congressmen from New York.

A majority of states being required, and with twenty-five states then composing the Union, the votes of thirteen states were needed to choose a president. If the House remained deadlocked past March 4, the day for inaugurating the new president, the vice president, in this case Calhoun, would assume the office. Few congressmen wanted that.

The remaining weeks of 1824 and early 1825 saw much superficial bonhomie in Washington. Jackson and Senator Eaton called on Adams (December 9). Adams invited Clay, Calhoun, Van Buren, and others to dinner at his home (December 23). Jackson, Adams, and others had dinner at the home of Joel Poinsett, whom both Adams and Jackson would later appoint to important diplomatic positions (January 4). There was the inevitable ball commemorating the victory at New Orleans, which all the candidates attended (January 8). Adams, Jackson, Van Buren, Clay, and Calhoun dined together once more (January 12).[104]

Behind the social niceties, however, there was rampant speculation. There were those, Daniel Webster later recalled, who claimed they could tell how a congressman would vote by the way he put on his hat. The city was treated to the unusual picture of the normally reserved secretary of state, John Quincy Adams, popping up at receptions and holding private meetings with congressmen. No, Adams told Congressman Scott of Missouri, he had no intention of giving printing contracts to any newspapers in Missouri other than those who already had them. And he would see what he could do for Scott's brother Andrew, a judge currently in trouble owing to having killed a fellow judge in a duel.[105] Yes, he told a group of Republicans, he fully regarded himself as one of them, but hoped to rise above parties. No, Adams told Webster and a handful of ex-Federalists, he did not hold a grudge against them for reading him out of the party in 1808. "Conciliation, not collision," he said, would be his principal aim if chosen president.[106]

Jackson, holding what he and his friends believed to be the winning hand, stood pat, publicly and privately condemning "intrigue" and "bargaining."

All eyes were on Clay, who had carried the electoral votes of only three states but who had congressional friends in many more. He was clearly enjoying himself. He recounted to a friend how advocates of the three candidates would sidle up to him: "I am sometimes touched gently on the shoulder by a friend (for example) of Genel. Jackson, who will thus address me. 'My dear Sir, all our dependence is on you; don't disappoint us; you know our partiality was for you next to the Hero; and how much

we want a western president.'" The same approach, with different arguments, was tried for Crawford and Adams.[107] In reality Clay had already
made up his mind. There was no way he could support either the invalid
Crawford or Jackson, the "military chieftain" of 1818. He admitted to
Francis Preston Blair, a Kentucky ally at the time, that Adams would not
have been his first choice "if at liberty to draw from the whole mass of
our citizens." But Adams did not pose a threat to either the office or the
nation. "Not so of his competitor, of whom I cannot believe that killing
2,500 Englishmen at N. Orleans qualifies for the various, difficult, and
complicated duties of the Chief Magistracy."[108]

Toward the end of December Jackson learned that Clay was against
him. He was not surprised. "Rumors say that deep intrigue is afoot," he
told William B. Lewis, "that Mr. Clay is trying to wield his influence with
Ohio, Kentucky, Missouri & Elonois [Illinois] in favour of Adams." As
for himself, he would remain on the high ground. "I would feel myself
degraded," he told John Coffee, another Tennessee intimate, "to be placed
into that office but by the free and unsolicited voice of the people—Intrigue
may stalk around me, but it cannot move me from my purpose."[109]

At a New Year's dinner honoring the ubiquitous Marquis de Lafayette,
Clay asked to meet with Adams. He did so on Sunday, January 9, a
meeting that would have profound consequences for both men. Pro-
phetically perhaps, the churchgoing Adams had returned from a service that day in which the biblical text for the sermon was taken from
the book of Ecclesiastes 7:23: "I said I would be wise, but it was far
from me." After Clay asked a few desultory questions about Adams's
plans "without any personal consideration for himself," Clay told his
former rival that "in the question to come before the House between
General Jackson, Mr. Crawford, and myself, he had no hesitation in saying that his preference would be for me."[110] There follows in Adams's
manuscript diary an extraordinary and intriguing gap in the narrative,
in which Adams's editor son Charles Francis Adams explained many
years later that his father intended to give fuller details, suggesting
that "the extreme pressures of business and visiting" no doubt inter-
fered.[111] Up to then, relations between Clay and Adams had been far less
friendly than those between Adams and Jackson. Clay had been one of
Jackson's leading critics, and Adams perhaps the general's most important defender. Now, faced with a choice between two men whom he had
opposed for many years, Clay allied himself with the Yankee instead of
the frontiersman.

Following his session with Adams, Clay proceeded to go about persuading his congressional friends to support the secretary of state, even if it meant contradicting the apparent wishes of their own constituencies. This was particularly true in his own state. The Kentucky legislature had just passed a resolution urging its congressional delegation to support Jackson, the fellow westerner, over Adams. Kentucky voters had predictably rallied to Clay in November, but Jackson had run a respectable second, whereas Adams had not been on the ballot at all. Indiana had voted for Jackson, and Missouri and Ohio for Clay. Would the speaker be able to bring them around for Adams? "Intrigue, corruption, and sale of public office is the rumor of the day," Jackson sputtered in late January. "How humiliating to the American character that its high functionaries should conduct themselves as to be liable to the interpretation of bargain & sale of the constitutional rights of the people!" Yet a week before the House voted, Adams told President Monroe that Jackson's election was still "more probable" than his own.[112]

The House met on February 9, 1825, with Clay in the speaker's chair. It was a moment of high political drama matched only once or twice in the nation's political history. The speaker first announced that no candidate had received the necessary majority of electoral votes and then directed the House to proceed immediately to its vote. Daniel Webster, the ex-Federalist, and John Randolph of Virginia, the unpredictable Radical, were appointed tellers. In those days the roll was called from North to South. Thus there were no surprises when all six of the New England states lined up with Adams; when Tennessee, Pennsylvania, and New Jersey stuck with Jackson; and when Virginia and Georgia went for Crawford. But the strength of Clay was felt when Kentucky, Ohio, Louisiana, and Missouri—none of whom had voted for Adams—came out in his favor. With support from New York, Maryland, and Illinois, Adams had the necessary thirteen votes on the very first ballot. "It was impossible to win the game, gentlemen," Randolph told the Jacksonians. "The cards were stacked."[113]

"The election is over," declared an angry Jackson the next day. "Thus you see here, the voice of the people of the west have been disregarded, and demagogues barter them as sheep in the shambles, for their own views, and personal agrandisement."[114] Letters flowed in from his friends. "I have not the language to express to you, the deep sorrow, and mortification I feel in the result of the late Election, by the Representatives of the People (falsely so styled) in their choice of a President of the US," wrote John Pemberton, an aggrieved supporter who undoubtedly spoke for thousands. Pemberton was particularly incensed at Louisiana's vote for Adams. "Louisianeans! Degraded—Ungrateful Men!! to vote against you! you!! who under God, they are indebted for their soil! The Protector of the Chastity of their wives and daughters!! You—who saved them from the brutal lusts of a mercenary soldiery!!!"[115] Jackson's nephew exploded. "What a farce!" he wrote. "That Mr Adams should swear to support the constitution of the U States which he purchased from Representatives who betrayed the constitution, and which he must distribute among them as rewards for the iniquity."[116]

Jackson kept whatever resentment he privately felt at the result carefully controlled in public. The evening after the House vote, at a huge reception honoring the president-elect, so the story goes, he greeted Adams accompanied by a "large, handsome lady on his arm." The general was most gracious, offering his left hand to Adams, "for the right, as you see, is devoted to the fair. I hope you are very well, sir." Adams stiffly responded, "Very well, sir. I hope General Jackson is well." Observers marveled at the Tennessean's composure, given the situation and his reputation. Adams wrote in his diary that Jackson's conduct was "placid and courteous."[117]

In the weeks following the House vote before his inauguration, observers thought they saw signs of distinct uneasiness in the president-elect. When Daniel Webster officially delivered the result of the House vote, Adams reportedly sweated profusely and was clearly uncomfortable. When he and his family attended a theater performance a few days later his reception was less than friendly. In truth, Adams was troubled. Unlike Jackson, Adams had come down from his Olympian perch, abandoned the Mute Tribune ideal, and "intrigued" for the office through his meeting with Clay and with dozens of congressmen. He had moved the minute hand on the watch.

Yet what was his alternative? Clay had come to him, not he to Clay. Was he to reject his offer of support? He honestly believed himself to be better qualified both through education and experience than any of the candidates, and by the standards of the day he was. He had been a senator and a cabinet member and had capably represented the United States abroad in four different countries. He had personally known all five of his predecessors. And he was genuinely upset at the prospect that a Jackson presidency, combined with Calhoun's vice presidency, would exclude the North from both offices. Yet he admitted that the outcome of the election had not ended "in a manner satisfactory to pride or just desire; not by the unequivocal suffrages of a majority of the people; with perhaps two-thirds of the whole people adverse to the actual result."[118]

Within forty-eight hours of his election by the House Adams informed President Monroe that Henry Clay was his choice for secretary of state. Monroe was not sure this was wise, but said nothing.[119] Then all hell broke loose. Ever since Clay had made his preference for Adams known, there had been allegations that the new president had in effect "bought" the presidency through a "corrupt bargain" with the speaker of the House. One of the charges came from George Kremer, a semiliterate Pennsylvania congressman whose leopard-skin jacket helped contribute to a certain reputation for eccentricity. Stephen Simpson's Jacksonian *Columbian Observer* had already printed the accusation—without attribution—twelve days before the House vote on the presidency. Clay promptly called on the author to come forward like a man—with the clear implication that a challenge to a duel would follow. Kremer's semicomical repute prevented this, and besides, he quickly denied any intent to impugn Clay's character. A congressional investigation ensued and failed to produce any evidence against Clay. With the House vote pending, even the pro-Jackson congressmen were reluctant to make any statement that could alienate potential supporters. But the news of Clay's nomination coming after the House vote seemed to confirm the charge. "Expired at Washington," said a Jackson paper, "on the ninth of February, of poison administered by the assassin hands of John Quincy Adams, the usurper, and Henry Clay, the virtue, liberty, and independence of the United States."[120] "So you see," Jackson fumed, "the Judas of the West has closed the contract and will receive his thirty pieces of silver. His end will be the same."[121]

It had been Adams's hope that he could fulfill Monroe's desire to put an end to partisanship and promote national unity. "My great object will be to break up the remnant of old party distinctions and bring the whole people together in sentiment as much as possible," he wrote in his diary.[122] To this end, he hoped to put together a cabinet that would both reflect a balance of sections and include the followers of his former rivals. He even went so far as to ask Crawford to stay on as treasury secretary. Crawford declined, probably to Adams's relief. He asked Samuel Southard of New Jersey, the navy secretary and a Calhounite, to stay on, which he did. He thought of offering Jackson the post of secretary of war; he was told the general would have none of it. (Besides, the thought of Jackson and Clay in the same room, let alone the same cabinet, was enough to give one pause.) William Wirt of Maryland, another Calhounite, agreed to stay on as attorney general. With two vacancies yet to fill, Adams nominated Pennsylvania's Richard Rush, his successor as minister to Great Britain, as treasury secretary, and James Barbour of Virginia, a former Crawfordite, as secretary of war. John McLean of Ohio, thought to be a Calhounite, agreed to stay in the politically sensitive post of postmaster general, although it was not yet a cabinet position. With himself from New England, Southard and Rush from the middle states, Clay and McLean from the West, and Barbour from the South, Adams had produced a well-balanced cabinet, or so he thought. Conspicuous by their absence, however, were any Jacksonians or any representative from the Deep South.

Adams's inaugural was held in the House chamber (Statuary Hall in the present Capitol building). There, in the presence of the newly sworn Vice President Calhoun, Speaker Clay, President Monroe, Senator Andrew Jackson, and most of Congress, Adams read his Inaugural Address. William Plumer Jr., an Adams admirer, told his father that the address was "worthy of the man & of the place." True, the new president appeared at first to be "a little agitated—but soon recovered his self possession, & spoke with great clearness, force, and animation."[123] The address was a plea for unity, now that "the baneful weed of party strife" had withered away. He praised both Federalists and Republicans for their past contributions. "The candid and just," he declared, must admit that both parties had "contributed splendid talents, spotless integrity, ardent patriotism, and disinterested sacrifices," while both "required a liberal indulgence for a portion of human infirmity and error." Those days of partisan rancor, he hoped, had passed. There remained only one challenge that lay before those who had once embraced a political party. "It is that of discarding every remnant of rancor against each other, of embracing as countrymen and friends, and of yielding to talents and virtue alone that confidence which in times of contention for principle was bestowed only upon those who bore the badge of party communion."[124]

He raised a few eyebrows when he declared his conviction that national unity could best be promoted through an imaginative program of internal improvements. He was sure, he said, that "unborn millions of our posterity" would be grateful for what this generation could achieve, and he hoped that any "speculative scruple" about the limits of congressional power could be resolved "by a practical public blessing." This was the only hint offered in the address of Adams's own views on this particular issue, controversial as it was to many of his listeners.

To those who saw him as an elitist opposed to popular government, he reaffirmed the republican creed that "the will of the people is the source, and the happiness of the people is the end [i.e., the purpose] of all legitimate government." He went even further, describing the United States as a great "representative democracy." No president before him had ever used the word "democracy" in a public address. He then referred to the unusual circumstances of his election. "Less possessed of your confidence in advance than any of my predecessors," he confessed, "I am deeply conscious of the prospect that I shall stand more and oftener in need of your indulgence."[125] When he was finished, the president-elect turned to Chief Justice John Marshall, whom his father had appointed some twenty-four years earlier, and took the presidential oath. Afterward Jackson stepped forward and shook Adams's hand. It would be the last time they would shake hands in all the many years that lay before them.[126]

★ Chapter Four ★

At first Andrew Jackson did not hunger for the presidency. The strategy behind his nomination by the Tennessee legislature in 1822 and his election to the U.S. Senate a year later was to bar two men whom he distrusted from the office, rather than advance himself. Even after his candidacy caught fire beyond Tennessee, he was still prepared to see any outcome, favorable or not, provided there was no unrepublican "corruption" or "intrigue." The election of his former ally Adams with the help of his hated enemy Clay convinced him that the will of the people had been set aside through conspiracy. Many Americans were ready to agree.

As soon as Congress adjourned in March 1825 Jackson headed back to the Hermitage. (He stayed long enough to join thirteen other senators in voting against Henry Clay's appointment as secretary of state. Twenty-seven voted in favor, including Van Buren and Benton.) The closer he got to Tennessee the angrier he became. "Well, general," an old Pennsylvania friend commiserated, "we did all we could for you here, but the rascals at Washington cheated you out of it." Jackson agreed. "There was *cheating*, and *corruption*, and *bribery* too," he replied.[1] For the next three years the charge of "corrupt bargain" would be leveled at Clay and Adams, and after Jackson's triumph in 1828 would pass into American history, if not as a fact then at least as a legend.

Many years later, when all the principals were in their graves, Jacksonians such as Martin Van Buren and Thomas Hart Benton dismissed the charge (although they were perfectly willing to take political advantage of it at the time). Van Buren described Adams as "an honest man, not only incorruptible himself, but...an enemy to venality in every department of public service." Benton, in his own memoirs, said the same thing about Clay, his former friend.[2] In politics as in life, what is believed to be true often displaces the truth itself. There was nothing illegal or unconstitutional in the Adams-Clay alliance. Given their joint commitment to an expanded view of federal power regarding internal improvements and other aspects of the American System, it made sense. Adams's offer of the premier cabinet position to his longtime critic may have been politically naïve, but it was not corrupt. The blunder lay in Clay's acceptance, which, as one historian has put it, was tied to him like a tin can to a dog's tail for the rest of his career. Years later, while running for president himself, Clay admitted that it had been the worst mistake of his life.[3] Whether it automatically doomed the Adams administration is not clear. The result in 1828 had as much to do with events and decisions made after Adams was sworn into office as it did with his election by the House of Representatives in 1825.

Even before he was sworn into office Adams was warned of trouble ahead. If he appointed Clay secretary of state, a friend reported, Calhoun and his allies would organize themselves into opposition, with Jackson at their head. Already there were rumors that the two had dined together, along with their supporters. "Only New England states would support the Administration," said Adams's friend, "New York being doubtful, and the West much divided, and strongly favoring Jackson, as a Western man. Virginia is already in opposition, and all of the South decidedly adverse." It turned out to be a remarkably accurate, if premature, prediction. "The voice and power of the people has been set at naught," proclaimed Calhoun. Clay's appointment was "the most dangerous stab which the liberty of the country has ever received." His South Carolina ally, Congressman George McDuffie, was already preparing a proposed constitutional amendment whereby presidential electors would be chosen in districts by popular vote, stripping Congress of any role in choosing the president. "I am at least forewarned," noted the president-elect.[4]

In the meantime Jackson was receiving letter after letter encouraging him to run for president in 1828. Still playing the role of the Mute Tribune, he did not immediately commit himself. His saved his energy for attacks on Clay, "the Judas of the West." The former speaker's dismissal of Jackson as a "military chieftain" still stuck in his craw. "I am well aware that this term 'Military Chieftain' has for some times past been a cant phrase with Mr. Clay and certain of his retainers," he told Samuel Swartwout, an enthusiastic supporter from New York City. "Mr. Clay never yet has risked himself for his country, sacrificed his repose, or made an effort to repel an invading foe." Apparently "he who fights and fights successfully must according to his standard be held up as a 'Military Chieftain': even Washington could he again appear among us might be so considered." As for the new president, Jackson grumbled that his inaugural had been accompanied by "a pomp and ceremony of guns and drums not very consistent in my Humble opinion with the character of the occasion." Other than that he had little to say about Adams for several months. Swartwout, a close friend and ally of Aaron Burr, thought so much of his correspondence with Jackson that he had it published without Jackson's knowledge or permission. Jackson did not protest.[5]

By the following October Jackson had changed his opinion of the man who had so consistently supported him in the past. "Mr Adams is the Constitutional President, and as such I would myself be the last man in the Commonwealth to oppose him on any other ground than that of principle," he told Henry Lee, an admirer and scion of one of Virginia's first families. "I had esteemed him as a virtuous, able and honest man, [and even after his election] I manifested publicly a continuation of the same high opinion of his virtue." The appointment of Clay altered matters. After that, the general continued, "I withdrew all intercourse with him.... The private relations of life forbids an association with those whom we believe are corrupt or capable of cherishing vice when it ministers to selfish aggrandisement."[6]

Two weeks later the Tennessee legislature nominated Jackson for president in 1828. When he learned of it he hurried to the state capital at Murfreesborough. A simple letter of acceptance would have done the trick, but Jackson was demonstrating his flair for the well-timed gesture. Standing before a joint session of the legislature, he submitted his resignation from the U.S. Senate and filled his address with traditional republican rhetoric. Unless the people's will prevailed, he warned, "it requires no depth of thought to be convinced, that corruption will become the order of the day, and...evil may arise of serious importance to the freedom and prosperity of the Republic." Not only was his resignation dramatic, but it made good political sense. His election to the Senate had been a political ploy whose usefulness had since passed. His continued presence there would force him to take positions on issues that might weaken his support among many who might otherwise be his friends. And the resignation allowed him to maintain his distance from the nation's capital, the center of "intrigue and corruption."[7]

The Nineteenth Congress, elected the year before, assembled in Washington in December 1825. Topping the agenda for members of the House of Representatives was the election of a new speaker to replace Henry Clay. It was the first test of strength for the Adams administration. In those days the speaker controlled all committee appointments, and the election of a hostile speaker would not bode well for the future. As it was, the president's supporters organized effectively enough to elect John W. Taylor, a New Yorker and an enemy of Van Buren's Albany Regency, but the vote was very close.

On December 6 Congress received President Adams's first Annual Message. Now known as the State of the Union message, in the nineteenth century it was delivered to Congress in writing and read by a clerk. (Not until the twentieth century would presidents take advantage of the opportunity to deliver it in person before Congress, and in prime time.) Adams had labored long and hard over the message. He hoped to use the occasion not only to "report on the state of the union," as the Constitution required him to do, but to spell out his own understanding of "republicanism." In so doing he was about to lay out an extraordinary vision of the capabilities of government in what he had already called "a representative democracy."

Adams had never accepted the notion that liberty and power were always and inevitably opposed. Certainly it was true when power was wielded by absolutist monarchies and entrenched Old World aristocracies. Certainly it was true when Americans overthrew unchecked power in the hands of a British Parliament in which they had no representation. Now, however, the American people themselves were the rulers. "Individual liberty," he told a Massachusetts friend, "is individual power, and as the power of a community is a mass compounded of individual powers, the nation which enjoys the most freedom must necessarily be in proportion to its numbers the most powerful nation." He had admitted to his father while American minister in London, "My system of politics more and more inclines to strengthen the union and its government. It is directly the reverse of that proposed by Mr. John Randolph." It was unfortunate, he said, that "according to the prevailing doctrine our *national* Government is constituted without the power of discharging the first *duty* of a nation, that of bettering its own condition by internal improvement." He refused to believe that those who wrote the Constitution had been "so ineffably stupid as to deny themselves the means of bettering their own condition."[8]

He had kept these views to himself and to private correspondents while he was secretary of state, and his Inaugural Address contained only a few hints. Now, in his first Annual Message, Adams was more specific. With the end of the European wars, the emergence of new nations in Latin America, and the recovery from the Panic of 1819, the time had come for Americans to embark on a bold course of action that would prove to the rest of the world that liberty and power were no longer in opposition. It was, he admitted, "a perilous experiment." His cabinet counseled against it. They either doubted the constitutionality of some of his proposals or, given his precarious political position, questioned their timing. Adams listened to their comments but went ahead with his original plan. The Annual Message was a great opportunity, perhaps his only opportunity, to persuade, to inspire, and to move the nation forward to new ground rather than to restate and reinforce the "prevailing doctrine."[9]

Adams saved his main idea until the final paragraphs of the message. "The great object of civil government," he told Congress, "is the improvement of those who are parties to the social compact." He went on to propose an ambitious and startling package of measures that included an accelerated program of road and canal construction, the establishment of a new department of the interior, the creation of a national university, the financing of scientific expeditions of exploration and research, the creation of a naval academy, the enactment of a national bankruptcy law, the establishment of a uniform system of weights and measures, and the building of a national astronomical observatory. Regarding the last item, he noted that there were at least 130 observatories in the world—"lighthouses of the skies," he called them—but not one in the United States.

Adams closed his Annual Message with a peroration: "The spirit of improvement is abroad upon the earth." Improvement meant not only the physical creation of roads and canals. It meant improvement in the intangibles as well: in scientific research, in education, and in the arts. To those still influenced by eighteenth-century notions of republicanism he repeated his earlier, privately held view: "Let us not be unmindful that liberty is power; that the nation blessed with the largest portion of liberty must in proportion to its numbers be the most powerful nation upon earth." Had Adams stopped there he might have been on safe ground. But he went on: "While foreign nations less blessed with that freedom which is power than ourselves are advancing with gigantic strides in the career of public improvement," he continued, "were we to slumber in indolence or fold up our arms and proclaim to the world that we are palsied by the will of our constituents, would it not be to cast away the bounties of Providence and doom ourselves to perpetual inferiority?"[10]

The reaction was instantaneous. "Are we reading a state paper, or a school boy's Thesis?" asked Thomas Ritchie. "Sir," snorted another Crawfordite, "this administration I verily believe will be conducted upon as corrupt principles indeed more corrupt, than any that has preceded it." Now "the Crawford party will have to stand aloof." "The friends of states rights object to it as utterly ultra," declared Vice President Calhoun.[11] Former presidents Madison and Jefferson read the message and were not happy. "I see...with the deepest affliction, the rapid strides with which the federal branch of our government is advancing towards the usurpation of all the rights reserved to the States, and the consolidation in itself of all powers, foreign and domestic," Jefferson wrote to a fellow Virginian. Madison, as usual, was a bit more restrained. "All power in human hands is liable to be abused," he said, without any direct mention of the Annual Message.[12] Francis Preston Blair, long an ally of Henry Clay in Kentucky, defected to Jackson, as did Thomas Hart Benton, who years later recalled that the Annual Message defeated Adams's hope for abolishing political parties and, on the contrary, brought about "the reconstruction of parties on the old line of strict...construction of the constitution."[13]

The message convinced Jackson that Adams, whom he had once "never doubted of his attachment to our republican government," now was "not the man of real wisdom, that had heretofore been ascribed to him." His notion "that it would be criminal for the agents of our government to be palsied by the will of their constituents" could only end in despotism "if not checked by the voice of the people," he warned a North Carolina sympathizer. Unlike Adams, he had great confidence in the people. "Instead of building lighthouses of the skies, establishing national universities, and making explorations round the globe," he predicted, "their language will be, pay the national debt—[be] prepared for national independence & defence—then apportion the surpluss revenue amonghst the several states for the education of the poor—leaving the superintendence of education to the states respectively."[14]

The modern reader of Adams's Annual Message will note that nearly everything he advocated eventually came to pass. In many ways the message was, admitted Andrew Jackson's most thorough biographer, "a bold, courageous, and statesmanlike assertion of the government's responsibility to assist the advancement of the nation's intellectual and economic well-being."[15] It was both behind and ahead of its time. On one hand it reflected the more vigorous approach to governing that had been associated with the Federalists, and on the other looked forward to the Progressive Era in the early twentieth century, when government indeed would be viewed as a means for improving the human condition. But in 1825 the timing was poor and the phraseology inept. Many thought their political will had already been "palsied" by the outcome of the previous election. Adams's urging Americans to imitate Europe in "the career of internal improvement" enabled his critics to accuse him once again of a sneaking admiration for the effete, corrupt, and "monarchical" society of the Old World in which he had spent much of his adult life. Whatever merits the message may have had as a measure of the vision and integrity of John Quincy Adams, it was a political disaster. His injection of literary metaphors, as when he called astronomical observatories "lighthouses of the skies," brought only ridicule.

Although Adams consulted regularly with his cabinet, he had no close allies who were dedicated to his political fortunes and whose loyalties were unlimited. There were no counterparts to Eaton, Lewis, Houston, or the various members of the Donelson family who had been attached to Jackson since New Orleans, or even before. Adams had the political support, but not the personal devotion, of such capable leaders as Clay and Daniel Webster, whose own political futures rested on Adams's success. Webster, who had moved from his native New Hampshire to Massachusetts, had hoped to be rewarded for his loyalty by being named minister to Great Britain. Instead, Adams offered it first to DeWitt Clinton, who, secretly supporting Jackson and with his own designs on the presidency, turned him down. Adams inexplicably then turned to the elderly Federalist Rufus King, who had held the same post under his father in the 1790s. King took the post, but his age caught up with him and he was forced to resign. Then Adams appointed a Republican, the Swiss-born Albert Gallatin, who had been Jefferson's treasury secretary and Adams's colleague at Ghent in 1814. Gallatin's diplomatic experience was unquestioned, but his appointment gained the president nothing in terms of support at home. Webster swallowed his frustration and continued to support the administration. "Mr. Adams, during his administration," wrote Thurlow Weed, who had engineered Adams's victory in New York in 1824, "failed to cherish, strengthen, or even recognize the party to which he owed his election, nor as far as I am informed, with the great power he possessed did he make a single influential friend."[16] The irony, of course, is that while Adams was accused of conniving for the presidency through "bargain and corruption," he was steadfast in his determination not to use his powers to hold on to it.

Adams remained committed to his predecessor's quest to rid the presidency, if not the nation, of the "baneful weed" of partisanship. That commitment was tested very early in the administration, when Secretary Clay urged the removal of James Sterrett, a naval officer in New Orleans whom Clay claimed was "a noisy and clamorous reviler of the Administration." It was his position that "no officer...should be permitted to hold a conduct in open and continual disparagement of the Administration and its head." Adams disagreed. Removal merely "at the pleasure of the President," he told Clay, was inconsistent with "the principle...of removing no person but for cause." The alternative, he continued, would be "an invidious and inquisitorial scrutiny into the personal dispositions of public officers" that would "creep through the whole Union." The principle of rotation in office, he wrote on another occasion, "would make Government a perpetual and unremitting scramble for office."[17] Frustrated, Clay never again raised the issue directly with Adams, although others would.

As secretary of state, Clay turned his attention first to Latin America, whose independence from Europe he had long supported. He had clashed with Adams in earlier years over how much encouragement the United States should offer the colonies of Spain and Portugal; now, in 1825, independence had become reality for most Latin Americans. Clay suggested that the United States accept the invitation offered by the organizers of a proposed conference of Latin American republics, conceived by the great Latin American revolutionary Simón Bolívar, and scheduled to be held in Panama the following year. Adams agreed to make the recommendation in his Annual Message. It was in the interest of the United States, he and

Clay believed, to cooperate with the new nations to the south in establishing their place in the world. As it was to be only a consultative gathering of diplomats with no legal significance, Adams thought nothing about accepting the invitation and nominating two delegates and a secretary without consulting Congress. The delegates were neither ambassadors nor ministers with powers to negotiate. A U.S. presence at Panama would be a gesture of friendship to the new republics to the south and would provide an opportunity to promote American ideas on freedom of the seas and religious liberty. "We have laid the foundations of our future intercourse with the southern republics in the broadest principles of reciprocity and the most cordial feelings of fraternal friendship," Adams said.[18]

The Panama Conference, along with the Annual Message, became the basis for the emerging anti-Adams coalition. As soon as the message was published Congressman McDuffie wasted no time in introducing his amendment revising presidential elections. Not only did it call for the popular election of presidential electors by districts, but it changed the final selection process so that in the event of no candidate receiving a majority of electoral votes the choice would revert to the states, not to Congress, with the final list reduced to two instead of three.[19] McDuffie was by no means the first person to suggest that a revision of the Constitution was in order; Martin Van Buren had proposed much the same thing over a year before. With the lingering resentment over the result of the previous election, the alleged "corrupt bargain," coupled with the reaction against Adams's Annual Message, McDuffie's proposal took on new significance.

In an earlier day, McDuffie explained, restrictions on the popular vote may have been justified. No longer. The proliferation of newspapers, pamphlets, books, and communication in general had produced an informed electorate whose direct role could no longer be denied. Democracy, he said, was "the renovating, self-sustaining principle of our liberties."[20] In the Senate Missouri's Thomas Hart Benton lined up with the Jacksonians and offered the same proposal. Jackson, too, supported it, along with another amendment that would prevent the appointment of any congressman to the president's cabinet during the term for which he was elected. It was needed, he said, to preserve the separation of powers, but it was clearly aimed at Clay.[21]

Jackson's crony from the New Orleans days, Edward Livingston, now a congressman from Louisiana, went McDuffie one better, proposing to do away with the Electoral College altogether. Let the people vote directly for the president, he said: "Let them do that for themselves, which they are now compelled to do by an attorney." The ensuing debates forced the Adams supporters to defend the existing system. They praised the "symmetry and harmony" of the Constitution, and though admitting that the nation had been "deeply agitated" over the result the year before, denied that was a reason for change. The young congressman Edward Everett, an early protégé of John Quincy Adams, defended the system in a three-hour oration that exceeded in length, if not profundity, his speech at Gettysburg thirty-seven years later.[22]

Both Livingston's and McDuffie's proposals were doomed to fail: McDuffie's, for no other reason than that the district system would break up the power of the larger states, which, by voting as a unit, carried more weight than they otherwise would; Livingston's, because although few would admit it at the time, a direct vote of the people—meaning, of course, virtually all adult white males—would do away with the "three-fifths bonus" that the existing system awarded the southern slave states in the Electoral College. By the end of the first session of Congress the proposals were dropped. The debates nonetheless kept the result of the previous election before the public and placed those who opposed the changes, nearly all of whom had supported Adams, in the position of defending both the system and the result.

With the start of the New Year Vice President Calhoun saw to it that the Senate's Committee on Foreign Relations was stacked with allies of Jackson, Crawford, and himself.[23] The Committee's report on the Panama Conference was presented by Nathaniel Macon, the respected, strict constructionist Old Republican from North Carolina. It opposed U.S. participation in the Conference on both constitutional and practical grounds. It questioned not only the power of the president to accept the invitation in the first place, but the motives of the Conference as well, pointedly observing that Adams had omitted any discussion of the slave trade, which had been listed on the meeting's agenda. Tennessee's senator Hugh Lawson White, Jackson's successor, and South Carolina's Robert Y. Hayne, Calhoun's spokesman, chimed in with many anxious worries about the "peculiar institution" should U.S. delegates mix with black representatives from Haiti, the former slave colony. Americans should have nothing to do with any discussion "connected with slavery," declared Hayne, least of all with black Haitians. Others added warnings about the dangers of white Americans having to associate with "Africans" or "mixed bloods."[24] New York's Van Buren was a bit more subtle, contenting himself with a strict constructionist approach. It was "not within the Constitutional power of the Federal Government to appoint deputies," he claimed; he was supported by Benton. Others invoked the principles of Washington's Farewell Address and Jefferson's warnings about "entangling alliances."

Jackson joined in. "To be represented at a congress of Independent confederate nations, is an event, which I presume, the framers of our constitution never thought of," he told one correspondent. "Entangling alliances with none—that is our true policy." Again he focused his ire more on Clay, whom he blamed for the whole affair, than the president. "Mr. Adams is really to be pitied," he said, and predicted a possible "divorce between Mr. A. & Mr. C."[25] Adams watched the developments. At the end of January 1826 he noted the effort to "combine the discordant elements of the Crawford and Jackson and Calhoun men into a united opposition against the Administration. It is at an early stage of its progress, but it has already become complicated, and admonishes me to proceed with extreme circumspection."[26]

The Panama Conference was popular in the nation at large, however, and the anti-Adams forces were unsuccessful in blocking it, losing in the Senate by a vote of twenty-four to nineteen, and in the House by an even bigger margin, 132 to 60. They achieved their purpose nonetheless, as the delay alienated the Latin American leaders, and the holdup in funding prevented the delegates from arriving in time to make any difference. Indeed, one of them did not arrive at all, perishing of tropical fever on the way.[27]

In spite of their defeat the opponents did not let up. John Randolph, now a senator from Virginia, went after Clay, denouncing the Panama project as "a Kentucky cuckoo's egg, laid in a Spanish-American nest." It was the result, he continued, of "the coalition of Blifil and Black George— by the combination, unheard of until then, of the Puritan and the blackleg." This was a reference to two unsavory characters in Henry Fielding's novel *Tom Jones* and was obviously an allusion to Adams and Clay. Vice President Calhoun, then presiding over the Senate, should have called Randolph to order, but didn't. Adams ignored the insult. Clay, however, challenged Randolph to a duel, which ended with the Kentuckian firing a bullet into the Virginian's coat and the irrepressible Virginian firing into the air. Then they shook hands. According to Senator Benton, who was hiding in the bushes at the time, it was one of the last high-toned duels in Washington.[28]

Benton led the attack on patronage in the Senate, accusing Adams of using his appointive powers to build up a personal following that would guarantee his reelection in 1828. He proposed no fewer than six measures intended to rein in presidential authority, including limits on the powers of appointment, removal, and the publication of congressional acts and executive regulations. Senator Macon joined him, denouncing the "monstrous influence" of John Quincy Adams. Benton's proposals failed, as he knew they would, but like the attacks on the Panama Conference and the Electoral College, they were effective in building the case against the administration.

While Clay and others were chagrined over the president's refusal to use his appointive powers to aid his cause, his enemies were portraying him as a ruthlessly partisan manipulator. Adams's administration, "wretched & rotten," John Henry Eaton reported to the Hermitage, "is already crumbling, yes broken down and nothing can keep it up." He and the Tennessee delegation had already clashed with Adams over his appointment of a Jackson opponent, John Patton Erwin, to the Nashville Post Office. Erwin was the editor of the Nashville *Whig* and a brother of Henry Clay's son-in-law.[29] Incredibly, Erwin's appointment was proof to Jackson and others that the administration intended to use patronage to shore up its strength for 1828. "It displays a *littleness* that I did not suppose Mr Adams capable of, whatever I thought of Mr. Clay," Jackson told Sam Houston. "There is more corruption in Washington at present than is to be found in any Government under the sun," wrote a disappointed job applicant. Jackson vowed that if elected he would put an end to abuses of executive power.[30]

By the end of the first session of the Nineteenth Congress, the outline of the anti-Adams coalition was clear. Former Crawfordites Van Buren and Macon were allied with Calhounites McDuffie and Hayne and Jacksonians Benton and White. Still, an anti-Adams coalition was not yet the same as a pro-Jackson movement.

Upon his return to Tennessee in the spring of 1826 Senator Eaton hand-delivered a letter addressed to Jackson. "An issue has been fairly made...between *power* and *liberty*," wrote Vice President Calhoun, "and it must be determined in the next three years, whether the real governing principle in our political system be the power and patronage of the Executive, or the voice of the people." The vice president went on, "For it can scarcely be doubted, that a scheme has been formed to perpetuate power in the present hands, in spite of the free and unbiased sentiment of the country." Calhoun knew his man. The assertion of the ancient republican tension between power and liberty was bound to appeal to Jackson. "It will be no small addition to your future renown," he concluded, "that in this great struggle your name is found, as it always has been, on the side of liberty, and your country. Occupying the grounds that you do, there can be no triumph over you, which will not also be a triumph over liberty."[31] With that, Calhoun gave notice that he would postpone his own ambitions for at least four more years and join with Jackson against Adams.

Calhoun had been forced to rethink his position on many issues since his defeat by the Jacksonians in Pennsylvania in 1824. He could not compete with Adams in New England, nor with Jackson in the middle states. In addition, his own state of South Carolina, a Federalist stronghold in the 1790s, was undergoing a profound change of heart in both its political and intellectual perspectives. The Missouri debates over slavery's future in 1820 and an aborted slave rebellion in Charleston two years later told white South Carolinians that they were in a minority both in their own state and in the nation as a whole. As such, the assertions of federal power once made by Calhoun and his fellow nationalists now seemed threatening. A federal government strong enough to restrict slavery's growth in the West might in the future be strong enough to end it altogether in the South. Protective tariffs seemed to protect northern manufacturers at the expense of southern planters. Increasingly out of step with his own state, Calhoun would have to abandon either his earlier thinking or his political ambition. He was not prepared to do the latter. An alliance with Andrew Jackson against the "ultra" doctrines advocated in the president's Annual Message could provide the means by which he could not only survive but become president himself. Jackson, by his own admission, was not in the best of health, and a one-term Jackson presidency with Calhoun continuing as vice president would open a smoother path to the presidency than anything Calhoun had yet seen.[32]

Jackson took over a month before replying to his former superior. When he finally did, he repeated his disappointment with Adams. Until he saw the Annual Message, he thought "Mr Adams to have a tolerable share of common sense," and that he would avoid "the asperity which marked the struggle of 98 & 1800 [i.e., the Alien and Sedition Acts and Jefferson's defeat of his father]." Such had not turned out to be the case, however, and the administration seemed intent on using patronage and deception, "precisely where the enemies of freedom in all ages have placed the foundations of power." Then he took up Calhoun's suggestion: "I trust my name will always be found on the side of the people, and as their confidence in your talents and virtue has placed you in the second office of the government, that we shall march hand in hand together in their cause."[33] Thus began the alliance between Jackson and Calhoun that would lead to their joint success two years later. Jackson still did not know of Calhoun's attacks on him in Monroe's cabinet. When he did, it would lead to the most fiery confrontation between a president and a vice president in American history.

All of this lay in the future in the spring of 1826, as congressmen made their way home and the nation began preparations for observing the fiftieth anniversary of the adoption of the Declaration of Independence. From old cities like Boston, Massachusetts, and Charleston, South Carolina, to frontier towns like Chillicothe, Ohio, and Salem, Indiana, citizens prepared toasts and tributes, banquets and balls in honor of the nation's founding. The three surviving signers of the Declaration—John Adams, Thomas Jefferson, and Maryland's Charles Carroll—along with former presidents Madison and Monroe, were invited to Washington to be honored for their contributions to the Early Republic. All of them declined, owing to age and poor health.[34]

On July Fourth President Adams made plans to attend the ceremony in the Capitol building. He rode, appropriately enough, in a separate carriage from that of Vice President Calhoun. There he listened to an undistinguished oration and returned to the Executive Mansion, where he received "citizens and strangers" who wished to pay a call. Similar orations, often followed by public dinners and flowery toasts, took place throughout the nation. Toasts honored "the Day," "Patriots and Sages," "the Republican Form of Government," and "the Constitution." Sometimes "the President of the United States" was offered, but infrequently by name. Partisanship occasionally could be discerned. In Jackson's Nashville, after a reading of the Declaration, glasses were raised to *The next presidential election*—All power is inherent in the people; their will be done." In Charleston John Randolph was honored for his attack on Adams and Clay. Congressman McDuffie was also honored with an altered line from *Macbeth*: "Lay on Macduff, and damn'd be he who first cries hold, enough." On the other hand, banqueters in Vincennes, Indiana, toasted "Internal Improvements and Domestic Manufactures." The president, oblivious to such things, contented himself the next day with a close examination of the cultivation of silkworms and the planting of live oaks, the latter in keeping with a resolution recently passed by the House of Representatives.[35]

The next day Adams received word of "a strange and very striking coincidence." Thomas Jefferson had died on the Fourth of July 1826—fifty years to the day after the promulgation of the Declaration of which he was the principal author. Forty-eight hours later he opened a letter from Quincy informing him that his own father was dying and not likely to survive. On his way to Baltimore he learned that John Adams, too, had died on the Fourth. Most Americans agreed with him that "the time, the manner, the coincidence with the decease of Jefferson, are visible and palpable marks of Divine favor." The news set off another round of ceremonies and testimonials, including a thundering two-and-a-half-hour performance by Daniel Webster in Boston, during which, according to Adams, the entire audience sat "mute." Several weeks later Jackson presided over a commemorative meeting in Nashville.[36]

In the long run, the passing of the two Founders, inspiring as it may have been to most Americans, did not work in Adams's favor. In recalling the earlier days, it was difficult to avoid the fact that it was the Republican Jefferson who had limited the Federalist Adams to one term, allegedly over the very same issues of liberty and power that threatened the reelection of his son. Jackson sensed this. "Is the death of Mr. Adams a confirmation of the approbation of Divinity," he asked a friend, "or is it an omen that his political example as President and adopted by his son, shall destroy this holy fabric created by the virtuous Jefferson?" Upon leaving his father's empty house for Washington that fall, Adams reflected that in time he would be settling there for good, "probably within three short years."[37]

Such gloomy Adams-like pessimism was not, however, a trait of Henry Clay, who had spent much of the year trying to repair whatever damage had been caused by the charges of the "corrupt bargain." After a number of appearances in Kentucky he was convinced that the worst was over. "I have no fears for the future," he told his brother-in-law after Congress adjourned. A month later he assured Webster that Adams would "be re-elected by a vote of more than two-thirds of the Union."[38]

However, the complaints about the president's appointment policy—or lack of it—continued to flow in. Former congressman Henry Warfield of Maryland, who voted for Adams in the House election of 1825, was typical. "Be assured Sir," the agitated Warfield wrote, that if Adams persisted in ignoring his allies, his political influence "will blast and wither like the lightning of Heaven." An applicant for a federal appointment himself, Warfield sarcastically said that he didn't mean to offend Adams by supporting him.[39] He still did not get the appointment. Another former congressman, Joseph Bellinger, complained from South Carolina that Jackson had the support of "every civil officer of the General Government here." The administration had to decide whether to continue to allow their enemies to remain in office. Supporters were expecting some sort of reward, and Bellinger recommended a likely prospect for appointment as collector of the port of Charleston. He didn't get the appointment either. "I can not understand this policy," another Charlestonian complained.[40] Clay did what he could. Not having much influence over appointments or removals, he did have some authority in awarding lucrative printing contracts to newspapers for the publication of federal laws and regulations, the target of Benton's proposed legislation. In the first year of the administration Clay took contracts away from ten out of eighty papers, and ultimately from over seventy—an unprecedented number for the time.[41]

No one had more appointments and contracts at his disposal than John McLean of Ohio, the postmaster general. Beginning with McLean's tenure under Monroe, the number of post offices had increased by approximately 70 percent.[42] Eventually Clay, Webster, and others began to suspect McLean, a Calhounite, of using his power to favor opponents of the administration. They demanded that he be fired. McLean denied the charges and insisted on his loyalty. After discussing the matter with him Adams refused to let him go, though he later became convinced that McLean was guilty of "deep and treacherous duplicity." The Ohioan was a "double-dealer" whose "words are smoother than butter, but war is in his heart."[43] The problem was that McLean was extraordinarily competent, having introduced measures that made the Post Office one of the most efficient branches of the government. Significantly he was the only member of Adams's cabinet to avoid criticism from the opposition. After his election Jackson continued McLean in his post and later appointed him to the Supreme Court.[44]

Eighteen twenty-six was a congressional election year, and for the first time in American political history many contests were conducted with an eye toward the presidential election two years down the road. The new Congress would not meet until December 1827, when there would be another opportunity to elect a speaker of the House. The Twentieth Congress would be in session through all of 1828, the last year of Adams's term, and control would be critical. Clay and Webster knew this, as did the Jacksonians Eaton, Lewis, Houston, and indeed Jackson himself. The president, apparently unconcerned, took his time returning to Washington from Quincy following the death of his father.

Clay was confident that the administration's men would prevail and that Adams would continue to be supported in the House of Representatives by a friendly speaker.[45] But the administration's opponents proved to be better organized. The voters in Waterford, New York, for example, were urged to support no one but "an open, avowed and devoted friend of Andrew Jackson" in order to avoid any repeat of the 1824 election, which had resulted in placing a man in office by virtue of "a bargain, paralleled only by the history of an Iscariot."[46] Daniel P. Cook, who had been Illinois's sole representative in 1825 and who had cast the state's vote for Adams, went down to defeat, according to one observer, owing to his opponent's doing "nothing for many months previously, but ride through the state, and visit the people in their own houses."[47] Adams's sole supporting congressman from Missouri was likewise defeated. In Ohio some friends of Adams unwisely supported a Jacksonian candidate purely for family reasons, and in another district three pro-Adams candidates ran against one Jacksonian. The same thing happened in one Kentucky district, and two others were lost as well, giving the Jacksonians a majority of the congressional delegation in Clay's own state. The same lack of coordination occurred in New York. Daniel Webster lamented that nowhere else had the cause been so "badly managed." In Philadelphia pro-Adams Republicans and pro-Adams Federalists refused to work together. These losses were offset in part by favorable outcomes in New Jersey and Maryland, but the overall result would not be known for another year.[48]

Martin Van Buren pondered his options. Still smarting from the result of the Crawford debacle and his insistence on sticking to the congressional caucus in 1824 when hardly anyone else wanted it, he had not given up on his plan to reconstruct the old party divisions that he believed were the best means of preserving republicanism from its enemies. Adams's Annual Message, as Benton noted, resurrected Van Buren's earlier plan to "revive the old contest between federals and anti-federals." The question for the Little Magician was which of the remaining contenders in 1824 would offer him the best chance of success in 1828. Crawford was slowly recovering from the stroke he suffered in 1823, but now had little support outside of his own state. Calhoun, ensconced in the vice presidency, perhaps was thinking of advancing himself in 1828, but his record, embracing as it did an expansive view of federal power, made him an unlikely choice. Clay's attachment to the American System hardly qualified him. That left Jackson, whose hatred of Van Buren's friend Crawford had once been almost as great as it had been for Clay. A Jackson-Crawford alliance would take some finesse.

Although he had distinguished himself by opposing the Adams administration on the Panama Conference and other matters, Van Buren still refused to take a stand on the presidential question. "We...lay upon our oars, and will not lightly commit ourselves," he advised a Regency leader.[49] There were several reasons for this. In the first place, there were problems in his own state, where DeWitt Clinton, his longtime rival, was cruising toward reelection in a year in which Van Buren himself was a candidate for reelection to the U.S. Senate by the state legislature. Second, many of his Radical allies who had supported Crawford in 1824 still did not trust Andrew Jackson, whose reputation for hotheaded arbitrariness they saw as wholly inconsistent with their strict construction views. "Nothing can be gained...in principle," said one Radical, "by turning out Adams and electing Jackson."[50] Editor Ritchie had been particularly scathing in his attacks on Jackson in his *Enquirer* ever since the Florida episode in 1818 and had yet to be convinced. Third, Van Buren did not fully trust Calhoun. The South Carolinian had gone ahead and set up his own opposition newspaper, the *United States Telegraph*, earlier in the year, whereas Van Buren would have preferred someone less attached to Calhoun, possibly Ritchie. Van Buren continued to wait upon events, a trademark that would contribute to his success in the long run.

What was missing from the Jackson movement was any clear enunciation of principles that could distinguish it from the administration other than righteous indignation at the outcome of the previous election. "If Gen Jackson & his friends will put his election on old party grounds," Van Buren wrote to an old friend in Virginia after the results of the 1826 elections were in, "preserve the old systems, avoid if not condemn the practices of the last campaign, we can by adding his personal popularity to the yet remaining force of old party feeling, not only succeed in electing him but our success when achieved will be worth something. We shall see what they are willing to do." He was prepared, he said, to "go over" to Jackson, but he told the Regency leadership late in 1826, "We will support no man who does not come forward on the principles & in the form in which Jefferson & Madison were brought forward."[51]

In 1826 the Albany Regency held on to control of the New York state legislature, which meant Van Buren's reelection to the U.S. Senate was assured. With his seat no longer in doubt, he was ready to make his move. In December he sat down with Vice President Calhoun and offered not only his personal support of the Jackson effort but that of the Radicals who had once supported Crawford. This meant, in Van Buren's count, most of New York's electoral votes (New York had recently changed its means of selection from the legislature to a popularly elected district system), as well as Crawford's old strength in Virginia and Georgia. He promised to visit Richmond and bring Ritchie and the *Enquirer* into line, followed by a tour of the South and a meeting with Crawford himself. Adding the electoral votes of New York, Georgia, and Virginia to those of the Jacksonians in the rest of the South and most of the West gave the general more than enough electoral votes in 1828. Calhoun agreed. The two shook hands and, as Van Buren later recalled, "united heart and hand" to support Andrew Jackson and defeat John Quincy Adams.[52]

As promised, Van Buren composed a lengthy letter to Ritchie in Virginia, laying out the reasons for Radical support of a Jackson candidacy, sharing it with Calhoun and others before sending it off. Van Buren repeated his conviction that only through an organized political party could true republicanism be preserved. Continuation of an Adams presidency, with its commitment to nonpartisanship, would erode the orthodox republican ideology that had once bound Ritchie, Crawford, and himself in a common cause. Jackson might win the election solely on the basis of his great personal popularity, but a victory without reference to any set of political principles might be no better than another four years of Adams. On the other hand, the New Yorker continued, a Jackson victory obtained "as the result of a combined and concerted effort of a political party, holding in the main to certain tenets & opposed to certain prevailing principles, might be another and far different thing."[53]

He then returned to his favorite notion: "We must always have party distinctions," he told the editor, "and the old ones are the best of which the nature of the case admits. Political combinations between the inhabitants of the different states are unavoidable & the most natural & beneficial to the country is that between the planters of the South and the plain republicans of the north. The country has once flourished under a party thus constituted & may again." Not only that, argued the Magician, but the combination of southern planters (i.e., slaveholders) with northern republicans would discourage sectionalism and defuse what he pointedly referred to as "the clamour against Southern influence and African slavery." Given the growing population trends in the North, a purely North-South geographic rivalry would be disastrous for Ritchie's own section. But "party attachment in former times furnished a complete antidote to sectional prejudices." Party loyalty could and should trump sectional loyalty. After thinking it over, Ritchie and the *Enquirer* came out for Jackson in the spring of 1827. It was time, the editor told William B. Lewis, to "cleanse the Augean stable—circumscribe the sweep of the Genl. Government within its constitutional limits, and in fact restore the good old Republican era of the Jeffersonian school."[54]

Van Buren's conversion to the cause was relayed to the general and his friends in Nashville. Sam Houston, who was about to leave Congress to become governor of Tennessee, knew Van Buren and was delighted. "Your friends who know him best are satisfied with his course and are pleased with it," he told Jackson. Although they had met casually during Jackson's brief senatorial term, Van Buren and Jackson had not been particularly close, given the Magician's support of the despised Crawford and Jackson's tribute to DeWitt Clinton in 1819. Van Buren moved to remedy this by opening up a correspondence, first with William B. Lewis and eventually with Jackson himself. Just to ensure that nothing went wrong, he sent a New York ally, James A. Hamilton, to Nashville to keep an eye on matters and report back as needed. (Curiously, Hamilton was none other than the son of Alexander Hamilton, the arch-Federalist whose "aristocratic" ideology Van Buren's alliance of southern planters and northern "plain republicans" was organized to combat.)[55]

In the meantime the Nineteenth Congress continued to dismember Adams's Annual Message. The plan for a national university never made it to the floor of either house of Congress, although every president since 1787 had favored the idea. The naval academy went down to defeat under a combined attack of anti-intellectualism and republican "simplicity." Public virtue was threatened, a North Carolina congressman told his fellows, by a naval academy that would have "a tendency to produce degeneracy and corruption of the public morality, and change our simple Republican habits." Opponents also objected to appropriating seven thousand dollars for four professors. Even the existing academy at West Point came under fire as a "monarchical institution" and "one of the very creatures of royalty." Although it had been revealed that during the War of 1812 the British had had better naval charts of the American coast than the Americans themselves, no comprehensive survey plan was adopted. A proposed research exploration of "the South Seas" likewise remained unfunded. There would be no national bankruptcy act for some time.[56]

By the time the Nineteenth Congress finally adjourned in the spring of 1827, the Jacksonians, if not Jackson himself, had staked out ground that seemed to support Van Buren's intent to resurrect the ancient conflict between "federals and anti-federals." Whatever momentum there had been for constitutional nationalism in the Madison and Monroe years had exhausted itself in many parts of the country, especially in the South. The aftermaths of the Panic of 1819 and the Missouri debates had done their work. A South Carolinian declared, "The term National was a new word that had crept into our political vocabulary, a term unknown to the origin and theory of our Government."[57]

Wisely Jackson himself never publicly committed to Van Buren's blueprint for resurrecting the partisanship of the 1790s. Many from northern and western states who favored Jackson also favored federal funding of internal improvements—at least in their own districts. While opposing any "national" blueprint along the lines of the Annual Message, they were ready to support selected individual projects. Riverbeds needed to be dredged, harbors needed to be improved, existing roads needed to be extended, and private canal companies were clamoring for federal financial aid. Northern and western Jackson supporters quietly joined with the Adams administration in funding these measures, while continuing to disparage the president himself and his Annual Message. (One project in Ohio was even funded twice.)[58] But southern Jacksonians were less impressed. South Carolina's legislature passed a resolution stating that it was unconstitutional for the citizens of one state to be taxed for constructing roads and canals in another.[59] If the Jackson effort were to succeed, these differences would have to be resolved, or, more likely, concealed.

True to his promise, Van Buren set out to tour the South as soon as Congress adjourned. His first stop was in Charleston, where he attended a dinner honoring Calhoun's friend Robert Y. Hayne. He then took a steamboat to Savannah for a meeting with Crawford. After some hesitation, the former treasury secretary agreed to support one former rival,

Jackson, but balked at supporting the other, Calhoun. They agreed to dis-agree on that question, and Van Buren spent the rest of his stay conferring with other Georgians, setting forth his arguments in favor of the Jackson-Calhoun ticket. He then made his way back to Washington, stopping and attending dinners wherever he could and sending regrets when he could not. The southern mission consumed nearly two months.[60]

Having been burned in 1824 by his stubbornness regarding the con-gressional caucus Van Buren readily abandoned it in favor of partisan conventions in 1828. He hoped that local, county, and state conventions could be pyramided into a symbolic national convention of Republicans, who would nominate Jackson and Calhoun for the presidency. Calhoun and others were dubious, if for no other reason than that not all states were as enthusiastic about Calhoun as they were about Jackson. A truly national nominating convention would have to wait.

Van Buren's journey and its mission were no secret. "There are intrigues on foot," the Washington *National Intelligencer* told its readers, "to place the election of President and Vice President of the United States within the control of a Central Junta in Washington, of which Mr. Van Buren's happy genius is the ascendant influence." The Little Magician planned to introduce "his system of party discipline, and to procure the rejection of nominations, not upon the question of honesty or fitness for trust, but upon the test of persons' having voted one way or another at a preceding election." The result, the editors warned, would be "to substi-tute the regular operation of the Government, and to control the pop-ular election by means of organized clubs in the States, and organized presses every where."[61] The *Intelligencer* was not alone in following Van Buren. "The Buck tail or Republican party are beginning to move in New York," a South Carolinian reported to Andrew Jackson at the Hermitage. "Van Buren the first man in that State is *zealously cordially* and *entirely* with us."[62]

President Adams was watching him too. "Van Buren is now the great electioneering manager for General Jackson," Adams confided to his diary in the spring of 1827, and he had "every prospect for success." Van Buren, he thought, was like another New Yorker, Aaron Burr, who had made a similar tour of the South before uniting with Thomas Jefferson to defeat Adams's father in 1800. "There is much resemblance in char-acter, manners, and even person, between the two men." Yet the smiling Van Buren, who prided himself on maintaining friendly relations with his political opponents, did not hesitate upon his return from his mission to invite Henry Clay to visit New York or to stop by the White House for a friendly chat with the man he was planning to defeat. Adams sensed what lay ahead. "My own career is closed," he wrote the day after Van Buren's visit. "My duties are to prepare for the end, with a grateful heart and unwavering mind."[63] The Magician agreed. "You may rest assured," he told one of his friends, "that the re-election of Mr. Adams is out of the question."[64]

★ Chapter Five ★

The word "campaign" is a military term. It implies leadership, orders, a hierarchical structure, and above all a willingness on the part of the rank and file to place common cause above individual interest. The penalties for disobeying orders in a political campaign are far less stringent than in a military one, and individuals in a political campaign will always have their eyes on their interests as well as those of the candidate or party, yet most successful political campaigns follow as closely as possible the military model. "To manage men," said a Jacksonian organizer, "is as much a science as to manage armies."[1] It probably was no coincidence that the first truly national political campaign for the presidency was run on behalf of a military figure.

In the presidential election campaign of 1828 can be found the elements, sometimes rudimentary, of most elections to come: coordinated media, fund-raising, organized rallies, opinion polling, campaign paraphernalia, ethnic voting blocs, image making, even opposition research, smear tactics, and dirty tricks. Most, but not all, of these innovations were introduced by the Jacksonians, who time and again proved that they had grasped the significance of the shifting tectonic plates that lay beneath the political landscape better than their opponents. They recognized that the expanding electorate needed to be handled in new ways. They accepted, and for the most part embraced, the role of organized political parties in a republic. They understood, too, what effective political operatives in future elections would also come to understand: that although particular issues can be important, nothing in a presidential election is more important than the image of the candidate. In the end it was the image of Andrew Jackson, the Hero of New Orleans, the outsider untouched by "intrigue and corruption" in Washington, the defender of true republicanism in the face of its "aristocratic" enemies, that would prevail. It was one of the most powerful presidential images in American political history. Combined with the campaign put together on his behalf and the lack of an effective response by his opponents, it proved to be unbeatable. "Say what you will," an Adams supporter ruefully conceded after it was over, "these Jacksonians are excellent politicians."[2]

"Without a paper," Martin Van Buren once told a fellow New Yorker, "we may hang our harps on the willow. With it, the party can survive a thousand convulsions."[3] He was right. Partisan newspapers were hardly new, as anyone knew who could recall the angry politics of the 1790s. But the creation of a network of newspapers, coordinated among the editors who published them, was an innovation of the Jackson campaign, one that clearly differentiated it from its opposition and one that would be followed in presidential campaigns in the future.

Between 1800 and 1828 the number of newspapers in the United States had tripled. *Niles' Weekly Register* reported approximately six hundred of them, many, if not most, with a clearly partisan intent. Fifty were dailies, 150 were semiweeklies, and about four hundred were weeklies.[4] At a time when it cost an ordinary citizen as much as twenty-five cents to send a one-sheet letter through the mail, a newspaper could be sent for less than two cents. Moreover, every editor could send one copy of his journal to every other editor in the country free of charge. This meant that in an age in which news could still travel no swifter than a fast horse, newspapers were dependent on one another to circulate and recirculate the news. Aiding the accelerated transmission of news and partisan propaganda was a steady improvement in the quality of post roads, as well as an increased number of post offices. In a society in which literacy was already high, the combined effect of new roads, cheap newspaper postage, an expanding network of editors, and the establishment of new post offices contributed to the new political culture.[5]

Ironically, given the limited government, strict construction views of many of Jackson's supporters, a good part of the expenses connected with the election of 1828 was borne by the federal government and, through it, the American taxpayer. Not only was postage cheap, at least for newspapers, but the congressional "franking privilege," which allowed congressmen and senators to communicate with their constituents through the mails at no personal expense, was virtually unlimited at the time. All they had to do was affix their signature to the item, and off it would go. This meant that partisan material—newspapers, broadsides, books, pamphlets, and other forms of political propaganda—could be sent out to states and districts free of charge. Thomas Ritchie happily reported that many Jacksonian congressmen were placing their signatures on plain wrapping paper, which, after being sent to partisans in the congressman's home district, could be used to wrap campaign materials and then be deposited in the mail. By this means the *United States Telegraph*, with a subscription list of twenty thousand, was printing and circulating twice that many copies by the spring of 1828.[6]

Both the Jackson and the Adams campaign benefited from these developments, but the Jackson campaign benefited more. Three Jacksonian newspapers, each representing an element of the new coalition, stood at the top of a remarkably organized journalistic pyramid. The *United States Telegraph*, edited by the Calhounite Duff Green, was published in Washington itself. From Virginia came the Richmond *Enquirer*, edited by Thomas Ritchie, the former Crawfordite. In New York the Albany *Argus*, edited by Edwin Croswell, had long been the mouthpiece of Van Buren's Albany Regency. To these three could be added the Concord (New Hampshire) *Patriot*, edited by the former Crawfordite Isaac Hill, New York City's *Evening Post*, edited by the former Federalist William Coleman, and of course the Nashville *Republican*.

These newspapers constituted the summit, but Jackson's allies in and out of Congress were active in subsidizing, promoting, and contributing to dozens of other newspapers located in the hinterlands. In North Carolina alone, nine new papers had been set up by the summer of 1827, and eighteen were added in Ohio. No section of the Union was ignored, not even Adams's own New England. "We have organized our fences in every quarter," boasted New Hampshire's Jacksonian senator Levi

Woodbury, "and have begun & shall continue without ceasing, to pour into every doubtful region all kinds of useful information." Jackson's friends were expected to shore up newspapers when they needed it. When Stephen Simpson's *Columbian Observer* showed signs of financial distress, Senator Eaton responded with a gift of fifteen hundred dollars.[7]

For the first time newspaper editors themselves emerged as effective partisans. Duff Green, whose daughter was married to Calhoun's son, is only one example. Both an editor and a politician, when he was not editing the *Telegraph* he was corresponding with dozens of fellow editors, inquiring about the state of opinion around the nation. While editorial objectivity for newspapers had never been thought needed or even desirable, the election of 1828 saw editors—such as Green in Washington, Hill in New Hampshire, and Kendall and Blair in Kentucky—not only emerge as partisans but go on to hold important elective or appointed positions themselves. This new breed of editor had never been comfortable with the antiparty rhetoric of the Monroe variety and, in the words of one scholar, combined "rhetorical brutality, fanatic zeal, and intense competitiveness, along with a moral code flexible enough to accommodate ideological inconsistency or a bout of opportunism regarding public affairs and printing contracts." At least seventy editors would be appointed by President Jackson to federal offices; others received lucrative printing contracts.[8]

The Adams administration was unable to match the opposition in newspaper support. Many papers, perhaps even a majority, were sympathetic, but they lacked both the circulation and the aggressiveness of a Green, a Ritchie, or a Hill. It was a matter of quality, not quantity. The closest thing to a national newspaper in the 1820s was Hezekiah Niles's Baltimore-based *National Register*. Niles himself was personally sympathetic to Adams, but he was more concerned with promoting the American System than he was with the fortunes of any particular candidate, and thus the columns of the *Register* were filled with extended encomiums in favor of internal improvements, the protective tariff, and the organized efforts for their promotion. Under the slightly dismissive heading "Elections and Electioneering," one could read occasional items in the *Register* regarding the election taken from other journals. The Washington-based *National Intelligencer*, which had supported Crawford in 1824, came around to Adams in 1827, but only after Van Buren, in a blatantly partisan move, led the effort to shift the Senate's printing contract to the *Telegraph*. Even then, the *Intelligencer* saw itself as soaring above pure partisanship. Its editors, Joseph Gales and William Seaton, loftily stated that they sought to present "all facts truly upon the evidence...and misrepresent no man or measure" simply because of politics. Clearly, as events would show, this would not be typical of campaigning on either side in the election of 1828.[9]

The only other pro-Adams newspapers of note were the Washington *National Journal*, which went through three editors during Adams's presidency; New York City's *American* and *National Advocate*, neither of which were a match for Coleman's *Evening Post;* and the Richmond *Whig*, no match either for Ritchie's *Enquirer*. As one student of the press in 1828 has remarked, Jacksonian journalists seemed to enjoy the give-and-take of editorial combat more than their opponents did and entered into the lists with a certain amount of glee and gladiatorial enthusiasm.[10]

A second innovation established by the Jackson campaign was its coordinated direction. Calhoun, Van Buren, Eaton, and Benton met regularly while Congress was in session and corresponded when it was not. As a group they represented all sections of the Union. At first their problem was one of overenthusiasm, as unofficial pro-Jackson committees emerged, anti-administration resolutions were published, and tirades against the "corrupt bargain" of 1825 erupted. Many such committees had already been established, such as the Democratic Committee of Vigilance and Superintendence, formed the year before in Philadelphia, "to accomplish through the agency of corresponding committees a perfect understanding among the friends of ANDREW JACKSON in all the States," or when twenty citizens in Cincinnati came together in 1826 to promote the general's candidacy and to correspond with like-minded committees throughout Ohio and the Union. Harnessing this enthusiasm without stepping on too many toes required delicacy on the part of the leadership, but by the end of 1827 there were few cities or counties that did not have some form of Jackson committee engaged in organizing Jackson meetings. Armies are broken down into battalions, regiments, companies, and platoons; the Jacksonians aspired to a similar design. One partisan boasted that, "with the cooperation of about half a dozen, intelligent and zealous friends," he had organized "a plan, or System of Committees, from a Principle or Central Committee...down to Sub-Committees into every ward of the Town, and Captains Company in the Country." In rural areas Jacksonians sometimes were organized by school districts.[11]

Recognizing that the coming election would involve men who had never before cast a vote for president, the Jacksonians developed innovations intended to raise voter participation to new levels. Hickory Clubs sprouted in a number of towns; hickory trees were planted, usually followed by a rally of enthusiasts brandishing hickory poles. (The trees would still be around twenty years later.) In the South, knowing that crowds would be there in advance, the Jacksonians scheduled their meetings when men were already gathered for militia musters or court meetings. "Meetings will now take place all over the state," one southerner assured another, "perhaps in every county."[12]

These meetings required coordination, which became the responsibility of county "committees of correspondence." In most cases they organized carefully staged county "conventions," consisting of delegates elected from the towns, often made up of as many as could afford the trip. The county conventions in turn chose delegates to state conventions, whose numbers were calculated according to the state's population or congressional representation or some combination thereof. The committees were connected to one or more of the three leading papers: the *Telegraph*, the *Argus*, or the *Enquirer*. The election of 1828 was the first in which a majority of the states held nominating conventions.

The conventions tended to follow an established pattern that would be repeated for generations to come. First the faithful would sit through a number of speeches, one or two of which would be selected for later publication. Resolutions would be proposed and adopted. Toasts would be offered, followed by dinner. Then the speeches and resolutions would be reported and approved in friendly presses and denounced, dismissed, or ridiculed by their opponents. The Jackson meetings, said the pro-Adams *National Journal*, somewhat hopefully, were not genuine expressions of opinion, but were "designed to lead the people astray." The *National Intelligencer* agreed: "They seek to ensure victory, by raising a shout that victory is already won."[13]

The Adams partisans organized conventions of their own, sometimes even ahead of the Jacksonians, but their efforts were often stilted and lacked their opponents' enthusiasm. An Adams committee was formed in Indiana, but it met only once, whereas the Jackson committee there met six times.[14] There was no coordinated group of Washington leaders to match the Jackson effort. Clay and Webster carried most of the burden. Clay, however, spent too much of his time defending himself against the "corrupt bargain" charges, and Webster's earlier Federalism made him an easy target for the orthodox Republicans. In the House of Representatives the cause was upheld by Edward Everett of Massachusetts and

John W. Taylor of New York. No attempt was made to put together an alliance of westerners, southerners, and northerners. (Indeed, with the exception of Clay, Adams had no prominent advocate from either the South or the West.) Adams's cabinet did what they could. Navy Secretary Samuel Southard was particularly effective, traveling throughout Maryland, Delaware, and his own state of New Jersey. For this he and others were denounced by the Jacksonians, who loudly complained of the "juggling or traveling Cabinet." (The *Telegraph* was particularly indignant. The president was allowing his secretaries, it complained, to "neglect the business of the nation, for the purpose of making electioneering journies, attending barbeques, and addressing inflammatory harangues to the people with a view to the perpetuation of his power: thereby degrading the dignity of the office and corrupting the morals of the community.")[15]

Paralleling the Jacksonian leadership in Washington was an informal "central committee" in Nashville, headed by John Overton. The committee had two purposes: to fend off and refute attacks on the candidate and to provide counsel and advice when needed. As soon as they heard about it, the administration press promptly dubbed it the "white-wash" committee. No similar group was created on behalf of Adams, in Massachusetts or anywhere else.

And there was the question of money. Both campaigns would see not only the mushrooming growth in partisan newspapers but an accompanying avalanche of additional printed material, including books, pamphlets, addresses, broadsides, and even the first examples of campaign buttons, ribbons, and other political paraphernalia, all of which required cash in unprecedented amounts. Vice President Calhoun suggested that each friendly congressman and senator be given financial responsibility for his district or state and for seeing to it that the *Telegraph* be circulated within it. Those who couldn't afford it would be advanced funds from those who could, upon a promise to repay later. It is not clear to what extent Calhoun's plan was implemented. It is clear, however, that Duff Green picked up an impressive eleven thousand dollars from Massachusetts Jacksonians, who, realizing they could probably not carry their state, were willing to help those who stood a better chance elsewhere.[16] Much of the money was raised in the New York–Philadelphia area by men who were hardly "plain republicans." The Mechanics and Farmers' Bank of Albany, New York, was firmly controlled by the Albany Regency, and its managers were continually pressed by Van Buren to feed the needs of the movement.

Particular individuals had their own needs as well. Amos Kendall had been a friend of the Clay family in Kentucky for many years, and had even tutored some of Clay's children. He had vigorously supported Clay for president in the 1824 election. After Clay loaned him fifteen hundred dollars, the editor assumed that his friend, now secretary of state, would find a job for him in Washington that would allow him to pay off his debt. He was mistaken. Clay's job offer came nowhere near the amount needed, and after Clay brought suit for payment the two parted company. It was another of Clay's misjudgments, resulting in Kendall's defection to Jackson. Van Buren was able to find help, and Kendall's difficulties were solved.

The Jacksonians knew that the broader the base of participation in presidential elections, the greater the opportunity for fund-raising. Taking part in a pro-Jackson rally or convention often came at a price. Participants were expected to contribute small amounts to cover the cost of printing the orations that were the offshoots of the meetings. "Public" dinners were held, often at a cost of five dollars per plate, not a small sum in 1828. One estimate has suggested that it may well have cost over one million 1828 dollars to elect Andrew Jackson president.[17] But the administration was not far behind. "The course adopted by the Opposition," Clay told Webster, "in the dissemination of Newspapers and publications against the Administration and supporting presses, leaves to its friends no other alternative than that of following their example." He added, "Our friends who have the ability should contribute [to] a fund for the purpose of aiding the cause." Webster, with his contacts in the New York and New England business communities, became the administration campaign's unofficial treasurer. It is impossible to estimate, given the lack of records, the exact extent of fund-raising by either campaign.

Finally, following the newspaper network, the coordinated leadership, and the fund-raising, there was the role played by the candidates themselves. So far as Jackson was concerned, the days of the Mute Tribune were over. Whatever doubts he might have had about the propriety of seeking the office he laid aside. He forgot most of his old quarrels (Clay always excepted), reached out to former foes, embraced new friends, and concentrated on winning the office. He "threw himself into the fray as no previous presidential candidate had." Visiting congressmen and others were welcomed. From the Hermitage came a stream of private letters, carefully couched to avoid any implication of self-promotion but encouraging correspondents to fight the good fight against intrigue and

One of the many "correct views" of Andrew Jackson's victory at New Orleans. Jackson and the Americans are off in the distance; General Pakenham's death is displayed front and center. Note the unusual American flag at the top. *Courtesy of the Collections of the Library of Congress*

Andrew Jackson, in full uniform, sword in hand and horse at the ready, posed for this portrait by John Wesley Jarvis shortly after his controversial invasion of Florida in 1818. *Courtesy of the Metropolitan Museum of Art, Harris Brisbane Dick Fund, 1964 (64.8). Image © The Metropolitan Museum of Art*

Although it says "President of the United States" underneath, this Asher Durand engraving was taken from a Thomas Sully portrait of John Quincy Adams as secretary of state. He has a book in his lap and a number of maps strewn around him, indicative of his success in diplomacy with other nations. *Courtesy of the Collections of the Library of Congress*

John C. Calhoun was President Monroe's secretary of war when John Wesley Jarvis painted this portrait in 1818. Jarvis captured the intellectual intensity that would characterize Calhoun's entire career. *Courtesy of the Yale University Art Gallery. Gift of John Hill Morgan, B.A. 1893, LL.B. 1896, M.A. (Hon.) 1929*

A very young Henry Clay, perhaps already contemplating a run for the presidency, posed for this portrait by Charles Bird King in 1821. *Charles Bird King, "Henry Clay," 1821, oil on canvas, 36 1/8 x 28 1/8 in (91.76 x 71.44 cm), Corcoran Gallery of Art, Washington, D.C., Museum Purchase, Gallery Fund*

In the early nineteenth century most men and women did not smile for their portraits, possibly because they had bad teeth. The young Martin Van Buren seems to be on the verge of breaking this custom in this portrait, painted by Francis Alexander in the early 1820s. *Courtesy of the White House Historical Association (White House Collection)*

Although a stroke in 1823 effectively ended William H. Crawford's political career, he lived long enough to join with his longtime rival Andrew Jackson to help defeat President John Quincy Adams in 1828. This portrait was painted by John Wesley Jarvis shortly before Crawford's illness. *Courtesy of the Pennsylvania Academy of the Fine Arts, Philadelphia. Gift of Charles Roberts*

"A Foot-Race." This cartoon was probably created in the summer of 1824, before the election results of that year. It shows John Quincy Adams and William H. Crawford out in front, with Andrew Jackson closing in. Henry Clay is falling behind, and John C. Calhoun is nowhere to be seen. The man on the far left is saying "Huzza for Jackson," while old John Adams is saying "Huzza for my son Jack." Note the stereotypical Irishman and the foppish French aristocrat center right. *Courtesy of the Collections of the Library of Congress*

REPUBLICAN
ANTI-CAUCUS TICKET.
For President,

JOHN QUINCY ADAMS,

For

VICE-PRESIDENT,

Some tried and approved Patriot.

TICKET.
Col. Stephen Wright, *Norfolk.*
Dr. Henry W. Holleman, *Surry.*
Dr. John W. King, *Dinwiddie.*
Edward R. Chambers, *Lunenburg.*
Col. John Clarke, *Halifax.*
Benjamin Hatcher, *Manchester.*
Col. William B. Lynch, *Lynchburg.*
Col. James Callaway, *Franklin.*
John M. Martin, *Nelson.*
William B. Randolph, *Henrico.*
Philip Harrison, *Fredericksburg.*
Christopher Tompkins, *Mathews.*
Robert Lively, *Hampton.*
Hancock Eustace, *Stafford.*
John Shackleford, *Culpeper.*
Capt. John P. Duval, *Fauquier.*
John Rose, *Leesburg.*
Hon. Hugh Holmes, *Winchester.*
Col. Jacob Vanmeter, *Hardy.*
Thomas J. Stuart, *Staunton.*
Pere B. Wethered, *Greenbrier.*
Peter Mayo, *Abingdon.*
Enos Thomas, *Mason.*
John S. Barnes, *Monongalia.*

To sweep the Augean Stable.

FOR PRESIDENT,

Andrew Jackson.

FOR VICE-PRESIDENT,

JOHN C. CALHOUN.

ETHAN ALLEN BROWN, of Hamilton
ROBERT HARPER, Ashtabula.
WILLIAM PIATT, Hamilton.
JAMES SHIELDS, Butler.
HENRY BARRINGTON, Miami.
THOMAS GILLESPIE. Green.
THOMAS L. HAMER, Brown,
VALENTINE KEFFER, Pickaway,
ROBERT LUCAS, Pike.
JOHN M'ELVAIN, Franklin.
SAMUEL HERRICK, Muskingum.
GEORGE SHARP, Belmont.
WALTER M. BLAKE, Tuscarawas.
BENJAMIN JONES, Wayne.
WILLIAM RAYEN, Trumbull.
HUGH M' FALL, Richland.

The rebellion against the caucus system of choosing presidential nominees is reflected in this pro-Adams broadside for 1824, aimed at Virginians. Note the absence of any named vice presidential nominee. *Courtesy of the Collections of the Library of Congress*

"Sweeping the Augean Stables" was a recurring theme for the Jackson cause in both 1824 and 1828. Here is the successful ticket of Jackson electors in Ohio for 1828. *Courtesy of the Collections of the Library of Congress*

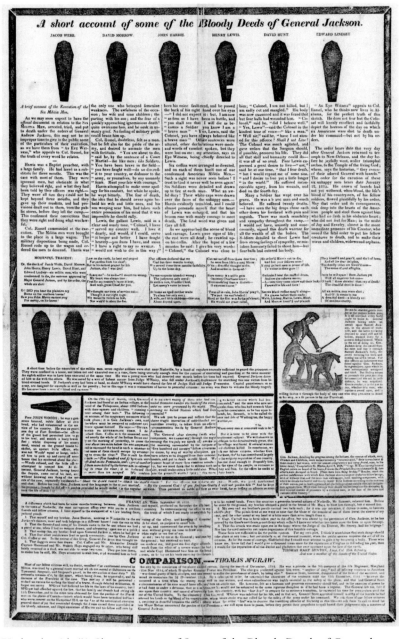

Under the title "A Short Account of Some of the Bloody Deeds of General Jackson," John Binns's "Coffin Handbill" was one of the most widely circulated items of its kind in 1828. Its effect is unclear. A hasty reader might conclude that Jackson personally executed several militiamen in 1815, when in fact he merely signed off on sentences already declared by a military court. *Courtesy of the library of the American Antiquarian Society, Worcester, Massachusetts*

"The Pedlar and His Pack" is actually Charles Hammond, weighted down by coffins, presumably those in the "Coffin Handbill" of John Binns. Henry Clay is on the left and President Adams on the right, desperately trying to hold on to the presidential chair. *Courtesy of the Collections of the Library of Congress*

HUZZA!
For Gen. Jackson!!

Undeniable and conclusive Reasons why General Jackson should be elected President of the United States, founded on the most unquestionable authority, and selected from high-minded, consistent, and republican authors.

1st REASON—Because he was the Friend and Defender of the immortal Washington, as *conclusively* appears from the following facts:

On the 17th of December, 1796, the Congress of the United States, of which Gen. Jackson was then a member, had under consideration the answer to the Speech of Gen. Washington. The concluding sentence of the Address was as follows—" For our country's sake, for the sake of republican liberty, it is our earnest wish, THAT YOUR EXAMPLE MAY BE THE GUIDE OF YOUR SUCCESSORS, and thus after being the ornament and safeguard of the present age, become the patrimony of our descendants." A motion was made to 'strike out this sentence, and the ayes and nays being called, GEN. ANDREW JACKSON VOTED FOR THE STRIKING OUT!!

2d REASON—Because he is the Candidate of the Democratic Party, and its able and strenuous supporter—which is fully confirmed by his late letter to PresidentMunroe, advising him to appoint FEDERALISTS to office, for the avowed purpose of BREAKING DOWN THE REPUBLICAN PARTY—but which is more fully confirmed by the support yielded him, by that bold and consistent deefnder of the peoples' rights, and real *Old Hickory* of Democracy—William Coleman, Editor of the Evening Post.

3d REASON—Because in public and private life he has given proof of his respect for the laws and constitution of his country—as fully appears from the reasons which follow, comprising the most brilliant and prominent events of his life.

4th REASON—Because the first conspicuous act of his life in Tennessee may be found at the race ground and the cock pit— At such places he was a leading and conspicuous actor ; and it is a notorious fact, that he was scarce ever known to leave the ground without participating in quarrels, generally of the most violent, rancorous and deadly nature. His whole life has been a scene of confusion, and no man can point to a single day in which he has been at peace with the world. The above particulars are given by Col. Thomas H. Benton, (now an *honourable* member of the Senate from Missouri,) at the commencement of the last Presidential Election. Col. Benton is now one of the General's advocates.

5th REASON.—Because he has showed himself, under various circumstances, master of *himself*, and capable of subduing his passions to wholesome restraint ; it being an acceded requisite, that he who is entrusted with the government of *others*, should have learned how to govern *himself*.

How eminently qualified the General is in this particular, is illustrated by the statement of Col. Benton of Gen. Jackson's attempt to *assassinate* him at his lodgings in Nashville, with pistols and dirks, " the truth of which," the Col. asserts, " he is ready to establish by judicial proof." "As for the name of *courage*," continues the Col. in his statement, " God forbid that I should ever attempt to gain it by becoming a BULLY."

6th REASON—Because, in the pride of conscious innocence and *integrity*, he has ever shown himself ready *quietly* to submit his

public acts and conduct to the investigation of the constituted authorities of the nation.

The General's proud consciousness of rectitude of conduct, and his willingness to submit it to the ordeal of a public examination, is happily illustrated by his peaceable demeanor while his public acts were under investigation in the Senate of the United States. In this investigation Mr. Eppes, the son-in-law of the patriot Jefferson, took an active part, who was selected by Gen. Jackson as the particular object of his vengeance ; and he swore with his usual profanity that he would *cut off his ears* in the midst of the Senate. Intent on this foul purpose, he proceeded to the door of the Senate Chamber, where he was met by the gallant Decatur. Having previously heard of the General's threats of violence, he fearlessly intercepted his entrance, and frankly told him, that " the persons of our Senators are sacred when engaged in their deliberations, and it is *our* duty to protect, and not to assail them." Whilst Decatur thus kindly remonstrated, Jackson hastily interrupted him with the following remark : " I have made it a rule in life, Sir, to be revenged of all insults, and I am not now to be diverted from my purposes. By the eternal G—d I will enter the Senate Chamber, and flog the d——d rascal." Decatur slapped his hands together in his own peculiar manner, and fiercely observed,—" you shall not enter that door, Sir, *unless it be over my dead body*."

7th REASON—Because he is THE CANDIDATE OF THE SOUTH, and is supported by the enemies of DOMESTIC INDUSTRY, who in their public speeches and addresses declare that all duties laid by Congress for the PROTECTION OF DOMESTIC MANUFACTURES ARE UNCONSTITUTIONAL, AND MUST BE REPEALED !

8th REASON—Because the SOUTHERN STATES have furnished us Presidents for *thirty two years*, and the Northern States, embracing a much larger free population, have furnished them only for eight years.

9th REASON—Because he is the friend and champion of the *Citizen Soldier*—the benefactor, and kind arbiter of the rights, liberties and lives of MILITIA MEN—as fully appears from his having caused 200 militia men of his own state to be ignominiously punished, six of them with DEATH, against the positive law of the land, and under circumstances shocking to humanity.

10th REASON—Because the Flying Comet, *alias* Martin Van Buren, and his tail, C. C. Cambreleng, a native of Tar River, N. Carolina, have pledged and sold the Electoral votes of the independent state of New-York, for the purpose of driving from office the man of the North who acted with and had the confidence of Washington, Jefferson, Madison and Munroe.

11th REASON—Because a grave Senator, pending the last Presidential Election, declared [" if he (General Jackson) should be elected President, he would surround himself with a pack of *political bull dogs*, to bay at all who *dared to oppose his measures. For myself* (listen to the colonel how valiantly he talks)—*for myself, as I cannot think of legislating with a brace of pistols in my belt, I shall, in the event of the election of Gen Jackson, resign my seat in the Senate, as every independent man will have to do, or risk his life and honour !! !"*

A clever diatribe against Andrew Jackson in 1828, this broadside may have misfired. Only the careful reader would realize that the "Huzzas" are sarcastic, aimed at Jackson's vote in 1796 against the resolution of thanks to George Washington, as well as other alleged transgressions. *Courtesy of the Collections of the Library of Congress*

PRESIDENCY!!!

This is the House that We built.*

TREASURY.

This is the malt that lay in the House that WE Built,

John Q. Adams,

This is the *MAIDEN* all forlorn, who worried herself from night till morn, to enter the House that We built,

CLAY,

This is the *MAN* all tattered and torn, who courted the maiden all forlorn, who worried herself from night till morn to enter the House that We built.

WEBSTER,

This is the *PRIEST*, all shaven and shorn, that married the man all tattered and torn, unto the maiden all forlorn, who worried herself from night till morn, to enter the House that We Built.

CONGRESS,

This is the BEAST, that carried the Priest all shaven and shorn, who married the man all tattered and torn, unto the maiden all forlorn, who worried herself from night till morn, to enter the House that We Built.

CABINET,

These are the *Rats* that pulled off their hats, and joined the Beast that carried the Priest all shaven and shorn, who married the man all tattered and torn unto the maiden all forlorn who worried herself from night till morn to enter the House that We built.

"OLD HICKORY,"

This is the *Wood*, well season'd and good, We will use as a rod to whip out the RATS, that pulled off their hats and joined the Beast that carried the Priest all shaven and shorn, who married the man all tattered and torn, unto the maiden all forlorn, who worried herself from night till morn, to enter the House that We Built.

NEW-YORK.

This is the *state*, both early and late, that will strengthen the Wood well seasoned and good, to be used as a rod to whip out Rats that pulled off their hats, and joined the beast that carried the Priest all shaven and shorn, who married the man all tattered and torn unto the maiden all forlorn, who worried herself from night till morn to enter the House that We Built.

EBONY & TOPAZ.

* *The People.*

Using an old nursery rhyme about "the malt that lay in the House that Jack built," Jacksonians turned it against President John Quincy Adams, Henry Clay, Daniel Webster, and others, who were trying to hold on to the "the House that WE built." Note the mention of "Ebony and Topaz" at the bottom. *Collection of The New-York Historical Society (negative #47611)*

MURDER WILL OUT!!
Truth is mighty and shall prevail!

Four years ago I charged General Andrew Jackson, in an address printed and published in Nashville, with various acts of cruelty and dishonesty when acting officially. His cruelty has been established beyond doubt by the Documents furnished from the War Department, in ordering the execution of six innocent militia men and twelve regular soldiers, the first on the 22d and the other order for the twelve dated the 28th January 1815, in the midst of his rejoicing in New Orleans and after the defeat on the 8th Jan. and retreat of the enemy. Seven or eight of these regulars were shot almost in secret near this place by a few men, separately, at one stake, their blood running together and they were buried in one grave. They shot the first man, named Jones, about 12 o'clock (he had to be shot twice) and did not finish the butchery of the whole until near night. A part of these regulars were poor men from Dixon county, who first volunteered for a short time, but a dispute arising respecting the length of their term, they were frightened to enlist; but considering themselves treated ill, they attempted to procure their liberty by desertion in a fit of desperation. They soon repented, and of their own accord went and delivered themselves up to Col. Joslin of the militia, whom they knew, and he delivered them to their officers in Nashville. Jackson ordered a Court Martial; they were found guilty, and notwithstanding their voluntary surrender to Col. Joslin they were ordered to execution by an order from Jackson, dated at New Orleans, in the midst of his rejoicings, without giving the President of the United States time to interfere and pardon them according to his duty.

As to the charge of dishonesty, I have just completely trapped him. I charged him with contriving ways to get land slipped into his own or his friends' hands when he was acting in a public capacity as Commissioner to treat with the Indians. This I offered to prove in the case of Colbert's reserve on Tennessee river, by evidence of James Jackson, if he would call on him to speak out and shew papers which I believe he holds, in General Jackson's own hand writing, and signed by him. I did prove the guilt and connexion of John Coffee, Surveyor General and kinsman of General Jackson, and that of Andrew Jackson the General and Commissioner, and James Jackson, a private gentleman, as well as that of Senator Eaton, by a chain of circumstances of irresistible weight, to their faces, and have published the same to the world. I do not think that Eaton was to have had much, if any, of his pay out of the reserve. The three others named above, Andrew Jackson, James Jackson, and John Coffee, were to have had all, or nearly all, of the reserved land. The whole of this villainy, I am confident, can be proved if Gen. Jackson would *call on* James Jackson to speak *all* he knows and show *all* the papers he has in possession on the subject. I have travelled 200 miles to catch in this town of Nashville, at this time, James Jackson and John Coffee, who live in Alabama, and Senator Eaton and General Andrew Jackson, who live near this place within three hours ride, and also to catch all of their eighteen Committee gentlemen. all of whom I have found here present, or in the immediate vicinity; and I have been here at the City Hotel thirteen days, charging them to their faces in print and by word of mouth with this monstrous act of villainy, and I have been and continue to so charge; and I have offered, and I hereby again offer to be shot on the Public Square in Nashville, on condition that James Jackson's evidence shall be called for by General Jackson and heard, and a fair exhibition by him of every thing in his power concerning the above transaction. And I further offer to acquit all of guilt unless it is irresistibly and conclusively proved.

General Jackson and his Committee have not dared and will not dare to make the call, and I hereby PROCLAIM the whole affair to the WORLD in all its nakedness. May God save our country!

JESSE BENTON.

City Hotel, Nashville, Oct. 13th, 1828.

"Murder Will Out!" Unlike his brother, Missouri's senator Thomas Hart Benton, Jesse Benton never relented in his hatred for Andrew Jackson following his and his brother's brawl with him in Nashville in 1814. In this broadside, published in late 1828, Jesse accuses Jackson of butchery, cruelty, and dishonesty. *Courtesy of the Collections of the Library of Congress*

Methought the souls of all that I had murder'd came to my tent. Act. 5. Sc. 3.

RICHARD III.

At a time when Shakespeare's plays were part of the popular culture, Adams partisans had no hesitation in likening Andrew Jackson to Shakespeare's villainous Richard III. Jackson's face is composed of the bodies of his alleged victims. *Courtesy of the library of the American Antiquarian Society, Worcester, Massachusetts*

"Protector and Defender of Beauty and Booty" is the caption hanging over this painting by J. Wood of Philadelphia, used for a Jackson campaign poster in 1828. *Courtesy of the Collections of the Library of Congress*

VICTORY OF NEW-ORLEANS, JANUARY 8, 1815.

JACKSON BALL.

—◦◦◦—

solicited to attend a Ball in commemoration of the VICTORY OF NEW-ORLEANS, and the election of **GEN. ANDREW JACKSON,** to be held at STOCKING's EAGLE TAVERN, on the EIGHTH OF JANUARY, in this City, at half past 6 in the evening.

       O. WISWALL,
       J. D. MONELL,
       T. E. BEEKMAN,
       S. ANABLE,
       H. STEEL,
       J. W. EDMONDS,
       C. GARDNER,
       C. MITCHELL,
       B. F. DEUELL,
       JAS. CLARK,
           Managers.

Hudson, December 18, 1828.

Andrew Jackson's supporters in New York were invited to celebrate his political victory in 1828 at a banquet celebrating the fourteenth anniversary of his military victory in New Orleans in 1815. Similar banquets had been held all over the country the year before. *Collection of The New-York Historical Society (negative #80723d)*

"The President's Levee, Or All Creation Going to the White House" was intended by Robert Cruikshank as a caricature of Andrew Jackson's inaugural reception. Actually, it is a rather sedate view of what turned out to be a fairly raucous event, although the horse at center right seems to be out of control. *Courtesy of the Collections of the Library of Congress*

A somewhat idealized portrait of Rachel Jackson, painted by Ralph E. W. Earl in 1831, three years after her death. Earl was a favorite of the Jacksons, living at the Hermitage before the election of 1828 and occupying a studio at the White House during Andrew Jackson's presidency. *Courtesy of The Hermitage: Home of President Andrew Jackson, Nashville, Tennessee*

Andrew Jackson reluctantly dressed up and posed for this 1845 daguerreotype, possibly by Mathew Brady, only two months before his death. *Courtesy of the Collections of the Library of Congress*

A photograph of a daguerreotype of John Quincy Adams, taken by Mathew Brady at his New York studio, probably in 1847. Adams had suffered a stroke the year before and had less than a year to live. *Courtesy of the Collections of the Library of Congress*

A group of young admirers of Andrew Jackson and his statue in Jackson Square, New Orleans, in the 1890s. *Courtesy of the Collections of the Library of Congress*

corruption so that the voice of the people might be heard and the country restored to its republican ways.[18]

Beyond these platitudes, however, Jackson remained silent on specific questions such as tariff reform and internal improvements. His allies counseled him to say as little as possible on these or any other issues. Senator Benton advised him to refer all inquiries to his voting record in Congress, which was bland enough to satisfy—or perhaps confuse—practically anyone. South Carolina's Calhounite senator Robert Y. Hayne agreed: "During the two years of your service in the Senate, and frequently since, your opinions have been publicly expressed," and that was enough. To go any further might risk exposing differences within the Jacksonian coalition. Van Buren warned that in his experience, taking positions on specific issues before an election almost always backfired. "Our people do not like to see publications from candidates," he said. "It is a singular point that in almost every case in which they have (with us) been attempted on the eve of an election they have operated agt. the cause they are intended to serve."[19] In other words, the Jackson campaign followed two separate but parallel tracks: one promoting the general's heroic image, the other following Van Buren's proposed alliance of southern planters and northern "plain republicans."

Although he had been warned from the very first day of his administration of the likelihood of a Jackson-Calhoun-Crawford coalition against him, President Adams continued to insist that the office he held was and should continue to be above politics. He was the last president to so believe. With the election approaching, he was again importuned to use his appointive power to the administration's advantage. He refused. "My system has been, and continues to be, to nominate for re-appointment all officers for a term of years whose commissions expire, unless official or moral misconduct is charged against them." Yet he complained, "I am importuned to serve my friends and reproached for neglecting them, because I will not dismiss, or drop from Executive offices, able and faithful political opponents to provide for my own partisans."[20] For the new breed of politician there was no such thing as an "able and faithful political opponent."

His friend and protégé Edward Everett had his doubts. In every election, he told Postmaster General McLean, there are winners and losers. The winners enjoy and benefit from the result, and the losers resent it. "For an administration then to bestow its patronage, without distinction of party, is to court its own destruction." President Adams was following that course. "And what has been his reward? A most furious opposition rallied on the charge of corrupt distribution of office, and the open or silent hostility of three-fourths of the office-holders in the Union."[21]

In the spring of 1827, while Van Buren was building support for Jackson in the South and Calhoun was meeting with congressional leaders, an article appeared in an Ohio newspaper that would signal yet another twist in presidential politics. "In the summer of 1790," wrote Charles Hammond, editor of the Cincinnati *Gazette*, "Gen. Jackson prevailed upon the wife of Lewis Roberts [*sic*] of Mercer county, Kentucky, to desert her husband, and live with himself, in the character of a wife."[22]

Jackson's friends in Nashville knew that there were three issues most likely to provoke his volatile temper: his personal honor, his military reputation, and, above all, the honor of his beloved wife, Rachel.[23] They were both alarmed and outraged at Hammond's charges: alarmed because they feared they might be true, and outraged because the domestic arrangements of presidential candidates had never been the target of campaign literature before. (A possible exception was the accusation in 1803 that President Thomas Jefferson had sired more than one child by his mulatto slave, Sally Hemings. It had no effect at all on Jefferson's reelection, although John Quincy Adams, much to his later regret, had published some rather snide poetry on the subject. In 1828 his enemies did not fail to remind the public of this.)[24]

The Nashville group now had its first serious challenge. Jackson's image had been built around his spotless innocence in the face of the corruption that had infected politics. He was poised to cleanse the fetid atmosphere in the nation's capital. Now he was in danger of being revealed as an adulterer and home wrecker. With Jackson's hairtrigger temper, any attack on Rachel was virtually guaranteed to set it off. And although he almost always first cleared his correspondence with Eaton or Lewis, there was still the risk that at some point his anger would boil over, with unhappy results. Eaton was particularly anxious. "Every thing I have to say is, be cautious—be still—be quiet," he said, "& let your friends fight the arduous battle that is before them; they will call for you when wanted." He urged Jackson to focus on his own affairs. "Weigh & bale your cotton & sell it," he later said, "and if you see anything about yourself just throw the paper into the fire...& go on and *weigh the cotton*." If Jackson would "forbear all political letters, enquries & discussion," all would be well.[25]

John Overton, who had lived with Jackson at Rachel's mother's boarding-house in the 1790s, took charge of the case. With Jackson's help he assembled the relevant documents and published a defense of both Jacksons in the *United States Telegraph*. The Jacksons, he claimed, had married with the understanding that Lewis Robards (not Roberts) had obtained a divorce from Rachel. Then they moved to Natchez. When they discovered that there had been no divorce, they were married a second time, after the divorce from Robards was finalized, thus leading to the confusion. This became, and has remained, the standard Jackson defense. The problem was, and has remained, that no record of the first marriage exists.[26]

Although the Nashville group had no choice but to respond, the effect, as is often the case, was to refocus attention on the charges rather than on the rebuttal. "If General Jackson should be elected President," asked one partisan, "what effect, think you, fellow-citizens, will it have on American youth?" Anticipating the counterattack, Hammond then detailed his case in a new pamphlet, titled *Truth's Advocate and Anti-Jackson Expositor*. This time he included the divorce verdict from the foreman of a Virginia jury in 1790: "We the jury do find that the defendant, Rachel Roberts [*sic*], hath deserted the plaintiff, Lewis Roberts [*sic*], and doth still, live in adultery with another man." Hammond then asked his readers, "Ought a convicted adultress and her paramour husband to be placed in the highest offices of this free and christian land?"[27]

Jackson's allies in Ohio and elsewhere rallied to his defense, not always helpfully. A Cincinnati journal thundered that the charges were a "BASE, WANTON, AND MALIGNANT FALSEHOOD." A Pennsylvania paper tried to dismiss them: "Suppose all this to be true;—which bye the bye is INFAMOUSLY FALSE—but suppose it is true," what was to be gained by "dragging" Rachel into the public arena? Jackson had imbibed the "frank and generous spirit" of the frontier, said another, "and perhaps partook of their faults." The Nashville *Republican* tried to help by explaining that after deserting his wife, Lewis Robards threatened to return to Tennessee and carry her back, whereupon Rachel moved to Natchez with Jackson. This only made things worse. "A wife whose husband is jealous of her," chortled Hammond, "seeks refuge among strangers, in company with her suspected paramour! And this is evidence of her innocence. What monstrous absurdities the world is expected to swallow where Gen. Jackson is concerned."[28]

Hammond then escalated the attack. "General Jackson's mother was a COMMON PROSTITUTE," he charged, "brought to this country by the British soldiers! She afterwards married a MULATTO MAN, with whom she had several children, of which number General JACKSON is one!!!" A Kentucky newspaper carried matters yet another step further, likening Jackson's wife to a "dirty, black wench." Thomas Arnold, a renegade Tennessean, piled on with another pamphlet claiming that Jackson "tore from a husband the wife of his bosom."[29]

When Jackson learned that editor Hammond was an ally of Clay, he had no trouble linking the hated Kentuckian to the attacks on his wife. When he learned that Hammond had indeed visited Clay earlier in the year, he immediately contacted Senator Eaton in Washington and pointedly demanded an investigation. Eaton confronted Clay, who admitted that Hammond had visited him but denied any involvement in the attacks. Jackson was not convinced. "I will curb my feelings until it becomes proper to act," he told Sam Houston. He knew that he was being provoked by his enemies. "They calculated that it would arouse me to some desperate act by which I would fall prostrate before the people, [but] for the present my hands are pinioned."[30]

Duff Green, however, retaliated on his own. He had no desire, he unctuously told the readers of the *Telegraph*, "to trace the *love* adventures of the Chief Magistrate [Adams], nor to disclose the manner, *nor the time*, at which *he*, his brother-in-law, and his father-in-law before him, led their *blushing* brides to the hymenial altar." Hoping for Jackson's approval, he reported his efforts. "The effect here was like electricity," he reported. "The whole Adams corps were thrown into consternation." He received no encouragement from Jackson. It might be appropriate to throw in a few facts when relevant, Jackson replied, but he insisted, "Female character should never be introduced or touched by my friends, unless a continuation of attack should continue to be made against Mrs. J. and then only, by way of *Just retaliation* upon the *known guilty.* . . . *I never war against females* and it is only the base and cowardly that do." Green backed off from further attacks on the Adams family's private life, but others would take up the cause. Six months later Isaac Hill published a pamphlet accusing Adams of procuring a young American woman for the lusts of Czar Alexander.[31]

In the meantime there was more trouble. Earlier in the year Jackson had learned through a secondhand source that Navy Secretary Southard had suggested at a dinner that not only did Jackson not deserve the glory he had obtained at New Orleans, but that Jackson had been on his way home at the time and had had to be recalled by the secretary of war, James

Monroe, who, Southard was supposed to have said, really deserved the credit for the victory. It did not take long for the Hero of New Orleans to react to this alleged outrage. Off to Washington went another letter, this time to Congressman Sam Houston, enclosing a personal note that was to be delivered to Southard himself. Houston was to wait for a reply, one of the first steps to a potential confrontation. "Say to him from me," the old duelist wrote, "that from the high and honorable station he fills I expect a prompt, and categorical answer from him." He suspected the Adams cabinet of "secretely intimating slanderous things of me." "This I mean to expose, and put down, one after the other, as I can obtain positive proof."[32]

Jackson's note was so menacing that Houston, after conferring with Eaton and others, suggested that he, not the general, write to Southard. Jackson would have none of it. He forwarded a second letter, this time a little less confrontational, which was then handed to the navy secretary. Southard quickly denied any intention of impugning Jackson's honor or reputation, protesting that he had intended only to reassert the role played by Monroe, which he thought had been overlooked. He told Jackson, "[Your victories] form a part of our national glory which I have no inclination to tarnish." Jackson grudgingly accepted Southard's explanation, pointedly suggesting that he should take extra pains to stick to the facts while on future "electioneering tours" and "wine drinkings."[33]

Like any Tennessee gentleman, Andrew Jackson enjoyed entertaining guests at the Hermitage. One of them was Carter Beverly, a prominent Virginia planter, who in May 1827 probed his host's thinking about the "bargain and corruption" two years before. In response—possibly after one of his own "wine drinkings"—Jackson went further than he had ever gone before. Not only had there been "corruption," he said, but he himself had been approached by one of Clay's emissaries with a "bargain" of their own. If Jackson would promise *not* to reappoint Adams as his secretary of state, the general was told, Clay and his friends would make him president "in one hour." Consistent with his practice, Jackson told Beverly, he indignantly rejected the offer. "Before I would reach the presidential chair by such means of bargain & corruption," he later said, "I would see the earth open & swallow both Mr. Clay & his friends, and myself with them."[34]

Without consulting his host, Beverly shared this potentially explosive anecdote with a friend in North Carolina, who passed it on to a local paper. Soon it appeared in Green's *Telegraph*. Clay quickly denied the charge. Brought reluctantly into the spotlight, Jackson had to admit that he could not be sure he was approached with Clay's knowledge, and he did not disclose the name of the alleged representative. Clay then challenged Jackson to name him, which Jackson finally did, citing Congressman James Buchanan of Pennsylvania, a former Federalist but now a Jackson supporter.[35]

Jackson's problem was that Buchanan (who would go on in the 1850s to become one of the nation's more undistinguished presidents) was a meddling self-starter who had been operating entirely on his own. The general was not pleased. "You are aware of the position which you occupy," he pointedly told the congressman, "and which I trust you will Sustain when properly called on." Buchanan then had to admit that he "had no authority from Mr. Clay or his friends, to propose any terms to General Jackson in relation to their votes." The general was annoyed, but the congressman was a key part of the Jackson campaign in Pennsylvania, and so the matter was dropped.[36]

Buchanan's admission threatened to derail the campaign, but Clay and his friends soon threw away their advantage by pushing things too far. The pro-Clay Kentucky legislature passed resolutions in his support. Clay then went about assembling testimony from a variety of old friends who were ready to swear that in the spring of 1825, on his way back to Tennessee, Jackson was already fuming over the result, charging "bargain and corruption" even then. Senator Benton, a Jackson ally in 1828 but a Clay ally back in 1824, acknowledged that Clay had told him even before he went to Washington that he would support Adams, so there could not have been a bargain. The letters and recollections were published in early 1828. Once again, however, the effect was to focus more attention on the charge than on the rebuttal. It is doubtful whether either Clay or the administration benefited.[37]

The organizational strength of the Jackson movement became clear when, in December 1827, the Twentieth Congress met to elect a new speaker of the House of Representatives. The result meant trouble for the Adams administration. John W. Taylor, who had narrowly been chosen two years earlier, went down to defeat at the hands of Andrew Stevenson, a Jackson supporter. As many feared, the administration had been out-organized by the opposition in the congressional elections the year before. Van Buren's skill as an organizer of the transsectional alliance of southern planters and northern "plain republicans" was made clear as well, when a majority of the Empire State's congressmen voted for Stevenson, a Virginian, instead of Taylor, their fellow New Yorker.

"There is a decided majority of both Houses of Congress in opposition to the Administration," Adams told his diary, "a state of things which has never before occurred under the Government of the United States."[38] Until then Adams had been restrained in his comments on Jackson, the man he had once said he could never contemplate without reverence, whom he had defended in 1818 and again in 1820, and whom he had once considered as a running mate. Now he let loose his frustration. It was quite possible that the Tennessean would be the next president, he admitted in a conversation with Clay, but it would be impossible that "his Administration should give satisfaction to the people of this Union." The man was "incompetent both by his ignorance and by the fury of his passions," he said. Warming to his subject, the president predicted that Jackson would be "surrounded and governed by incompetent men...and the Administration would go to wreck and ruin."[39]

The Jackson campaign's skillful coordination was demonstrated again when, on January 8, the thirteenth anniversary of the Battle of New Orleans, rallies and banquets in his honor were held in nearly every state capital. To top it off, Jackson himself was persuaded to make a highly publicized visit to the Crescent City, timed to arrive precisely on January 8. The visit and the rallies combined to present the first truly organized "media event" in American political history.

Jackson's return to New Orleans stemmed from an innocent invitation from the Louisiana state legislature. The background is unclear because the legislature was not in Jacksonian hands. But the majority could not afford to be caught in a position of hostility to the Hero of New Orleans and so joined with the Jacksonians in support. Then they proceeded to deny any public funding for the visit, forcing the Jacksonians to dig into their own pockets.[40] "I wish to avoid every thing that could draw over me the imputation of electioneering," Jackson naïvely told William B. Lewis, whom he put in charge of arrangements. Leaving the Hermitage at Christmastime, he boarded the steamboat *Pocahontas* at Nashville on December 29 and proceeded slowly downriver to the Mississippi and then to Natchez. Accompanying him were his wife, Overton, Lewis, and a number of veterans of the battle. Also among the party was James

Alexander Hamilton, acting as Van Buren's representative and occasional spy. The voyage flirted with disaster when Jackson, annoyed at the frequent crisscrossing of another boat in front of the *Pocahontas*, grabbed a rifle and threatened to shoot the pilot of the offending vessel. According to Hamilton, it took Rachel's intervention to calm the general down.[41]

The entourage arrived at Natchez on January 4, to be greeted by booming cannons and an immense throng of well-wishers, who escorted them to a dinner and a ball in Jackson's honor. Wishing to arrive at New Orleans precisely on the eighth, the party reembarked at midnight. They were met by a second boat, sent up from New Orleans and loaded with the city's arrangement committee. Both boats descended the Mississippi, arriving as planned. By this time the *Pocahontas* had been dressed up with twenty-four flags, one for each state, and Jackson took his place on the fantail of the ship, in full view of the crowd assembled on the shore. He and Rachel disembarked, greeted by veterans of the battle and by a group of "respectable ladies" of the city, who escorted them to their hotel. Jackson met with the governor and members of the legislature and proceeded to the nearby Catholic church for a solemn *Te Deum*. Four days of celebration followed. Speeches were given in both French and English, songs were sung, and the great battle recalled over and over.[42]

Virtually every newspaper in the nation reported the event. Estimates of attendance for the four days ran as high as thirty-five thousand.[43] "The crowd on the banks of the river was immense," reported one enthusiastic correspondent. It was "like a Dream," wrote another. "The windows, the balconies, even the roofs of the houses the decks, tops and rigging of the ships were covered with spectators. Their shouts when the general touched the shore were as loud as the artillery." The cheering stopped as soon as Jackson spoke. "Every one seemed eager to catch the sound of his voice. He spoke of his own deeds with modesty, of his surviving companions with affection, and of the dead with fond regret." Several delegations from a number of states had accompanied him, and he had a reply ready for each one. "We had a harmonious & happy meeting with all our friends & compatriots," Jackson later wrote to Edward Livingston. "The concourse was unusually great."[44]

Not everyone was impressed. Among the French-speaking element in New Orleans there was still resentment against Jackson's high-handedness in 1815, his treatment of his critics, and his suspension of habeas corpus even after it was known that the war was over. Stung by criticism that it had unwittingly been co-opted into the presidential campaign, the

Louisiana legislature adopted a resolution insisting that the invitation had been made "*solely* in compliment to the military services rendered...in defence of Louisiana, and not for *political* purposes, or in any way to express an opinion on the approaching election of president of the United States." A subsequent poll claimed that a majority in both houses was still for Adams, not Jackson.[45]

"Pompous pageantry," a peevish President Adams indignantly confided to his diary. Jackson's high-flown rhetoric, delivered "in an ambitious and court-dress style," convinced the president that they had been written by someone else. "Some of his impudent jackals fell into ecstasies in the newspapers at his eloquence and fine literary composition, and they were boldly claiming for him the reputation of an elegant writer," he complained. (Adams was wrong. The text of his address may be found in Jackson's papers, written in the general's nearly indecipherable scrawl.)[46] It made no difference. Whatever Adams or the Louisiana legislature chose to believe, the New Orleans visit was a brilliant stroke, reminding the nation once again of the glorious outcome of the battle and its Hero.

On that very day Jacksonians in Ohio, Indiana, Virginia, New Jersey, New York, Kentucky, Massachusetts, Mississippi, North Carolina, New Hampshire, and the District of Columbia met to hear speeches toasting Jackson and denouncing Adams. Even in Boston more than four hundred brave Jacksonians assembled at historic Faneuil Hall. "With one voice," Nathaniel Greene told his audience, "the whole nation at this moment is yielding the homage of grateful hearts to the hero and civilian who has 'filled the measures of his country's glory.'" Acknowledging that in Massachusetts the Jacksonians faced an uphill battle and risked social ostracism, Greene nevertheless plunged on, pleading for the election of "the farmer, the civilian, the hero of Tennessee." The oration was followed by a special ode, titled "Wreaths for the Chieftain," a public dinner, and a noisy salute of twenty-four guns on the Boston Common, repeated for effect at sunset.[47]

In Concord, New Hampshire, Isaac Hill led off the proceedings with a blistering attack on the Adams administration. The faithful then marched to a hall where they found replicas of the Battle of New Orleans, complete with depictions of frontiersmen in coonskin caps firing across cotton bales at British regulars, scrolls comparing the Declaration of Independence with the "Declaration of War 1812," and portraits of Jefferson, Madison, and of course the Hero himself. Glasses were raised in honor of the veterans of the Revolutionary War (several of whom were present), the

"Democracy of the country," and Greek independence. The day ended with a ball. The local Adams paper uncharitably suggested that many of the ladies in attendance were prostitutes.[48]

In Troy, New York, the local Baptist church was filled to capacity to hear a similar oration by Francis Yvonnet. After congratulating his audience on the progress that had been made in the past half-century (especially in removing the Indians from eastern New York), he moved on to the main item, rehearsing in detail Jackson's career, concluding with a rousing defense of the Jacksons' marriage. "Never before," he proclaimed, "has this peaceful land been inundated with such a torrent of slander and scurrility, as has been drawn out against this disinterested patriot."[49] Green's *Telegraph* spent most of January reporting on the banquets and rallies throughout the nation, celebrating the "anniversary of the most brilliant achievement in the history of our country."[50]

Simultaneously, the Jacksonians opened fire in Congress, which organized itself into "a virtual committee for the defeat of the president."[51] Andrew Stevenson, the new speaker of the House of Representatives, had the power to appoint all committees for the Twentieth Congress, and he had no hesitation in stacking them against the administration. On January 8, while the Jackson meetings were taking place in most of the states, Congressman James Hamilton of South Carolina moved to inquire into the feasibility of having a painting of the Battle of New Orleans hung in the Capitol rotunda, along with the depictions of the American Revolution. A few weeks later another congressman claimed that as American minister abroad Adams had padded his expense accounts; he proposed a congressional investigation. The old charges that Adams had opposed the Louisiana Purchase in 1803 and had been willing to sacrifice western interests at Ghent in 1814 in favor of New England's right to fish off the Grand Banks of Newfoundland were trotted out again. Isaac Hill's pamphlet making the charge that Adams had pimped for the czar of Russia made its entrance as well.

Earlier in Adams's term, John Adams II, in his capacity as his father's personal secretary, had delivered to Congress a report on White House expenditures. In it he listed as a public expense fifty dollars for a billiard table, plus eleven dollars for cues and balls. Then as now, billiards carried with it the suggestion of smoke-filled rooms, gambling, alcohol, and raucous male behavior. Was it possible, huffed a North Carolina congressman, "to believe that it was ever intended by Congress, that the public money should be applied to the purchase of gaming tables and gambling furniture?" Such an expense, he declared, could only "shock and alarm the religious, the moral, and reflecting part of the community." The man whom John Randolph had once ridiculed as a "puritan" now was presented as a gaming wastrel, frittering away the public's trust while lining up his best shots at a billiard table.[52]

The president's supporters floundered in their response. Some speculated that perhaps the items had been purchased in connection with General Lafayette's visit, or that they were intended to provide exercise for Mrs. Adams. The editor of the pro-Adams *National Gazette* in Philadelphia noted, unhelpfully, that a billiard table was "a common appendage in the houses of the rich and great in Europe, and by no means uncommon as such in the United States." Such defenses only played into the hands of the opposition, already busy fashioning the image of Adams as a closet aristocrat who in fact had spent too much time "in the houses of the rich and great in Europe."

Had there been a "central committee" of Adams defenders, similar to that which surrounded Jackson in Nashville, the charges would have gone nowhere, for the reality was that John Adams II had botched his report. The money indeed had been spent, but it came out of the president's pocket, not the public's. Adams corrected the record as soon as he learned of his son's mistake and thought no more of it. In the absence of any public refutation of the charges, however, they continued. The amount itself may have been insignificant, Amos Kendall told his readers, but "if the people tolerate the *trifling* expense of a billiard table, balls and chessmen, out of public funds, what may they next expect?" Rallies were held in Virginia and Ohio protesting the "gambling apparatus" acquired by the president at taxpayers' expense and the "erection of *Billiard Tables*, and costly and extravagant furniture in the President's House." At least two pro-administration congressmen blamed their defeat for reelection on the controversy.[53]

No one has argued that the outcome of the election of 1828 turned on the question of Adams's fondness for billiards, nor on the wild accusations of Isaac Hill. But the controversies demonstrated that an effective political campaign requires defense as well as offense. Hill's allegations, accusing Adams of providing the czar of all the Russias with young female companionship, were based on a distorted account involving one of the Adamses' domestic servants. Martha Godfrey had attracted the czar's attention not because of her charms, but because of her letters home describing his reputation for gallantry, which the Russian post office had opened. Amused, the czar (and the czarina) quietly arranged for the naïve

Martha to accompany the Adams family to a children's party so they could observe her for themselves. There was nothing more to the story, yet Hill's charges were never publicly rebutted. Even in the primitive communication system of the 1820s rumors and innuendoes could have a life of their own unless promptly confronted. The Jacksonians understood this. Adams, and the friends of the administration, did not.

In the meantime Adams grimly soldiered on. The same man who in the winter of 1824–25 moved easily from one Washington dinner to another, granting interviews to all, assuring the inquisitive that he would not threaten their interests, now seemed intent on shunning almost every opportunity to enhance his cause. He refused an invitation to participate in a commemoration of the fiftieth anniversary of the Battle of Bunker Hill in his own state of Massachusetts. He declined another invitation to travel to a German-speaking area in Pennsylvania to help open a canal and "to show myself among the German farmers and speak to them in their own language." One of the few American public officials of the time who was fluent in German, Adams nonetheless told his friends, "This mode of electioneering suited neither my taste nor my principles." When he was invited to attend a cattle show and agricultural fair outside of nearby Baltimore, he frostily responded in biblical prose: "Seest thou a man diligent *in his* business?" Such an appearance might lead to others, he feared: "From cattle-shows to other public meetings for purposes of utility or exposure of public sentiment, the transition is natural and easy. This is no part of my duty."[54]

Even his wife, the English-born Louisa Catherine Adams, who had never seen the United States until after she married him, was critical. "If he would only lend himself a little to the usages and manners of the people," she told one of her sons, "without hiding himself and … rejecting their civilities, no man could be more popular because his manners are simple, unostentatious, and unassuming." Her husband disagreed. "My journies and my visits, wherever they may be, shall have no connection with the Presidency." Traveling home to Quincy in the summer of 1827, he pleaded with friends and family not to let anyone know he was on his way.[55]

In contrast to Jackson, Adams seemed unable to respond to crowds, even friendly ones. Early in his term he accompanied Lafayette to Virginia, on one of the hottest days of the year, for a visit to yet another former president, this time James Monroe. Large crowds turned out to see them both. Adams was uncomfortable. "I have no pleasure in these scenes," he later wrote.[56] When he passed through Philadelphia two years later, several thousand people assembled at a wharf just to see the president of the United States, many wanting to shake his hand and give three cheers. He responded with a one-line speech: "God bless you all." There was no disorder, he remarked to his diary, as if there were some danger that the crowd would run amok. He hoped that his slight pleasure at the event came from no "vain or unworthy sentiment of exultation." In the same city a year later another large crowd turned out to greet him on his way home to Quincy. They again gave him three cheers, and many followed him to his hotel. This time his speech was longer. "Fellow-citizens," he said, "I thank you for this kind and friendly reception, and wish you all a good night." That was it. To say more would be to "electioneer," to engage in Jacksonian "pompous pageantry."[57]

Not only was Adams unwilling to help himself, but he was unwilling to help others. He declined to contribute to the administration's cause in Kentucky, describing expenditures for newspapers, handbills, and pamphlets as "altogether venal."[58] (Besides, he confessed, he couldn't afford it.) He noted with a mixture of amusement and amazement that a candidate for the Kentucky governorship had to "travel round the State and offer himself to the people and solicit their votes." When a pro-Adams group in Kentucky sought information to refute the old charge that he had opposed the Louisiana Purchase, he turned them down. He discouraged his son from contributing to a German-language newspaper in Pennsylvania supporting the administration.

Instead of issuing directives and suggestions to those working for his reelection, he concentrated on the duties of his office. What spare time he had was often consumed in reading the classical authors, debating the fine points of Cicero's orations with his youngest son, Charles Francis Adams, and puttering about the executive mansion, experimenting with tree seedlings. Only in his diary did he pour out his frustrations and anxieties over the changes in the American political atmosphere, and in his own fortunes.

Several of his biographers have suggested that Adams's reticence stemmed from his realization that, after all, the "reward" of the presidency had not come without connivance. There may have been no corruption in early 1825, but there certainly had been some bargaining. The Macbeth policy—"If chance will have me king, why, then chance may crown me, without my stir"—had been jettisoned, if only for a few days. The reward he had sought often seemed to turn to ashes in his mouth. "I can scarcely conceive a more harassing, wearying, teasing condition of existence," he confided to his diary in March 1827. "It literally renders life burdensome." A few months later he complained of an "uncontrollable dejection of spirits, insensibility to the almost unparalleled blessings with which I have been favored." Such thoughts did not lead to the combative frame of mind needed to win his reelection.[59]

Viewed objectively, if that were possible, the Adams administration's record was easily defensible. Yet according to Daniel Webster, "We are on the eve of a new election of President, and the manner in which the existing administration is attacked might lead a stranger to suppose that the chief magistrate had committed some flagrant offence against the country, had threatened to overturn its liberties, or establish a military usurpation."[60] The nation remained at peace, the economy was sound, the national debt was being retired, and Secretary Clay, in spite of chronic poor health and the distractions of answering his critics, was in the process of negotiating no fewer than nine commercial treaties with foreign powers, more than in any comparable period before the Civil War. There was trouble, however, in two areas, and the result in each case worked to the advantage of the Jacksonians.

The first, ironically, lay in foreign affairs. Prior to independence, American trade with the West Indies (Jamaica, Barbados, and certain of the Leeward Islands) had been an important part of colonial commerce and an equally important source of supplies for the islands' sugar planters. Indeed, the disruption of that trade by the British had been one of the contributing factors to the coming of the War of 1812. When the British closed the traffic to outsiders, Adams, as secretary of state, persuaded Congress to impose retaliatory duties on certain kinds of British shipping until they changed their minds. That was in 1823. In retaliation for the retaliation, the British now moved to close *all* American trade with their colonies, except Canada. The potential for economic disaster was enormous, and the Jacksonian opposition took advantage of it. Those who had once hinted that Adams's Federalist background made him soft on Britain now attacked him for his hard-line position in demanding free trade with its colonies. "Our diplomatic President," they snickered, had single-handedly wrecked trade with Britain. Following an unsuccessful attempt to repeal the Act of 1823, the issue lay unresolved, but discontent continued within the commercial community.[61]

The second matter involved Indian affairs. Shortly after he assumed office Adams learned that one of the treaties negotiated by the federal government with the Creek Indians in the state of Georgia, in which the Creeks had agreed to give up their lands and be moved west of the Mississippi, was fraudulent. The agents of the Creeks had been bribed by state and federal officials. Adams had ratified the treaty, not knowing the details. The Creeks responded by assassinating those responsible and refused to abide by it. The Georgians, led by their governor, proceeded to survey the lands anyway and prepared to remove the Creeks. One of the "five civilized tribes" of the old Southwest (the others being the Cherokees, Chickasaws, Choctaws, and Seminoles), the Creeks had become mostly farmers by the 1820s. They continued to occupy valuable land, rich in potential for cotton and other cash crops, and the white Georgians meant to have it, one way or the other. When James Barbour, Adams's secretary of war, suggested that the implementation of the fraudulent treaty be delayed until a new and fairer one could be negotiated, the governor of Georgia breathed defiance and threatened violence against any federal official who might intervene on behalf of the Indians. The controversy threatened to become the most serious federal-state confrontation since the Whiskey Rebellion of the 1790s.

Up to then, Adams had not been a particular friend of the American Indian. At Ghent in 1814 he had denounced the British attempts to set up a neutral homeland for the natives, and four years later he had come to Jackson's defense following his execution without trial of two Indian leaders. Now the threats to American expansion from both the British and the Spanish were gone, and the farm-owning Creeks seemed no different from the whites. The former hunters, Adams remarked, were now hunted themselves, "like a partridge on the mountains." However, there was little hope that the Jacksonian opposition would support any interference on behalf of the Creeks. In fact, a special Senate committee, headed by Benton, predictably condemned the administration and justified the Georgians. Finally, a revised treaty was negotiated, not much better than the first, and the Creeks were given the option of submitting to the white man's rule in Georgia or leaving for the trans-Mississippi West.[62]

Although he had little use for the Georgia governor (a former Crawfordite), Jackson made his position clear in a letter to one of that state's congressmen: "[The Indians] cannot be long fostered and preserved where they now are—They can only be perpetuated as tribes, or nations, by concentrating them west of the Mississippi," where they would be protected from "the encroachments of the whites, without violation to state rights, or the rights of citizens."[63] The removal of the Indian from the "encroachment of the whites" would be first on the agenda of the Jackson administration. In the election of 1828 the name of John Quincy Adams would not even appear on the Georgia ballots.

There were weaknesses in the Jackson campaign, but Adams and his administration failed to take advantage of them. The most glaring was the friction between the increasingly militant opponents of the American System in the South and its advocates in the West and North.

More than any other section, the West supported the federally sponsored road building and canal digging that would turn the frontier into prosperous farms and towns. People in sparsely populated Illinois wanted a canal to connect the Chicago River with the Illinois River. Indianans wanted a road from Lake Michigan to the Ohio. Westerners knew that as a senator Jackson had voted for a modest internal improvements measure in 1824 and hoped he would continue his support as president. Protectionists knew that he had supported a "judicious" tariff in 1824 and looked to him as an ally. This was especially true in the most protection-minded state in the Union, Pennsylvania, where Jackson had triumphed in both the electoral and popular votes in 1824, and where his partisans hoped to repeat their success in 1828. Samuel Ingham, a Pennsylvania congressman whom Jackson would eventually appoint to his cabinet, assured his friends that as president the Tennessean would raise the tariff "everytime he touched it." Jackson, not Clay, many of his Pennsylvania supporters claimed, "will give expansion to the American System."[64]

At the same time Vice President Calhoun and the South Carolinians were planning to use Jackson to roll back the economic nationalism of the postwar years, especially the tariff, which they had concluded protected one sector of the economy at the expense of the others. Once one of its staunchest advocates, Calhoun was now convinced that the tariff was not only unfair but unconstitutional as well. If the trend continued, threatened one of his more extreme allies, the South would be forced, as the phrase had it, to "calculate the value of the Union."[65]

At the same time, a growing number of southerners had become convinced that any expansive and "latitudinarian" view of federal power threatened slavery and its future. The power to build a road or dredge a harbor might imply as well the power to free a slave. Henry Clay, the principal advocate of the American System that embraced the extension of federal power, was now secretary of state—and possibly next in line for the presidency—and Clay was allied with Adams, the nonslaveholding northerner who was the author of the infamous Annual Message of 1825. How to satisfy Jackson's pro-tariff supporters in the North and West without antagonizing the increasingly agitated South was a challenge to the coalition of planters and "plain republicans" envisioned by Van Buren. This was why Jackson's advisors, both northerners like Van Buren and southerners like Hayne, insisted on his continued ambivalence.

Here was an opening for the administration. In the summer of 1827 delegates from northern and western states gathered at Harrisburg, Pennsylvania, calling for an increase in the protective tariff. It was presided over by Joseph Ritner, the German-speaking leader of the state House of Representatives. The Harrisburg Convention, as it came to be called, promptly drew fire from northern Jacksonians, who saw behind it—correctly—the hand of Secretary Clay, who had hoped to organize the meeting around the "friends of D.M.I.I. [Domestic Manufactures and Internal Improvements] and the Admin." Most of the delegates to the Convention indeed were administration supporters; nonetheless no move was made to endorse the president. Had the convention done so, Jacksonians from the manufacturing states would have been placed in a dilemma: either to restate and reemphasize their own protectionism and alienate their southern allies, or remain silent and lose support to the Adams administration.[66]

With no endorsement of Adams, the northern Jacksonians escaped the trap. Joseph Ritner announced his support for Jackson. Clay and others were convinced that an opportunity had been lost. "Why should the President omit giving an opinion on so important a Measure?" plaintively asked one of Clay's allies. Adams had the answer. He did not want to "appear to interfere improperly for the purpose of exercising an influence over the House."[67] He barely mentioned the tariff at all in his Annual Message for 1827. The only concession to Pennsylvania was the substitution of Philadelphia's Richard Rush, then serving as treasury secretary, for Calhoun as the vice presidential nominee on the Adams ticket. It was not enough. A better choice would have been Clay, who would have solidified the commitment to the American System and provided a sectional balance as well. Clay, however, declined.[68]

The northern Jacksonians now sensed their own opportunity and crafted a tariff bill especially designed to benefit Pennsylvania, Kentucky, and Ohio, whose electoral votes would be crucial to Jackson's election. The proposal increased duties on imported items produced in those states: hemp and flax, as well as iron, molasses, and other raw materials. Some historians have argued that the bill was only a symbolic gesture by the Jacksonians and was never intended to pass because its advocates expected the commercial-minded New Englanders to combine with the South to kill it. In a dangerous game of bluff, southerners deliberately voted to raise duties even further, making the bill as obnoxious as possible to the Yankees. They miscalculated. The New England economy since the war had moved steadily away from the sea and toward the factory, and the New Englanders gave the bill enough votes for it to pass.[69]

The southerners promptly dubbed the bill "the Tariff of Abominations." John Randolph was heard to mutter that the Tariff of 1828 referred to "manufactures of no sort, but the manufacture of a President of the United States." President Adams quietly signed it into law and, predictably, was denounced in the South while receiving no credit in the North. New Hampshire's Senator Woodbury told South Carolina's Senator Hayne that the whole issue was threatening the Jackson cause and urged "the propriety of keeping things quiet at least for the present."[70] Vice President Calhoun went back to South Carolina and attacked the tariff in an anonymous publication entitled *The South Carolina Exposition and Protest*, spelling out for the first time the doctrine later to be known as "nullification." A state, Calhoun argued, upon finding a law to be in violation of the Constitution, was not obligated to enforce it. He did not inform his running mate of his authorship.[71]

In fumbling their opportunity to divide and conquer, partisans and supporters of the Adams administration lost their chance to compete with the Jacksonians on the basis of political principles or ideology. As the election year moved into its final months, such volatile issues as tariff protection, internal improvements, Indian affairs, and foreign policy faded away and were replaced by the competing images of Andrew Jackson and John Quincy Adams. It proved to be an uneven competition.

★ Chapter Six ★

You've heard, I s'pose of New Orleans,
Tis famed for youth and beauty
They're girls of every hue, it seems,
From snowy white to sooty,
Now Pakenham had made his brags,
If he that day was lucky,
He'd have those girls and cotton bags
In spite of Old Kentucky.
    Oh! Kentucky, the hunters of Kentucky!
    Oh! Kentucky, the hunters of Kentucky!
But Jackson, he was wide awake,
And was not scared at trifles,
For well he knew Kentucky's boys
With their death-dealing rifles,
He led them down to cypress swamp,
The ground was low and mucky,
There stood John Bull in martial pomp,

And here stood old Kentucky.
  Oh! Kentucky, the hunters of Kentucky!
  Oh! Kentucky, the hunters of Kentucky!

If there was any competition for an official Jackson campaign song in 1828, "The Hunters of Kentucky" would top the list. Written by Samuel Woodworth soon after the Battle itself, it was in fact less than accurate, given Jackson's criticism of the Kentuckians at the time. In his view the Kentuckians had arrived at New Orleans late, ill trained, and ill equipped. But no matter. In 1828 the song was published and republished throughout the nation, with great success.[1] (There was no counterpart in the Adams campaign.)

It was one of many demonstrations of a new form of presidential campaigning. "Nicknames, slogans, humorous and lighthearted attacks, intimate glimpses of friends and foes, peppered from time to time with familiar biblical and Shakespearian references," emerged, along with imaginative approaches to propaganda. The use of graphics, boldface newspaper type, cartoons, campaign emblems, nursery rhymes, and what one historian has called "the cadence and emphasis of spoken language" proliferated in ways not seen before.[2]

"This is the House that We built," proclaimed a pro-Jackson broadside, revising the lines of the well-known nursery rhyme. John Quincy Adams was "the maiden all forlorn, who worried herself from night till morn" to enter the people's House; Henry Clay was the "man, all tattered and torn, who courted the maiden all forlorn"; and so on. With considerably less humor administration partisans published a grotesque caricature of Jackson, made up of the corpses of his alleged victims, under the title "Richard III," underscoring a line from Shakespeare's play: "Methought that the souls of all that I murdered came to my tent" (Act 5, Scene 3). "HUZZA! For Gen. Jackson!!" shouted a sarcastic administration broadside that proceeded to list his misdeeds, beginning with his vote against the resolution of thanks to George Washington in 1796. Wild charges, inflammatory rhetoric, and outright lies were not new in presidential politics, as the combat between Federalists and Republicans in 1800 had proven, but previously they had been aimed at a relatively small electorate. Now a much broader and more numerous public was swept up in the campaigns. There were more meetings, more broadsides, more pamphlets, and more books (some recycled and updated from 1824) than ever before. Propaganda became the means for not only advocating a cause but mobilizing for it as well.

There were other precursors of the future. Partisans devised handbooks and manuals to guide voters. Medals were struck, to be worn as symbols of the candidates. Likenesses of the candidates appeared on plates, snuff boxes, and ladies' hair combs. There even were primitive attempts at polling, as straw votes were taken at weddings, militia musters, and aboard steamboats. The Jacksonians accused the Adams committee in Queen's County, Maryland, of attempting to poll every voter in the district to determine his leanings with the intent of pressuring him to the right side. In New York the Jackson committee appointed one person in each school district to list voters and their leanings and block unqualified voters. One of Clay's friends was worried that Tennesseans would sneak across the border to vote illegally in Kentucky's election, but consoled himself with the thought, "We shall have two or three thousand illegal ones of our own."[3]

Not all of the campaign was "humorous and lighthearted." Drawn with bold capitals and black borders, John Binns's "Coffin Handbill" was easily the most controversial item of all. Under the title "A short account of some of the Bloody Deeds of General Jackson," it displayed pictures of the coffins of the six Tennessee militiamen executed in 1814, claiming that they had been shot owing to a dispute over their term of service. Late in the campaign another anti-Jackson pamphlet appeared, entitled *Official Record of the War Department.* It was a collection of documents that seemed to prove that Jackson had indeed acted without authority in arbitrarily extending the militiamen's service to six months. If it were true that Jackson was responsible for the deaths of simple volunteers—Tennesseans, no less—for no other reason than a misunderstanding of their terms of service, it undermined his image as a noble, selfless patriot and portrayed him as a ruthless, vengeful, and violent misfit.

Missing from the "official" collection was a letter from Governor Willie Blount explicitly authorizing the six-month enlistment. Also missing was any acknowledgment that Jackson was several hundred miles away from the trial scene and was merely signing off on a sentence that had already been meted out by the military court. Predictably there was a howl of protest. "Why don't you tell the whole truth?" shouted Isaac Hill at a Jackson rally on the Fourth of July. "On the 8th of January, 1815, he murdered in the coldest blood 1,500 British soldiers for merely trying to get into New Orleans for Booty and Beauty." When an Adams parade in Philadelphia featured six coffins the *Telegraph* suggested they represented the president and his five cabinet members. Thurlow Weed, the New Yorker who worked zealously for Adams in 1824 and 1828, refused to circulate the Coffin Handbill.[4]

The controversy over the Jackson marriage continued. John Overton's earlier defense was republished, along with a new and more powerful *Vindication* attributed to Henry Lee. What might have been a crippling scandal was converted into a story of romantic love and heroic gallantry in the face of a cruel ex-husband on the hazardous frontier. In politics, as in other forms of competition, the best defense is often a good offense, and Jackson's partisans did not hesitate to go after his opponents. They wisely avoided any detailed discussion of the long-ago events, pointing instead to Rachel Jackson as the real victim of the attacks on her husband. An overzealous paper in Massachusetts published an article titled "The Great Western Bluebeard" whose abuse of Rachel was so excessive that the Jacksonians reprinted and distributed it on their own. "They invade the domestic sanctuary," cried a Jackson pamphlet, "and with reckless malice drag forth to the public view a virtuous and pious lady, to heap upon her venerable head their filthy slanders, because she is the chosen wife of the most illustrious of our warriors."[5] The Hero had been attacked by "the venal, the vulgar, and the vile," Jackson was told at a Fourth of July meeting in Carthage, Tennessee. "Even the sanctuary of your fire-side has been invaded—the happiness and comforts of your domestic and private relations have not been spared. It is a calumny unmanly in its motives, unnatural in its object, and unworthy in its means." Jackson was "the *gallant* protector of female innocence" at New Orleans and yet was now the target of a "fiend-like spirit of destruction," said an orator on January 8. In the long run, the attack on the Jackson marriage backfired. The issue certainly had little effect on the southwestern frontier, where the conditions had often condoned casual relationships without benefit of clergy.[6]

In the absence of specific issues the Jacksonians contented themselves with repelling the attacks on their man and emphasizing the country's need for "Jackson and Reform," a slogan that could mean anything from repealing the result of the previous election, to cleaning up the alleged "corruption" that had led to it, to restoring the "virtue" of the Jeffersonian era.[7]

Two competing but occasionally overlapping images emerged in the final months of the campaign. Adams's best claim lay in his lifetime of public service consistent with the best traditions of American republicanism. Jackson, too, could claim a career in public service, but one that included defending the Republic against its enemies on the battlefield as well as against internal enemies who sought to corrupt it. Each image contained weaknesses. For Adams, the circumstances of his election in 1825 made him vulnerable to questions about the validity of his commitment, and the sweeping nature of his 1825 Annual Message made him the target of those who clung to the liberty-versus-power version of republicanism. For Jackson, his success at New Orleans had to be balanced against the traditional suspicion that military heroes were often potential Caesars ready to destroy republics. As it turned out, however, in 1828 the Hero of New Orleans was transformed "from a potential Caesar to a potential saviour."[8]

The careers of both Jackson and Adams, stretching back to the 1790s, created opportunities for early versions of what would later be called "opposition research." In Jackson's case, the Adams forces went all the way back to the Tennessee Constitutional Convention of 1795. If the general were a true republican, why had he favored a property qualification for office holding? If he was a second George Washington, why had he opposed the resolution of thanks to the first Washington in 1797? If he was a true patriot, why had he consorted with Aaron Burr? If he was a true servant of the people, why had he resigned from every civilian position to which he had been elected or appointed?

They culled juicy items from old issues of New York's *Evening Post*, the Richmond *Enquirer*, and the Albany *Argus*, all of which now supported Jackson but had vigorously opposed him four years earlier. "Compare him to Adams, and with Crawford," Thomas Ritchie had warned in 1824, "and how inferior must he be." His election, Ritchie had declared, would be "a curse upon our country." In 1824 the editor of the Albany *Argus*, speaking for Van Buren's Albany Regency, declared confidently, "The fact is clear....Mr. Jackson has not a single feeling in common with the Republican Party." Even Isaac Hill said as late as November 1824, "The more we contemplate the character of the able, assiduous, and excellent statesman and patriot [Mr. Adams], the further we witness his progress in the diplomatic history of our country—the more we see to admire and applaud." The Massachusetts Central Committee published Jackson's endorsement of Adams in his letter to President-elect Monroe in 1816.[9]

Adams partisans derided the mixed and contradictory combination of Jackson's former allies with his former enemies. Yankees such as Isaac

Hill were linked with the southerners who were "calculating the value of the Union." The Jacksonian coalition, said Ezekiel Webster, was "composed of the shreds and patches, the odds and ends, the thrums and heeltaps of all parties and principles, of all interests and opinions." Federalists such as the secession-minded Timothy Pickering were joining hands with John Randolph of Roanoke. Other Federalists in the Jackson camp included William Coleman, editor of the New York *Evening Post*, and two sons of Alexander Hamilton, James and Alexander Jr. Other Federalists who supported Jackson were Delaware's Louis McLane, whom Jackson would later appoint to his cabinet; Maryland's Roger B. Taney, whom Jackson would later appoint chief justice of the United States; and of course Pennsylvania's James Buchanan, whom Jackson would not appoint to anything but who would later be elected president nonetheless.

But the administration forces were faced with a dilemma. When reviewing Jackson's entire career it was impossible *not* to mention New Orleans. The lopsidedness of victory, the strategic location of the city, and above all its psychological impact on the nation still resonated in the memories of nearly every eligible voter from Maine to Georgia, from New Jersey to Mississippi, and there was no getting around it. To denigrate it in any way would be foolhardy, yet at the same time they needed to warn of the threat posed by military heroes in other times and other places.

"We cheerfully accord to him his full share of glory which renders the anniversary of the 8th of January a day of joy and triumph to our land," the Virginia anti-Jackson convention told the public. The Hero of New Orleans was "a brave warrior and successful general," New York congressman Henry Storrs told a pro-Adams meeting. Jackson was "a brilliant and elevated soldier" who had a number of "splendid military achievements," acknowledged another pro-administration pamphlet. "The praises poured out on Gen. Jackson," conceded the author of yet another, "for the skill and courage displayed by him in defence of the city were merited."[10]

Having said all that, the anti-Jackson forces then attempted to turn his military career against him. The Virginia convention worried about the need for "the military [to be] subordinate to the civil power," noting Jackson's suspension of habeas corpus after his victory at New Orleans, the "cold-blooded massacre at the Horseshoe," "the decoyed and slaughtered Indians at St. Mark's," and "the wanton and unexampled execution of Ambrister." Administration delegates in Louisiana repeated Clay's earlier warning: "Rome had her Caesar, England her Cromwell, France her Napoleon.... Let us be wiser than those nations." Ezekiel Webster warned, "The besetting danger of Republics, is a proneness in our natures to pay a blind and indiscriminate homage to martial renown." Congressman Storrs, after complimenting Jackson for the victory at New Orleans, went on to conclude that if, with full knowledge of the total record, "the People of this country should call him to the Presidency, then our political institutions are a mockery and a cheat."[11]

"MURDER WILL OUT!! Truth is Mighty and shall prevail," proclaimed Jesse Benton from the city hotel in Nashville. The details of the brawl in 1814 were told and retold, not only by Jesse Benton but in anti-Jackson broadsides. As for the Jackson marriage, administration meetings usually avoided specific mention of the issue, contenting themselves instead with elliptical references, as when a New Hampshire convention piously wished that Adams's opponent was equally "distinguished for his private virtues, his talents, experience, or public service." Adams supporters in Maryland were called out to vote as "friends of religion and good morals." Delegates to a New York administration convention claimed that only the length of their address kept them from detailing "some of the vices, which make it [Jackson's election] so eminently sickening to virtuous sensibility." At the same time the delegates announced, "We disclaim all ill will towards General Jackson. We would not pluck one leaf from his brilliant chaplet."[12] More than one reader must have been confused.

Finally, Adams supporters attempted to take advantage of Jackson's frequent grammatical and spelling lapses in his letters, some of which found their way into print. "What will the English malignants...the Edinburgh and Quarterly reviewers,—who have hitherto defamed even the best writings of our countrymen, say of a people who want a man to govern them who cannot spell *more than about one word in four?*" asked an anonymous pamphleteer.[13]

The question and the implications behind it reveal just how much the Adams effort failed to recognize the shift in the political landscape. Jackson's orthography may not have been perfect, but neither was that of most Americans. And most of them cared little for the opinion of the "Quarterly reviewers" in Edinburgh or anywhere else. "We care not if *he spell Congress with a K,*" said Duff Green. "He may, notwithstanding, understand the rights and duties of that body, or of the people, or of himself, as well as if he had spelled it correctly." Jackson was defended by none other than the aging former secretary of state Timothy Pickering, aiming one last blow at the Adams family. Washington, too, he reminded voters, often misspelled words, as did the great Duke of Marlborough, who had led the English armies to victory over their continental foes more than a century before. "Deep reading and scholarship, it is well known in the United States are not essential in the head of our government, to insure its faithful administration," Pickering assured a fellow Jacksonian. "An immense quantity of learning may be acquired, much to the pleasure of the individual, but to little purpose as respects the public."[14]

John Quincy Adams was a republican "in the true sense of the term—one who looks to the permanent good of the whole Republic—whose mind soars above the groveling pursuits of party," claimed one pamphleteer.[15] "Mr. Adams is a scholar," the *Washington Journal* proudly noted. "Is he to be superseded by a man of no education?" Letters of praise and support from Washington, Jefferson, even from Jackson himself appeared in the Adams press. "If intellectual powers of the highest grade, and cultivated with almost unexampled assiduity and success, contribute to fit a man for the first office in our Nation," New Yorkers were told, "then, it must be admitted, that the choice of Mr. Adams...was eminently proper."[16]

But that was just the point. What if "intellectual powers of the highest grade" did not necessarily qualify a person for high office? "General Jackson has not been educated at foreign courts and reared on sweetmeats from the tables of kings and princes," a Jackson paper observed. He "had not the privilege of visiting *the courts of Europe at public expense,*" nor was he "dandled into consequence by lying in the cradle of state," said another. And where, asked Francis Baylies, another dissident Massachusetts Federalist, were Adams and Clay while Jackson was risking his life in defense of his country? "Enjoying the gala days of Europe, after the over throw of Napoleon. Mingling with kings and nobles, parading at courts with laced coats and feathers."[17]

The anti-intellectualism hinted at in the "Wyoming" letters of 1824, was broadened in 1828. "It has been frequently and justly remarked," declared a Jacksonian orator, "that a close application to books, and a consequent banishment from society and neglect of living models, render men ignorant of human nature." An *Address* published by the "Young Men" of New York City admitted, "Mr. Adams is possessed of *learning....*He may be a philosopher, a lawyer, and elegant scholar, and a poet, too, forsooth (we know he wrote doggerel verses upon Mr. Jefferson), and yet the nation may be little better off for all these endowments and accomplishments."[18] Writing in the New York *Enquirer*, the Albany Regency's Mordecai Noah agreed. "We hold this truth to be incontrovertible," he informed his readers, "that no person can have a correct knowledge of mankind who has led a life of entire abstraction from the great body of the people, and who relies for this information on the books he has read, and the scholastic theories that are taught."[19]

There were times when Adams played into the enemy's hands. Relaxing for once his inhibitions about public appearances, he accepted an invitation in December 1827 to participate in the commemoration of the defense of Baltimore thirteen years earlier. In accordance with custom, he proposed a toast. "Ebony and Topaz," he offered. "General Ross's posthumous coat of arms, and the republican militiamen who gave it." The audience scratched their heads. What was the meaning? Realizing that he had puzzled the group, Adams hastily explained that the allusion was taken from the French writer Voltaire's *Le Blanc et Le Noir*, in which *Blanc* (white) stood for the good Americans, and *Noir* (black) for the evil British invaders. The Jacksonian press was delighted. Once again Adams had shown himself to be an elitist steeped in European culture and out of touch with his own countrymen. Duff Green gravely observed that he would reserve comment on the toast because he was less conversant with "Oriental literature" than was Adams. "You great men have no privilege to commit [such] blunders," Charles Hammond told Clay.[20]

For Adams, the Era of Good Feelings was still the norm to which the nation should aspire and return. That had been the thrust of his Inaugural Address. He had hoped to carry forward the political cease-fire advocated by his predecessor and eliminate the "baneful weed" of partisanship. The Jacksonians dismissed Adams's nonpartisanship as a hoax. According to Samuel Ingham, a Pennsylvania Calhounite-turned-Jacksonian, Adams told friends as early as 1807 that the only way to undermine the progress of the "democratic party" was to infiltrate it. Jacksonians in Bucks County, Pennsylvania, agreed. His split with the Federalists and his alliance with the Republicans, they said, was only a scheme to "deceive the democratic party." Moreover, Duff Green claimed, not entirely consistently, by switching parties Adams violated "the principle of party fidelity, which, in this country, all parties do or ought to respect." Therefore, "he can justly claim the confidence of no party." The man was "devoid of sincerity," "an aristocrat," and "a pretended disciple of liberty" who "sought its ruin for the sake of arbitrary power; and therefore, in the estimation of all who deem liberty valuable, he must be pronounced a *traitor*."[21]

By 1828 the opposition, following the lead laid down by Van Buren, Green, and the Jacksonian press generally, had overridden the antiparty-ism of the Founders and embraced instead the notion that only through partisan competition could republicanism be preserved. "That *political parties* are inseparable from free government is a truth which experience has reduced to absolute demonstration," proclaimed Van Buren's Albany *Argus*. The Jacksonian press denounced "amalgamators" who were trying to fool the public.[22]

Even former president Monroe came under attack. His visit to Boston in 1817 was little more than a Federalist plot, New Hampshire Jacksonians were told. The proclamation of the Era of Good Feelings was the work of a "crafty aristocracy" that, in the election of the second Adams, had "restored to power the party which fell with the first Adams."[23] The Adams administration were either Federalists in disguise or cynical intriguers who, having managed to "palsy the will" of the voters in 1825, were out to do it again in 1828. True republicans had no choice but to sup-port the Hero of New Orleans. Adams's friends were caught in another dilemma. Their claim of nonpartisanship left them open to the charge that they were actually closet Federalists trying to deceive the people, but if they professed to be partisan Republicans in the tradition of Jefferson and Madison, they risked losing the support of those former Federalists whose votes were essential to victory.

If the administration partisans had difficulty dealing with Jackson's military accomplishments, they faced problems with their own candi-date as well. Conventions held on Adams's behalf almost never described themselves as "Adams conventions," but more likely portrayed themselves either as "administration" or "anti-Jackson" assemblages. Outside of New England, the president rarely played a role in either their addresses or their rhetoric. When he did, it was frequently in an off-handed, semi-apologetic, and occasionally even critical way.

A group of Missouri supporters explained, "Although we have no great personal predilections for Mr. Adams, and do not indiscriminately approve of his opinions and recommendations, we cannot withhold our approbation of the leading measures and general policy of the Admin-istration." It was true, admitted a New York partisan, that Adams was "a plain, unostentatious man—of somewhat scholastic, or as some have been pleased to say, of old-fashioned manners."[24] The Young Men's

Convention in New York explained Adams's notorious aloofness: "As is the case with most men who have been engaged in deep and recondite pursuits, his manners, have, at first, somewhat the appearance of coldness," but once he got going his conversation "instructs and fascinates the willing hearer."[25] Members of the Virginia anti-Jackson convention told their fellow citizens that they "offered no panegyric on the present Chief Magistrate," but that he clearly was the lesser of two evils. They conceded that Adams had "on one occasion, not perhaps with strict rhetorical propriety, used the expression 'pulsed [*sic*] by the will of our constituents.'" And though they regretted the president's "too liberal" interpretation of the Constitution, they were more concerned with "the destroying hand of his rival." The choice was between the *"positive danger* of electing Gen. Jackson, and the *possible inconveniences* of re-electing Mr. Adams."[26] Even Ezekiel Webster conceded privately that support for the president came "from a cold sense of duty, & not upon any liking of Mr. Adams." To his brother Daniel he added, "We do not entertain for him one personal kind feeling, nor cannot unless we disembowel ourselves like a trussed turkey of all that is human nature within us." With friends like these, John Quincy Adams had no need to look for enemies.[27]

At about the time of the "Ebony and Topaz" fiasco, a dispute broke out over which candidate, Jackson or Adams, could rightly assume the mantle of the departed Jefferson. There was conflicting evidence. Webster's account of Jefferson's criticism of the young Senator Jackson once again made the rounds. It was generally known, too, that the Virginian had always respected Adams, whom he had known as a teenager in Paris in the 1780s; his break with the Federalists in 1808 over Jefferson's embargo had only solidified that respect. And though he had praised Adams's defense of Jackson's Florida escapade, it was also known, or at least suspected, that Jefferson had shared many of the same reservations about Jackson's temperament held by his enemies.

At the same time there was little in the Annual Message of 1825 that could be styled "Jeffersonian." Nothing could be more hypocritical, the Jackson forces maintained, than for Adams, whose father had opposed Jefferson twice and had signed the infamous Alien and Sedition Acts, to claim to be a Jeffersonian. Ingham and others dredged up the "Publicola" essays, claiming that it had been Thomas Jefferson, not Thomas

Paine, whom Adams had mocked as the "Islam of democracy." William Branch Giles, the governor of Virginia, came out for Jackson in late 1827, publishing a letter written to him by Jefferson just six months before his death, expressing alarm at the Annual Message. Nowhere was Jackson mentioned, and Jefferson had asked Giles not to publish it. Giles did anyway. But he concealed a letter written the day before, in which Jefferson had expressed his personal admiration for Adams. Soon another governor, Edward Coles of Illinois, who had once been Jefferson's private secretary, joined in the dispute. Like Jefferson, Coles was philosophically opposed to slavery, but unlike Jefferson, he had freed his slaves and left Virginia. "One might as well make a sailor of a cock, or a soldier of a goose," Coles quoted his former employer, "as a president of Andrew Jackson."

It took Jefferson's grandson, Thomas Jefferson Randolph, to straighten out the dispute between the two governors. The facts seem to have been that in 1824 Jefferson preferred the strict constructionist William Crawford over all the others. But after Crawford's illness had become plain, Jefferson preferred Adams, the son of his old friend and rival, to the tempestuous and unpredictable Jackson. By 1825 the implications of the Annual Message forced Jefferson, with less than a year to live, to express the doubts he had shared confidentially, he thought, with Governor Giles. Eventually, Giles was forced to publish the earlier Jefferson letter praising Adams. Once again Adams himself did not respond in his own defense for more than a year, by which time it was too late.[28]

That he was the son of John Adams undoubtedly cost the president some votes. Ingham's *Exposition* used almost as much space attacking the father for his alleged monarchism as it did attacking the son. Ingham claimed that the younger Adams was "educated as a Monarchist" and hoped to "pave the way for such a change in the Constitution as would establish in the United States, an aristocratical and Hereditary Government."[29] Given the circumstances, the use of the term "hereditary" was particularly effective. The election, Duff Green told his readers, was a struggle against "a system, which is fast tending to monarchy, a struggle between the honest yeomanry of the country, and an aristocracy, that with monied influence and patronage for its aid, seeks to make every thing subservient to its own views, and to perpetuate *in certain families*, all the offices and honors of the government." Just as the great Jefferson had been subject to attacks by "John the first," Jackson was now the target of the friends of "John the second." "*Who Shall be President?*

The Hero of New-Orleans, or John the Second, of the House of Braintree?"
asked a Massachusetts Jacksonian.[30]

The replacement of Calhoun with Richard Rush as the administration's
vice presidential candidate meant that for the first and only time prior to
the Civil War two northerners were facing two southerners in a presidential campaign. Adams's northern background proved to be more of
a handicap for him in the South than Jackson's background would be in
the North. It helped, of course, that whereas beyond the Appalachians
Jackson could be presented as a western candidate, below the Potomac the
Hero's southern birth and slaveholding status was plain for all to see.

For Adams the problem was not merely that he was a northerner, but
that he was a *Yankee*, a New Englander, a descendant of Puritans, with all
of the accompanying negative stereotypes. These included a reputation
for religious fanaticism, calculating stinginess, and, above all, a dangerous
meddlesomeness in private affairs. "The very name of Massachusetts is
odious," observed a Charleston newspaper.[31] Jefferson himself had been
certain that New Englanders were marked "like the Jews, with such
perversity of character, as to constitute from that circumstance the natural division of our parties." References to the "universal Yankee nation"
could be found in southern (and western) newspapers and correspondence
throughout the 1820s.[32] Jacksonian orators and editorialists often derided
"the land of steady habits" and Yankees in general. A pro-Jackson congressman from Kentucky, in the midst of the debates over the Tariff of
1828, made no bones about it in a letter to his constituents. "New England
and Western interests are antipodes to each other," he said. Kentuckians
have nothing to expect from that region: "The yankees are uncompromising on money matters." Another southerner mourned that after escaping
"the taxation of Old England" the nation was now threatened "by imposts
contrived to glut the avarice of New England."[33]

Some of the administration's own rhetoric confirmed the Yankee
stereotype. "This is a business government," declared the Address of the
Central Committee in Massachusetts. "We find that the sober, thinking,
and especially aged people, with the young men, who aim to advance themselves by diligence, industry, devotion to business in their calling…are
almost unanimous for the Administration." Adams's friends were confident that in Pennsylvania "the German population has been too much
gratified by the unostentatious manners of the President, and the practical

business-like character of the administration, to wish for a change." On the other side, they said, were "the political managers, the unsuccessful politicians of all parties, the unreflecting, and the adventurers."[34] Did the eccentric and unstable slaveholder John Randolph denounce Adams as a Puritan and a Yankee? "I boast the honor of parentage from the descendents of Puritans," proclaimed Ichabod Bartlett, an appropriately named congressman from New Hampshire, "and desire to thank God, that *I am a Yankee*." But such sentiments were confined to east of the Hudson.[35]

Sectionalism and regionalism in most countries, including the United States, carry with them certain cultural assumptions about what constitutes the "good life." With these assumptions often come fear and apprehension as well. For many in the West and South the tightly controlled, community-oriented New England culture that had produced a John Quincy Adams represented the very opposite of the good life, threatening as it did the freewheeling individualism of the southwestern frontier that had produced an Andrew Jackson. From the Yankee point of view, Jackson was "bred and lived in a country comparatively a wilderness, where all law was feeble.... His temper and disposition, naturally fierce and arbitrary, being unrestrained, have grown more so as he advanced in life." This wild, undisciplined, and occasionally violent lifestyle of the southwestern frontier reminded many of the equally wild, undisciplined, and occasionally violent American Indian. "With their feelings," sniffed the Boston *Patriot*, "they would put *Tecumseh* into the Presidency, were he alive and eligible."[36]

The degree to which slavery and its future were on the minds of the campaigners of 1828 is unclear. Although both Jackson and Calhoun were slaveholders, they and their partisans made little public reference to it. Privately it was another matter. In his successful attempt to persuade Thomas Ritchie to join the Jackson cause, Van Buren had pointedly observed that it would be in the interest of southern planters to ally themselves with northern "plain republicans" in order to prevent "prejudices between free and slave holding states." In other words, slavery was best protected by an alliance of northerners and southerners committed to the states' rights philosophy put forth in the Virginia and Kentucky Resolutions of 1798. The alliance, so long as it held together, could be relied on to keep the slave question off the table. Ritchie and other southerners could not help but notice that many of Adams's supporters were the same men who had favored blocking slavery's expansion in 1820.[37] Duff Green assured a Kentucky correspondent that although "the antislavery party in the North is dying away," a Jackson-Calhoun victory would "put it to sleep for twenty years." "Upon this subject," he added, "I know more than I can communicate by paper."[38]

The antislavery movement was *not* dying, and Jackson's slaveholding status did not go unnoticed. Andrew Erwin, his perpetual enemy in Tennessee, claimed that the accounts at the bank in Nashville would prove not only that Jackson owned slaves but that he bought and sold them for profit.[39] The bank refused to release the records. An antislavery tract aimed at New Yorkers mocked the opposition's attempt to portray Jackson as the humble "Farmer of Tennessee" and asked whether "the great body of our intelligent farmers will consistently give their votes for such a character, or will, in preference, continue the wise administration of John Quincy Adams, whose religious and moral feelings have been employed with success in protecting our country from increasing and perpetuating the curse of slavery." Others pointedly asked why it was that New York Jacksonians such as Van Buren always seemed to support southern slaveholders in preference to "the only president selected from the northern states in thirty years."[40]

Both sides occasionally played the race card. To his fellow Jacksonians in Kentucky Congressman Henry Daniel explained that in 1824 the general was the clear choice of white people. Adams's support had included blacks and mulattoes, "who, in New England, are qualified voters." Not so, claimed a convention of Republican Young Men in upstate New York. In 1824 the votes for John Quincy Adams "represented a larger portion of the *free white population*, than those received by General Jackson, or by any other candidate."[41] These hints were few. If slavery and its future were part of a hidden agenda in 1828, it was, like most hidden agendas, difficult to prove.

Not since the election of 1800, when Federalists accused Thomas Jefferson of being a closet atheist, had religion entered a presidential campaign.[42] Following his father's death in 1826 Adams formally joined the parish church in Quincy. That church was one of many that had broken with the more orthodox Congregationalists and joined the movement toward Unitarianism. Unitarians denied the trinitarian concept of God as Father, Son, and Holy Spirit and embraced instead the notion of a single God; they questioned the divinity of Jesus as well. For many Christians, then and now, this was heresy bordering on atheism. In his sermon *The Duty of*

Christian Freemen to Elect Christian Rulers the strict Presbyterian Reverend Ezra Stiles Ely reminded his parishioners, "Presidents...are just as much bound as any other persons in the United States, to be orthodox in their faith, and virtuous and religious in their whole deportment." A correspondent informed the *United States Telegraph* that he could not possibly vote for Adams because he was a billiards player *and* a Unitarian. He did not say which was worse.[43]

The ever alert Van Buren was aware that a profession of faith would help his candidate. "Does the old gentleman have prayers in his house?" he asked James Alexander Hamilton. "If so, mention it modestly."[44] Writing from the Hermitage, Jackson reassured Reverend Ely of his orthodoxy. In a letter that eventually found its way into print, the general declared, "I have thought one evidence of true religion is, when all those who believe in the atonement of our crucified Saviour are found in harmony and friendship together." Ely need not fear his defecting to another sect: "I can assure you no change of circumstances, no exalted office can work a change on me. I will remain uniformly the same, whether in the chair of state, or at the Hermitage. My habits are too well fixed now to be altered."[45]

At the same time Adams came under fire from a different quarter. In his Fourth of July Oration in 1821 he had referred to the Roman Catholic Church as a "portentous system of despotism and superstition." He had also made some slighting remarks about the Church in his message to Congress on the Panama mission.[46] "Mr. Adams," wrote "Fenelon," a pseudonymous Jacksonian in Louisiana, "chose to declare that Catholicism is contrary to liberal ideas, that its principles are in opposition to free institutions." General Jackson, on the other hand, had attended a celebratory Mass in New Orleans following his great victory in 1815. To ensure that the Francophone Catholic population got the message, Fenelon's pamphlet was published in French.[47] Adams's supporters responded by listing the number of Catholics he had appointed to office and the amount of money he and his wife had contributed to Catholic charities. In the West, Adams was accused of hobnobbing with priests and conversing with them in Latin; in New England, Isaac Hill denounced him for traveling on Sundays, and in disguise at that.[48]

Adams's alleged anti-Catholicism became a Jacksonian rallying point for not only Francophones but many Irish Americans as well. In Charleston, South Carolina, the Jackson celebration on January 8 featured a toast by the local Catholic bishop. Religion was mixed with ethnicity, as both Protestant and Catholic Irishmen were urged to rally behind Andrew Jackson, "the son of Irish parents." A Jackson orator in Troy, New York, was proud that the "hapless island, the seat of so much persecution, and yet the theatre of sublime displays of heroism and magnanimity…was the native country of those who gave him birth." Boston Irishmen planted their flag on Broad Street and proclaimed their kinship with the general.[49]

The pro-Adams New York *Advocate* helped the Jacksonian cause with its blatantly anti-Irish stance. "When we look at the population of some districts of our country," an editorial lamented, "mixt up with the dregs of all nations; when we are told that we have among us *half a million* of Irishmen, and when we know that they are all linked together and move in a phalanx, we are constrained to say, that the character of our country is degraded with the connexion." The Jacksonian *Argus* happily reprinted the editorial. "Irishmen! Sons of Erin. Look at what follows, and if you have a drop of true Irish blood in you, let it boil as you read."[50] A more cautious anti-Jackson pamphlet suggested that the general had in fact been born in Ireland, hastily adding, "To have been born in Ireland implies no reproach." It then went on to criticize Jackson's participation in the Mass at the Catholic church in New Orleans, which "the republican and Christian cannot fail to regret." Another pointed at Jackson's Celtic background, hinting at the signs of "royalty" and "kingly power" when he attended Mass at the New Orleans cathedral "in full military pomp."[51]

Although in 1828 the majority of the electorate was Anglo-Saxon, neither side wanted to be publicly associated with the English, the historic ethnic adversary of the Irish, the Scots Irish, and the German. The ever imaginative Green accused Adams, the Unitarian, of secretly working to "unite church and state after the manner of the English monarch." Not to be outdone, Adams supporters in New York warned workers that the English expected to benefit from a Jackson victory and, with it, the end of tariff protection. The administration supporters in Massachusetts assured the voters there that the English favored Jackson because they wished to see "the principles, on which a republican government rests, proved to be fallacious."[52]

Matters threatened to turn ugly toward the end of the congressional session. John Adams II, while delivering official papers to Congress in the Capitol building, was attacked by Charles Jarvis, a young Jacksonian whom the young Adams had insulted at a White House reception a few days before. Jarvis pulled Adams's nose, a standard form of insult at the time. The cabinet, led by Clay, insisted that something be done. Congress appointed a committee to look into the matter. It concluded that a grave offense had indeed occurred, but that nothing could be done about it. Administration journals were outraged. "How will it tell abroad," asked Hezekiah Niles, "that a secretary of the president of the United States, known and acknowledged to have been in the discharge of *public business*, was waited for and assaulted while yet within the capitol? How shall we feel at home, if a future president should send his messages to congress by the hands of armed men?" The Jacksonian press dismissed the insult, rising to the defense of Jarvis. The young Jacksonian was merely retaliating for the earlier insult, and young Adams should have expected it. How could Jarvis have known, snickered Green, "that the baby, who was considered old enough to take charge of the contingent fund, and bear messages to Congress, would run blubbering to tell his daddy that he had had his nose pulled and his jaws slapped for his ignorance?" Clay and some others wanted to pursue the matter, but not the president. "Under this Congress it is doubtful whether any remedy for such brutality can be found," Adams said.[53]

Two years before the election Henry Clay's brother had warned him of what would happen once the Jacksonians got started: "You may as well attempt to control the current of the Mississippi."[54] The Fourth of July 1828 triggered another series of coordinated Jackson events. Jackson himself attended a dinner in Carthage, Tennessee, in the presence of a number of Revolutionary War veterans. Jacksonians in Albany, New York, were promised that electing the general would "bring back the republic to the purity and simplicity of the democratic days."[55] In Portsmouth, New Hampshire, more than 170 enthusiasts gathered and "partook of an excellent Dinner" under a banner with Jackson's name in large letters. The varied accounts of these and other banquets featured a series of printed and prescribed "regular toasts," followed by unscripted "voluntary toasts." At a rally in Warner, New Hampshire, there were at least thirty-two voluntary toasts offered, and, for those still standing, there were many more, which, the reporter not surprisingly confessed, "We were not able to recollect." In nearby Plymouth no fewer than 24 regular and 123 voluntary toasts were offered, although it was insisted that "no ardent spirits were used." Jacksonians across the border in Andover, Massachusetts, celebrated with "great hilarity and joys," although angered by "some of the most degraded of the opposition," who tried to spoil things by "purloining the Cannon procured for the occasion."[56]

While Jackson was at Carthage and his supporters were holding their Fourth of July banquets and tributes, John Quincy Adams was presiding over the groundbreaking for the Chesapeake and Ohio Canal. The project was intended to connect the Potomac with the Ohio River Valley, hoping to link the Atlantic Ocean with the nation's heartland, much in the manner of the Erie Canal to the north. Nothing could have come closer to the heart of John Quincy Adams than the possibility of connecting the two great rivers. Following his address he was to turn over the first ceremonial shovelful of dirt. But he hit a tree root on his first try. Adams promptly threw off his coat and attacked the offending root until he came up with his shovelful. The crowd loved it. The incident, according to the *National Intelligencer*, "produced a greater sensation than any other that day."[57]

Such displays of the human touch would have gone a long way to offset Adams's reputation for dour remoteness, to say nothing of boosting his campaign. They were, alas, few and far between. He continued to correspond with his youngest son, tend to his plants, and, with the arrival of warm weather, swim in the Potomac. In August he left for home. On his way he spent a night in Baltimore, where competing Jackson and Adams meetings were being held. The Jackson rally took place next to his hotel, keeping him up past his bedtime. "A stranger would think that the people of the United States have no other occupation than electioneering," he complained.[58]

As in 1824, voters had approximately a month to choose electors prior to the first Wednesday in December, when the electoral votes were to be counted. Complicating matters, only one state, New York, held its presidential election simultaneously with congressional, state, and local elections. The rest held local and state elections at different times. In Kentucky congressional elections were held a full year before the others. Ballots were provided by the candidates, not by state authorities, and in the South voting was often done viva voce, announcing one's choice in front of the officials and the public.

It was clear to most that, again as in 1824, the election would be decided in the so-called middle states: New York, Pennsylvania, and Ohio, the largest, second largest, and fourth largest states, respectively. Together they represented 80 electoral votes out of a total of 261. Pennsylvania and Ohio would choose their electors on a general ticket, winner-take-all basis.

New York had taken away the choice of electors from the legislature and given it to the voters, but on a district system. To win all of New York's thirty-six electoral votes would be difficult for either ticket. It became even more complicated following a series of events that had taken place in the western part of the Empire State.

In the summer of 1826 William Morgan, a renegade member of the highly secret but socially prominent Masonic Order, had infuriated its leaders by threatening to publish details of its secret rituals. In retaliation some of the Masons arranged for Morgan to be arrested and jailed on a series of trumped-up charges, after which he was to be released. Upon leaving jail in Canandaigua, New York, Morgan was apparently hustled into a waiting stagecoach and spirited westward toward the Canadian border. He was never seen again.

Morgan's kidnapping and presumed murder set off a firestorm in most of western New York, not so much because of the incident itself, but because of the growing suspicion that the Order had not only been behind Morgan's disappearance but was engaged in what a later generation of Americans would call a cover-up.[59] The alleged perpetrators of the kidnapping were indicted. Owing to obstructionism by Masonic judges, Masonic prosecutors, and Masonic juries, however, they were not convicted. Word spread that the Order was little more than a conspiracy against the people, committed to protecting its special privileges. Masons, a growing number of western New Yorkers had come to believe, were intriguers, betrayers of the common good, a corrupt and hidden aristocracy, the enemy of true republicanism.

Western New York, especially those counties along Clinton's Erie Canal, had been settled by transplanted New Englanders for at least a generation. It was pro–internal improvements, pro-Clinton, and pro-Adams. And though Van Buren's Albany Regency still held sway in the eastern part of the state and in New York City generally, the Regency's hold weakened west of Syracuse. The anti-Masonic movement disturbed Van Buren. Most of the Regency leaders in Albany were Masons, as was Jackson himself. Were the anti-Masonic backlash to grow, Jackson's chances in New York, along with those of the Regency, would be threatened. Complicating matters further was the fact that Governor Clinton, although popular in the pro-Adams counties in the west, was supporting Jackson, not Adams. Thus the two long-standing rivals, Van Buren and Clinton, were now vying for the leadership of the Jackson cause in New York State. Given Van Buren's past association with the Crawford effort in 1824, there was no reason to assume that Jackson would prefer him to Clinton, whom Jackson had always admired.

Then, suddenly, Clinton died in the winter of 1828, and Van Buren no longer needed to worry about the leadership of the New York Jackson movement. But he still had concerns about the anti-Masons. Thurlow Weed, the same editor who had played a role in Van Buren's failure to carry the state for Clinton in 1824, was now the editor of the anti-Regency *Anti-Masonic Examiner*, published in Rochester. The young William Seward, who four decades later would be Abraham Lincoln's secretary of state, was Weed's close ally. Both were supporters of Adams. After delivering a generous eulogy to his longtime rival in a Senate speech, Van Buren concluded that the most effective means for defeating the anti-Masons, and to help the Jackson cause as well, was to become a candidate for governor himself. In New York the election of 1828 would turn out to be a test of strength, not only for Andrew Jackson but for Van Buren and the Albany Regency.[60]

In Pennsylvania the contest would offer an example of ethnic politics, with both tickets competing for the largest non-English-speaking minority in the nation at that time, German Americans. The Pennsylvania Dutch, as they have been euphemistically called, had been settling in Pennsylvania for over a century. Many were in fact quite fluent in English, but nonetheless were more comfortable in the language of their ancestors. German-language newspapers abounded, particularly in southeastern Pennsylvania and in parts of New Jersey. In recognition of the German American potential, fully one-third of the fifteen thousand copies of the proceedings of the Pennsylvania Jackson convention in 1828 were printed in German. George Kremer, the eccentric congressman who was the first to accuse Henry Clay of a "corrupt bargain," was a German speaker, as was Joseph Ritner, who, after endorsing Jackson, reversed himself by election time and returned to the administration's side. Although President Adams had refused to make an appearance, the administration forces were aware of the German American potential. They printed German-language material in Philadelphia, but in this, as in most other matters, they lagged behind the opposition. They did manage to produce a poorly translated version of Binns's Coffin Handbill, which only puzzled its readers.[61]

Ohio, too, had a significant German American population, particularly in Cincinnati. When the Jacksonians celebrated the New Orleans victory in Columbus on January 8 they printed two thousand copies of the proceedings in German, compared to one thousand in English.[62] Four years earlier Clay had narrowly defeated Jackson in Ohio, and the administration pinned their hopes on Clay's association with the American System and its potential to carry the day again.

Clay's own state of Kentucky was also in play. It had already held its congressional election the year before, when several thousand Jacksonians marched through the streets of Louisville wearing hickory leaves in their hats.[63] Now the state was in the midst of a gubernatorial contest to be settled in August, two months before the vote for president. The election took on the aspects of a modern presidential primary, with both sides watching closely for clues. Administration partisans were apprehensive. One of them complained that his district had been "lined, fitted, and inundated" with Jacksonian propaganda, especially with copies of the *Telegraph:* "The Jackson men out do us in industry, and contributions."[64] Nonetheless, there was a glimmer of hope for the Adams partisans in Kentucky when their candidate was elected governor in August, although this was partially offset by the election of a Jacksonian for lieutenant governor. The state elections in Louisiana had also gone well for the administration, electing a governor and denying control of the state legislature to the Jacksonians.[65]

Later congressional elections were another matter. In Louisiana the two congressmen who had supported Adams in the 1825 House vote were defeated. Missouri's sole congressman and Adams supporter was beaten as well. In Ohio the results meant that its new congressional delegation would be eight for Jackson, six for Adams. Worst of all, in Pennsylvania twenty-five out of the twenty-six congressmen elected in October were said to be Jacksonians.[66] Still, the presidential vote had yet to be cast.

The new electorate called for new tactics to guarantee the maximum turnout. "To the Polls!" shouted Green's *Telegraph* in October. "The faithful sentinel must not sleep—Let no one stay home.—Let every man go to the polls—Let not a vote be lost—Let each Freeman do his duty; and all will triumph in the success of JACKSON, CALHOUN, and LIBERTY." The Adams men in Maryland were, predictably, a little more sedate. "We call upon you, friends of religion and good morals, young and old, rich and poor, to turn out on the 10th of this month....Let no man stay at home; but let each set an example worthy of the emulation of his neighbors: let the young and healthy assist the aged and sick in reaching the polls." There were other methods as well. Workers in the Ninth Ward in New

York City were warned that a Jackson victory would probably cost them their jobs because his southern allies would see to it that tariff protection would be ended. Did they want factories in New York, or "3000 miles across the Atlantic?"[67]

Maine was among the first states to report actual balloting for the presidency. Until 1820 it had been part of Massachusetts, and Adams had represented it as one of its senators. Privately the Jacksonians had conceded all of the "land of steady habits." But, unlike the rest of New England, Maine had adopted a district system for choosing its electors. A spirited Jackson movement in and around the city of Portland produced a slim majority in that single district, denying Adams a complete sweep of New England. The rest performed as expected, except that in New Hampshire Isaac Hill's strenuous efforts and no-holds-barred approach to electoral combat resulted in a record-breaking turnout and only a narrow victory for Adams. For the general's supporters the victory in Maine and the close result in New Hampshire were omens of good things to come.

And they did come. Jackson triumphed in Pennsylvania, just as he had four years before. The margin was astonishing, nearly two to one, the majority there being virtually equal to Adams's majority in all New England. Like a string of dominoes the states to the west fell into the Jackson column, beginning with Ohio and followed by Indiana and Illinois. To Jackson's delight Kentucky reversed the result of the gubernatorial election, going for him by better than 55 percent.[68] There was no contest at all in any of the southern states except Louisiana, where anti-Jackson sentiment still could be found among the Francophones. Even there, however, Jackson carried 53 percent of the vote. It was very close in New York, with Jackson receiving barely 51 percent of the vote. Under its district system he netted twenty electoral votes to Adams's sixteen. New Jersey, which had voted for Jackson in 1824, was the only state to reverse itself for Adams four years later, owing to the hard work of Secretary Samuel Southard and division among the opposition.[69] Adams did well in Maryland too, but under the district system had to split the state's eleven votes, six to five.

The final electoral vote was 178 for Jackson, 83 for Adams. The popular vote was proportionally closer—approximately 56 percent to 44 percent—yet that margin of victory would not be matched in any presidential election for the rest of the nineteenth century. Calhoun was reelected as well, although not by the same margin as Jackson in the electoral count, owing to lingering animosity from the Crawfordites in Georgia, who gave their votes to a third candidate.[70]

State	Popular Vote		Electoral Vote	
	Jackson	Adams	Jackson	Adams
Maine	13,927	20,733	1	8
New Hampshire	20,922	24,134		8
Vermont	8,350	25,363		7
Massachusetts	6,016	29,876		15
Rhode Island	821	2,754		4
Connecticut	4,448	13,838		8
New York	140,763	135,413	20	16
New Jersey	21,951	23,764		8
Pennsylvania	101,652	50,848	28	
Delaware	(electors chosen by legislature)			3
Maryland	24,565	25,527	5	6
Virginia	26,752	12,101	24	
North Carolina	37,857	13,918	15	
South Carolina	(electors chosen by legislature)		11	
Georgia	19,363	0	9	
Alabama	17,138	1,938	5	
Mississippi	6,772	1,581	3	
Louisiana	4,603	4,076	5	
Kentucky	39,397	31,460	14	
Tennessee	44,293	2,240	11	
Missouri	8,272	3,400	3	
Ohio	67,597	63,396	16	
Indiana	22,257	17,052	5	
Illinois	9,560	4,662	3	
Total	**647,276**	**508,074**	**178**	**83**

Some have suggested that better organization by the administration might have produced a different, or at least a closer result in the Electoral College. Administration supporters were successful in state elections in Kentucky, Ohio, Indiana, and Louisiana, which meant the Jacksonian majority in the next U.S. Senate would be reduced. The result in New York was much closer than Van Buren had expected. The Little Magician was elected governor, but only because the insurgent anti-Masonic party and the former Clintonians refused to work together. There was continued bickering in Pennsylvania between Republican supporters of the administration and former Federalists. Workingmen in New York City and Philadelphia were potential voters for an American System that claimed to protect their jobs, but they were ignored. Had John Quincy Adams been more circumspect with his Annual Message in 1825, had he been willing to promote his ideas more vigorously after delivering it, had he used his appointive and removal powers more aggressively, had he replaced Calhoun with a southerner or a westerner as a vice presidential candidate—had he done any or all of these things, the result might have been different. Jackson's margin certainly would have been smaller.[71]

The geographic distribution of support demonstrated continuity with the earlier contests between Federalists and Jeffersonian Republicans. Adams did best in most of the areas that had favored his father in 1800, and Jackson triumphed in the states that had favored Jefferson. The distribution helped to inflate Jackson's electoral count. Although he carried barely half the voters in the free states, he attracted well over 70 percent of those in the slave states. With the three-fifths bonus awarded by the Constitution to the slave states for their nonvoting slave "property," the two hundred thousand southern votes generated 105 electoral votes, whereas the four hundred thousand he received in the North netted him only 73.[72]

But there should be no denying the fact of Jackson's success. The three-fifths bonus may have inflated his electoral count, but he would have won without it. Had the general ticket system been applied to all the states, his margin would have been even more lopsided: 189 to 72. As it was, no presidential candidate had ever been supported by the effort organized on behalf of Andrew Jackson in 1828. A Kentuckian complained that while supporters of the administration dallied on their farms, Jacksonians were "swimming rivers and risking their lives to get to the polls." Another admitted, "They have their forces better disciplined, and can bring them to the pools [*sic*] with greater facility than we can."[73] In an earlier era, when transportation and communication was slow, polling places far apart, newspapers and post offices comparatively few, and those eligible to participate in a presidential contest limited, such coordination and energy would have been impossible. But the tectonic plates of politics had shifted, and Andrew Jackson was the first to benefit.[74]

Historians are in agreement as to the importance of the election of 1828, but not necessarily as to why. Were there genuine issues involved, or was it just an uneven contest between two campaign organizations? Was it a significant advance for democracy, or was it an ugly campaign in which, as one nineteenth-century historian wrote, it was more honorable to lose than to win?[75] Did Jackson's victory signal the rise of the common man, or was it a cynical exercise in unprincipled ambition, in which the only real winner was a new breed of professional politician? There is evidence to support any (and all) of these conclusions. Both campaigns broke new ground in getting out the vote, with each, as one participant wrote, "fairly in the field, under *whip & spur*."[76] Presidential election participation more than doubled from that of 1824, from 27 percent to 57 percent. It increased in every state but one, Adams's Massachusetts, where, in spite of their enthusiasm in January, the Jacksonians were unable to mount a serious challenge in November. (Lack of serious opposition in Tennessee, however, did not prevent voters there from turning out in record numbers to support their hero, nearly doubling the turnout in 1824.) In New York as well, spurred on by the anti-Masonic phenomenon, voters responded with a turnout of more than 70 percent. With the addition of Louisiana, Georgia, Vermont, and New York to the list of states choosing their electors by popular vote, only Delaware and South Carolina continued to deny the choice of electors to the people.[77]

The increase in presidential voter participation prefigured the turnout during the rest of the nineteenth century. Although on the national level participation dropped by a fraction when Jackson was reelected in 1832, it picked up again in 1836, and in 1840 reached 74 percent. Participation never went below 69 percent for the rest of the century.[78] Before 1828 voters took more interest in state and local elections than they did in the presidency. Afterward the pattern was reversed. Van Buren was right: increased partisanship meant increased competition, increased competition meant increased awareness of the issues, and the voters responded accordingly. Most agree that the era of mass political parties began with the election of 1828. But "mass political parties" does not necessarily mean "mass control." Skeptical historians have suggested that in spite of the new rhetoric and increased voter participation the election merely replaced "one ruling clique with another." Public conventions, with all of their hoopla, may indeed have replaced the private caucus, but the change meant little more than moving "from overt to covert elitism."[79]

"After 1828," writes one historian, "the classical ideal of nonpartisan leadership, which Adams and Monroe had shared with Washington and countless political philosophers, was dead—killed in battle with Old Hickory as surely as General Pakenham."[80] The election opened the door to a legitimization of organized political parties, so that "the ordinary citizen…could more effectively control the operation of government and shape public policy." Many of the techniques used by the Jacksonians— banquets, songs, parades, symbols—had been used before, but on state and local levels, rarely, if ever, for the presidency. For some this was not necessarily progress. After recording instances of violence at the polls, charges and countercharges of illegal voting, bribery, and intimidation, an early twentieth-century authority balefully concluded that such practices "all became the rule when the number of the voters and the ignorance of a large portion of them made these methods useful."[81]

"For all of the vulgarities and slander, the campaign of 1828 was not an unprincipled and demagogic theatrical," one historian has written. For him it was about "contrasting conceptions of politics," rooted in an earlier era, between the Jeffersonian commitment to limited government and the equally Jeffersonian commitment to education, enlightenment, and public service.[82] At the same time, Jackson's most thorough biographer has maintained that the 1828 result "represented a victory not only for a much beloved and trusted public figure but a demand for the restoration of morality and virtue to civic life." A more critical historian argues that "Adams stood for a vision of coherent economic progress, of improvement both personal and national, directed by deliberate planning. Instead of pursuing improvement, Jacksonians accepted America the way it was, including its institution of slavery." Jackson's popularity "rested to a large degree on military prowess, which of course is the oldest political appeal of all, and by no means democratic. If Jackson was the candidate of the 'common man,' as he was so often described, it was specifically the common *white* man."[83] Noting the sectional distribution of the vote, another historian noted some time ago that the election "may not have been a victory for virtue, but it was a victory for the South." Nonetheless, "Democracy Triumphant" is the title of a chapter in a recent biography of Old Hickory.[84]

Was Jackson a hero to the "common [white] man"? Certainly not in most of New England, nor in western New York State, nor in those parts of what is now the upper Midwest, settled as they were by Yankees or their descendants. Here the cultural traditions of Puritan Yankee New England held sway, and they did not favor a slaveholding duelist. Adams found support among Quakers as well, for whom his opponent's martial repute and slaveholding status could not be expected to carry much weight either.[85] Yet in other parts of the North Jackson drew strength from economically undeveloped regions, far from the "universal Yankee nation." He also attracted support from first-time voters, many of whom were immigrants, young, or both.

American political historians enjoy debating whether voting behavior is a product of socioeconomic status or ethnicity. The 1828 election provides ammunition for both points of view. Regardless of the voters' wealth, Jackson proved to be strong in areas settled by his fellow Scots Irish. He did almost as well among the German-speaking counties in Pennsylvania and all but one German community in Virginia. In New York State he was strongest among the Dutch-descended communities along the Hudson, of whom Martin Van Buren was a typical representative. For the next thirty years or more New York State politics would be a battleground between the Yankees beyond Syracuse and the Dutch "Yorkers" along the Hudson. In general, John Quincy Adams drew most of his strength from what has been called the "host culture," the descendants in the Northeast of the predominately Anglo-Saxon Protestant settlers of the seventeenth and eighteenth centuries.[86]

Did socioeconomic status play a role? The evidence suggests it did. One historian has argued that Jackson's support was the strongest among "the lower (though hardly the lowest) rungs on the social ladder."[87] These would include both isolated frontiersmen and working-class city dwellers. His greatest success outside of the South was in economically undeveloped regions that had no interest in the promise of the American System. Adams did better among the more economically developed regions of the North, predictably those settled by Yankees.

Some evidence suggests that the administration partisans would have agreed with a class analysis of the electorate. In New Hampshire the Jacksonians were dismissed as mere "acreless men." Those who turned out so see him in New Orleans were similarly portrayed as "low cartmen, dirty woodsawyers and contemptible bricklayers."[88] A friend of Henry Clay lamented, "The ignorant and degraded class of our population are all against us." Another noted that a Jackson rally in Ohio was characterized by free transportation that brought "the halt, the lame & the blind; nearly all drunk, to vote for Jackson." The friends of the administration, he noted smugly, "make no display, they are above imitating the vociferations of the rabble." There is no record of similar comments made by Jacksonians about their opponents.[89]

The question of political motivation—how and why people vote the way they do—is a complex one. Voters in the Early Republic did not vote as they did simply "because of their reactions to events or to issues decided on their merits alone." Votes sprang as well "from men's location in the social structure, their cultural heritage, and the kind of communities in which they lived."[90] Behind the innovations in political organization and motivation, behind the leap in voter participation, behind the election of a charismatic military hero over a placid former diplomat, there was an emerging clash of cultures whose outlines were only faint in 1828 but would come into focus and establish the parameters for politics for the next thirty years, maybe more. One perspective, put forth by Adams's Annual Message of 1825, maintained that it was the function of government to improve the economic, educational, and moral condition of the citizenry. The other, that of most Jacksonians, insisted that government's sole function was to protect liberty against power. This dichotomy has become the basis of American political dialogue ever since.

Van Buren's coalition—combining the supporters of Crawford, Calhoun, and Jackson—laid the groundwork for the nineteenth-century Democratic Party. It was not always the alliance between "the planters of the South and the plain republicans of the North" that he had once envisioned, but he did succeed in reviving the contest between the "federals and anti-federals." The Democrats would dominate presidential politics for the next thirty years, during which they would win six out of eight presidential elections. Jackson's victory also began an unbroken streak of elected presidents who were either southern slaveholders or northern sympathizers, a streak that would not be broken until Abraham Lincoln's victory in 1860.

It is ironic to some that the icon of American democracy for much of the nineteenth century would be Andrew Jackson, a slaveholder with an autocratic personality occasionally inclined toward violence, instead of John Quincy Adams, whose personal lifestyle was far more republican. Jackson's Hermitage was an elegant, well-maintained plantation covering hundreds of acres, benefiting from the labor of hundreds of slaves. The Adams family farm was, and is, far more modest. But in at least one sense, Adams's critics were right. His long absence from the country, though it weakened neither his republicanism nor his patriotism, made him insensitive to the changes in political culture that were going on all around him. John Quincy Adams was, as the historian George Dangerfield remarked, "a great man certainly, and possibly a very good one, but a President who had planned for the people, without ever trying to understand them."[91]

Epilogue

"The Enemyes of the Genls hav Dipt their arrows in wormwood & gall & sped them at me," Jackson's wife wrote to a close friend in July 1827. Rachel Jackson was a modest, unprepossessing woman who turned increasingly to religion in her later years. She and her husband never had any children of their own, instead adopting various Donelson nephews, along with Lyncoya, the Creek Indian orphan. In an age in which childlessness was thought to be unnatural, in Rachel Jackson's mind it may have been God's punishment.[1]

An observer once wrote disparagingly of Rachel's "dowdy clothes, inelegant shape, and healthy tanned complexion." Another, who saw her at New Orleans in 1815, described her as "a short, fat dumpling."[2] Even a friendly visitor to the Hermitage much later described Rachel as "a coarse-looking, stout, little old woman, whom you might easily mistake for [Jackson's] washerwoman, were it not for the marked attention he pays to her."[3] Like many women of the frontier, she was not averse to sharing a pipe of tobacco now and then with her husband. Jackson loved her passionately and was never comfortable in her absence.

Her husband's election in 1828 brought her little satisfaction. Her health was declining, and she did not look forward to moving to Washington. She confessed in early December, "Were it not for the many base attempts that have been made to defame the characters of my husband and myself, I could hardly be induced to leave this peaceful and delightful spot."[4] She suspected that her background was not suited to the comparatively sophisticated atmosphere of Washington society, with the "carding and vissitting" that had so annoyed her husband. We shall never know. On December 22, 1828, Rachel Jackson died of an apparent heart attack at age sixty-one.

Speaking after her funeral, Jackson said that although he could forgive his own enemies, he was not sure he could forgive those whom he believed had slandered his wife. This included the president of the United States, a charge that Adams vehemently denied. Jackson refused to make a courtesy visit to Adams upon his arrival in Washington. In response, Adams consulted his cabinet on whether he should attend Jackson's inaugural. Led by Clay, they advised against it, with only Rush, the treasury secretary, demurring.[5] It did not bode well for the future relationship between the two.

★ ★ ★

Contrary to Adams's prediction, Jackson's presidency did not "go to wreck and ruin." His precarious health notwithstanding, and to the surprise of nearly everyone, he served two full terms in office. No other president would do so until after the Civil War. Each of the two terms had its crises, but in nearly every instance Jackson was as victorious in politics as he had been on the battlefield. When he stepped down in March 1837 both the presidency and American politics had been permanently changed.[6]

The Framers of the Constitution never intended the presidency to have the power it presently wields. As good republicans, they were suspicious of power, especially executive power. Yet if power was an evil, it was a necessary evil in any realistic plan of government. It was therefore best placed, they thought, not in the hands of one man but in the hands of the people's elected representatives. Members of Congress, more than half of whom would be chosen every two years, were power's safest repository. The president, elected every four years through an intentionally cumbersome process and removable only under extraordinary circumstances, was charged with carrying out the people's will by enforcing the laws passed by the people's representatives. That the president too might claim to be the people's representative rarely, if ever, crossed the Framers' minds.

Jackson changed all that by the sheer force of his personality and his unerring instinct for gauging public opinion. He convinced himself that his victories in 1828 and 1832 made him, not Congress, better qualified to speak for the whole nation. No single congressman, no single senator, not even Congress itself could ever make that claim. Only a president can speak for the nation, and every successful president since Jackson has claimed to do so.

Jackson's presidency did get off to a rocky start. Among the hundreds who swarmed into the White House after his inaugural were many who expected to be rewarded for their support. A New England Jacksonian thought the invasion by those in search of rewards was "a disgraceful reproach to the character of our countrymen."[7] Yet the expectations for reward were the inevitable result of the changes that had taken place in American political culture during the 1820s.

At first Jackson's view on patronage was the same as Adams's. No one, he said, should lose his job because of opposition to his election. But at the same time, Duff Green and Amos Kendall were proclaiming that Jackson would "REWARD HIS FRIENDS AND PUNISH HIS ENEMIES."[8] By the following December the pressure from job seekers had become too great, and Jackson altered course. His first Annual Message set forth one of the prevailing doctrines of his presidency: that "the duties of all public officers are...so plain and simple that men of intelligence may readily qualify them selves for their performance." Therefore, "no man has any more intrinsic right to official station than another." By then he had fired thirteen district attorneys, twenty-three registers and receivers, nine federal marshals, twenty-five customs collectors, and 433 postmasters. Jacksonians called this "rotation in office." His critics called it "the spoils system," and the name has stuck ever since.[9]

Cracks appeared in the Jacksonian coalition within a few months. On the surface was what former president Adams called "the Eaton malaria," the controversy surrounding the refusal of most of the wives of Jackson's cabinet members to associate with Margaret O'Neale ("Peggy") Eaton, the new wife of Jackson's longtime friend (and now secretary of war) John Henry Eaton. Mrs. Eaton brought with her a less than spotless reputation, owing to a number of alleged dalliances while her first husband, a naval officer, was away at sea. He died mysteriously, a probable suicide. Peggy Eaton's snubbing by the cabinet wives could not help but provoke in Jackson's mind memories of his own late wife and the attacks on her. He rallied to Mrs. Eaton's defense. In his cabinet only Van Buren, whom Jackson had made secretary of state, stood by her and therefore by Jackson. Van Buren was a widower.[10]

Behind "the Eaton malaria" was a more serious disease. With the exception of Eaton and Van Buren, the other cabinet members were Calhounites, and the snubbing of Mrs. Eaton was led by Floride Calhoun, wife of the vice president. Relations between Jackson and Calhoun began to deteriorate almost immediately, over the Eaton affair as well as the president's discovery of Calhoun's attacks on him over the Florida invasion back in 1818–19. It was also becoming clear that Calhoun's allies in South Carolina were among the most vocal in challenging the constitutionality of the Tariff of 1828 and the right of the president to enforce it.

The short-run result was the resignation of Jackson's entire cabinet in 1831, giving him the opportunity to start over with a group of men whose personal loyalty was beyond dispute. Back in 1789 George Washington had experimented with a cabinet representing various points of view, as with Hamilton and Jefferson. This turned out to be less than successful. Monroe had chosen an all-Republican cabinet, but the personal and political rivalries within it worked against him. Adams chose his cabinet with regard to regional considerations and had reached out to former rivals or their adherents in hopes of removing the "baneful weed" of party strife. That had not worked out either. For Andrew Jackson, service in the cabinet henceforth would mean service to the president and to the president alone. If a member found himself at odds with the president on a policy matter, he would be expected to resign. As he later put it to a dissenting cabinet member before firing him, "A secretary, sir, is merely an executive agent, a subordinate."[11] Such has been the pattern ever since. Jackson strengthened his position further by relying on a smaller group of advisors—derisively dubbed the "Kitchen Cabinet" by his critics—who, not having any official status, were free to offer advice that the president could accept or reject without risk to them.

The tension between Jackson and Calhoun continued to mount. Calhounites in and out of Congress continued to proclaim the right of a state to "nullify" a law it believed to be unconstitutional. The more extreme among them persisted in "calculating the value of the Union." Jackson and Calhoun confronted each other at a famous dinner honoring the birthday of Thomas Jefferson on April 13, 1830. Called on to deliver a toast, Jackson offered, "Our Union, it must be preserved." Calhoun responded, "Our Union. Next to our liberties, the most dear." Relations continued to deteriorate. His hopes for succeeding Jackson dashed, Calhoun eventually resigned as vice president and took his place as a senator from South Carolina. Duff Green, Calhoun's faithful advocate, turned against Jackson, and the *Telegraph* was replaced as the administration's mouthpiece by the new Washington *Globe*, edited by Francis Preston Blair.[12]

Van Buren was the beneficiary of the Jackson-Calhoun split. It was allegedly his idea to have the cabinet resign over the Eaton affair in order to give the president a clean slate, and it was his allies who had arranged for the confrontation between Jackson and Calhoun at the Jefferson birthday dinner. Jackson rewarded Van Buren by appointing him minister to Great Britain, but the Little Magician was recalled after Clay and

Calhoun combined to have the Senate reject his appointment. This only strengthened the bond between Jackson and Van Buren.

When South Carolina attempted to nullify the Tariff of 1828 Jackson responded with a rousing proclamation defending national supremacy that could have been written by John Quincy Adams himself. He threatened to use federal force to invade South Carolina and punish anyone who resisted, including, presumably, Calhoun. Congress backed him up with a so-called Force Bill. At the last minute Clay and Calhoun once again worked together to produce a compromise that gradually lowered the protective tariff over the next eight years, and the South Carolina authorities grudgingly accepted it. (To save face, they then "nullified" the Force Bill.) In this instance the principle of national authority had prevailed over the claims of state sovereignty. Jackson's precedent would be cited twenty-nine years later, in 1861, when South Carolina was leading the charge to secession.[13]

Jackson was not always consistent regarding federal authority. The first item of business for the Twenty-first Congress in 1829–30 was the passage of an Indian Removal Bill. Under its terms the Cherokees in Georgia were given the choice of being moved west of the Mississippi or remaining in Georgia and subject to Georgia's laws. It wasn't much of a choice. Remaining in Georgia meant harassment, discrimination, and probable violence. Removal meant disruption, dislocation, and obvious hardship. Sympathizers of the Cherokees brought suit in the Supreme Court, which ruled in *Worcester v. Georgia* that Indians could not be subject to state laws, only federal treaties. Jackson ignored the decision, allegedly saying, "John Marshall has made his decision, now let him enforce it."[14] In addition to ignoring the Supreme Court's decision, Jackson announced to Congress that he would no longer enforce the Indian Intercourse Act of 1802, intended to protect the natives against white intruders. This selective use of federal authority has led critics to conclude that Jackson's presidency was an assertion of his personal authority, not that of the office of president or the federal government. Yet whether he intended it or not, the presidency was strengthened. Few remember *Worcester v. Georgia*, but many remember the Nullification Crisis.[15]

Jackson could use federal authority over the states when he chose; he also used it to assert presidential power over Congress. Until then the presidential veto had been used sparingly, and almost always in those cases in which the president believed the proposed law unconstitutional. John Quincy Adams had not used it at all. Jackson used it more than all of his predecessors combined, mostly in connection with internal improvement bills that he did not like.

Jackson vetoed Congress's rechartering of the Second Bank of the United States in 1832, setting off a political firestorm. His suspicion of banks in general has already been noted, but there was little indication prior to his election that he believed he had a mandate to overhaul the nation's entire banking system. In 1832 the president of the Bank of the United States, Nicholas Biddle, moved to renew the Bank's charter five years before it was due to expire. The confrontation that followed not only established new grounds for the use of the presidential veto but also helped define the issues in the presidential election of that year. Congress contained a pro-bank majority, as did Jackson's new cabinet. Biddle's defiance in moving to have the charter renewed five years early managed to provoke Jackson. Encouraged by his Kitchen Cabinet, he vetoed the renewal.[16]

The Constitution requires that when a president vetoes a bill he must inform Congress of his reasons. In contrast to his proclamation against South Carolina, Jackson rejected the nationalist reasoning in Chief Justice Marshall's *McCulloch v. Maryland* decision upholding the Bank in 1819, and instead restated many of the old strict construction arguments against it. While he was at it, he denied the Court's sole power to determine the constitutionality of federal laws and denounced the Bank as an unrepublican monopoly that threatened the livelihood of ordinary Americans.

He went further than that. Fifty thousand copies of Jackson's Veto Message were circulated throughout the nation and reproduced in dozens of newspapers. Apart from the debate over the Bank's constitutionality, the significance of the Veto Message lies in its intended audience. Technically aimed at Congress, it was in fact aimed at the American people. It became a central part of Jackson's campaign for reelection. Like successful presidents in the future, Jackson wrapped himself in the garb of the national interest by going after "special interests." Congress upheld the veto, with many who initially supported the recharter reversing themselves in the wake of Jackson's powerful rhetoric. Clay had hoped to use the Veto Message against Jackson in his attempt to deny him a second term. Once again, however, Clay misjudged the situation. He received even fewer electoral votes in 1832 than had Adams four years before.[17]

When Jackson ran for reelection in 1832 he did so as the unabashed leader of a political party, now calling themselves Democrats. Not only had the ideal of the Mute Tribune passed from the scene, but so had the animus against parties in general. The antipartyism of the Founders receded into the past. Appropriately enough, in 1832 Jackson chose Martin Van Buren as his running mate, the very man who had been the prime mover in the revival of partisan competition.

The haphazard means for choosing candidates that had existed in earlier times was replaced in 1832 by carefully organized national party conventions, just as Van Buren had hoped. Oddly enough, the first to do so were not Jackson's Democrats, but the rambunctious anti-Masons. Putting their anti-elitist and democratic rhetoric into practice, anti-Masonic delegates gathered in Baltimore in September 1831 and nominated William Wirt, John Quincy Adams's attorney general, for president. Clay's National Republicans followed suit, meeting in the same city in December. The Jacksonian Democrats came last, also holding their convention in Baltimore, in May 1832. The selection of candidates by private caucuses and cliques had passed from the scene, replaced on both the state and national levels by nominating conventions.

For the next twenty years two national parties, each with clearly defined yet flexible ideologies, contested for the presidency, for Congress, for governorships, and for many local offices as well. Jackson's Democrats clung to the Van Buren formula of states' rights and strict construction. His opponents, reacting against his assertion of presidential power, denounced "King Andrew the First" and began calling themselves Whigs, after the British party of the same name that had once opposed the royal prerogative. In the decade to come the Whigs did their best to carry forward the Adams-Clay tradition of using federal power to promote economic development and "improve" society. Yet if the outcome of presidential elections is any guide, the Democratic message, invoking as it did the Jeffersonian republican values, predominated. On the state level the Whigs had some success in the regions that had once favored Adams, but not until after the Civil War did the Adams-Clay tradition enjoy any national success. Even then it was under a new political party that called themselves Republicans.

Jackson's success as an outsider, separated from the intrigues of Washington, became the model for many presidential campaigns well into the twenty-first century. So did the image of the self-made man. When the Whigs finally elected a president in 1840 it was another general with little experience in government. The "Log Cabin" campaign of William Henry Harrison, allegedly the hero of the Battle of Tippecanoe in the War of 1812, was as devoid of specifics as was Jackson's in 1828. Profiting from an opponent's sneer that all General Harrison needed was a pension, some hard cider, and a log cabin to keep him happy, the Whigs turned the tables on the Democrats. Log cabin replicas replaced hickory poles in the streets of small towns. Contingents of young enthusiasts marched in parades, shouting "Tippecanoe and Tyler Too." This time it was President Van Buren who was accused of high living in the White House. Harrison easily routed the incumbent president. "We have taught them how to defeat us," lamented a Democrat after it was over.[18] Twenty years later a former Whig would be elected to the presidency from much the same background. Like Andrew Jackson, Abraham Lincoln "came out of the wilderness."

Much to his family's displeasure, John Quincy Adams could not stay out of politics after his defeat. In 1830 he did something no former president has done since: he was elected to Congress, first in that year and consecutively until his death in 1848. He fought the Jacksonians on virtually every important issue.[19] Only on the Nullification Crisis and certain aspects of foreign policy did he find himself in reluctant agreement with his nemesis. But it was Adams's emergence as the leading congressional critic of slavery and its expansion and, in the 1840s, the annexation of Texas that drew Jackson's greatest ire. The two ex-presidents attracted national attention in the last decade of their lives when the Jacksonians accused Adams of bungling his diplomacy as secretary of state in 1819, charging the New Englander with letting American claims to Texas slip away out of fear of too much growth to the south and west. Adams retaliated by demonstrating through his diary that Jackson himself had approved the terms of the Treaty of 1819. In the midst of the controversy Jackson opened a letter from one Adam Goodlett, urging him to make peace with "that gracious and good man John Q. Adams." Jackson would have none of it. "What," he asked in reply, "has John Q. Adams or Henry Clay ever done for this countries good—nothing, but much mischief."[20]

At the time Old Hickory had little more than a year to live. When he died in June 1845 tributes flowed from all parts of the nation. George Bancroft, a Harvard-educated Yankee who knew and liked John Quincy Adams but liked Andrew Jackson more, delivered the memorial oration before the assembled dignitaries in Washington. Jackson was, he said, "the servant of the people. In discipline stern, in a just resolution inflexible, he was full of the gentlest affections, ever ready to solace the distressed, and to relieve the needy, faithful to his friends, fervid for his country."[21]

Jackson may have been a hero, John Quincy Adams told his diary, but he was also "a murderer, and adulterer, and a profoundly pious presbyterian, who, in the last days of his life belied and slandered me before the world."[22] While historians dwell happily on the postpresidential reconciliation of John Adams and Thomas Jefferson, there was to be no such rapprochement between John Quincy Adams and Andrew Jackson.

Adams followed Jackson to the grave in less than three years. In February 1848, just as he was voting against a resolution of thanks to the generals of the Mexican War, he was stricken with a cerebral hemorrhage and died two days later. Leading the tributes was none other than the old Jacksonian Thomas Hart Benton. "Death found him at the post of duty," he told his fellow senators, "and where else could it have found him, at any stage of his career?"[23] Of those prominent in the election of 1828, Calhoun was next to go, but not before he launched an attack on the Compromise of 1850, supported by Clay, Webster, and others, to alleviate the growing sectional crisis over slavery and its future. Clay himself followed in 1852, along with Webster. Benton lasted until 1859. Martin Van Buren died in 1862, in the midst of the Civil War. The Little Magician's alliance of the planters of the South with the "plain republicans" of the North had fallen apart under the strain created by the crisis over slavery. The "plain" northern republicans had a new hero in an Illinois congressman who had been in the House chamber when John Quincy Adams was stricken. Abraham Lincoln's frontier background and determination to preserve the Union were similar to Jackson's, but his ideas on slavery and the role of government were closer to those of Adams. Surely his ranking among the greatest of American presidents is in part due to his absorbing the best qualities of both men.

Acknowledgments

It is not often that at the beginning of one's graduate training one gets to sit in seminars with two future Pulitzer Prize winners, but such was my good fortune half a century ago. Since then, the contributions of Jim McPherson and David Fischer to the historical profession, as well as connecting the broader public with the past, have been truly remarkable. I was pleased and flattered to be invited to make a contribution to their Pivotal Moments in American History series. They each read an early version of this book and saved me from enough errors to allow me, perhaps, to make new ones.

Most of my teaching career took place in the Department of History at the State University of New York's College at Brockport. There I met with my second instance of good fortune, which was to interact with and learn from an unusual band of dedicated teacher-scholars who, in spite of the perils in which public colleges and universities often find themselves, and notwithstanding the curricular and bureaucratic demands forced on them by outsiders, never wavered in their commitment to their students and to their discipline. I became a better teacher, and a better scholar, as a result of my many years with them.

Two colleagues in particular contributed to whatever merits this book has. Owen (Steve) Ireland and Kathleen Kutolowski spent more time going over the manuscript than I had any right to expect, detecting repetitions, fuzzy reasoning, passive voice, and glaring ignorance. Like Jim and David, Steve and Kathy shared their own expertise as friends, scholars, and craftsmen. If I didn't always follow their advice, I may pay the consequences later.

But the good fortune eclipsing all others has been my marriage to Anne Hruska Parsons, the origins of which began at Grinnell College in Iowa over half a century ago. Since then we have traveled together to three continents, been part of four college communities, and raised two sons. At the same time Anne established a career of her own, not only as a mother but as a teacher, counselor, computer whiz, and academic community leader. Her encouragement and enthusiasm for this and other works of mine—including lectures, scholarly essays, and cranky letters to the editor—have never wavered, for which my gratitude and love extends well beyond my ability to express it. At long last, this book is for her.

Castine, Maine, 2008

Notes

Prologue

1. Margaret Bayard Smith, *The First Forty Years of Washington Society,* ed. Galliard Hunt (New York, 1906), 284; Robert V. Remini, *Andrew Jackson and the Course of American Freedom, 1822–1832* (New York: Harper & Row, 1981), 173, hereafter cited as *Jackson and Freedom.*
2. Edwin A. Miles, "The First Peoples' Inaugural—1829," *Tennessee Historical Quarterly* 38 (Fall 1978): 299.
3. Smith, *First Forty Years*, 271–291.
4. Frances Trollope, *Domestic Manners of the Americans* (London: Folio Society, 1974), 113; Miles, "First Peoples' Inaugural," 296.
5. Alexis de Tocqueville, *Democracy in America* (New York: Harper & Row, 1966), 436.
6. Quoted in Remini, *Jackson and Freedom*, 156–57.
7. Quoted in George Dangerfield, *The Era of Good Feelings* (London, 1953), 424.
8. Quoted in Remini, *Jackson and Freedom*, 147.
9. *Niles' Weekly Register,* November 22, 1828; Smith, *First Forty Years,* 257.
10. Smith, *First Forty Years,* 291.
11. Remini, *Jackson and Freedom*, 177–78; *National Intelligencer*, March 5, 6, 1828; Erik Eriksson, "Official Newspaper Organs and the Campaign of 1828," *Tennessee Historical Magazine* 8 (January 1925): 247.
12. John Quincy Adams, *The Memoirs of John Quincy Adam,* 12 vols., ed. C. F. Adams (Philadelphia, 1874–77), 8:78 (December 3, 1828), 8:105 (March 4, 1829).
13. Walter Dean Burnham, *Critical Elections and the Mainspring of American Politics* (New York: W. W. Norton, 1970), 1–7, and the same author's essay, "Party Systems and the Political Process," in

William Nisbet Chambers and Walter Dean Burnham, eds., *The American Party Systems: Stages of Political Development* (New York: Oxford University Press, 1975), 293–95, mention 1828 only in passing, but it would seem to fit the criteria for a "critical election."

14. Andrew Burstein, *The Passions of Andrew Jackson* (New York: Knopf, 2003), 225; David Hackett Fischer, *The Revolution of American Conservatism* (New York: Harper & Row, 1965), 49; Edward Pessen, *Jacksonian America: Society, Personality, and Politics* (Homewood, Ill.: Dorsey Press, 1978), 97–99.

15. Charles G. Sellers Jr., "The Equilibrium Cycle in Two-Party Politics," *Political Opinion Quarterly*, Spring 1965, 31.

16. Ronald P. Formisano, "The Concept of Political Culture," *Journal of Interdisciplinary History* 31 (Winter 2001): 393–426, and *The Transformation of Political Culture: Massachusetts Parties, 1790s–1840s* (New York: Oxford University Press, 1983). See also the introduction to *Beyond the Founders: New Approaches to the Political History of the Early American Republic*, ed. Jeffrey L. Pasley, Andrew W. Robertson, and David Waldstreicher (Chapel Hill: University of North Carolina Press, 2004).

Chapter One

1. Commissioned shortly after Jackson's death in 1845, the first edition of the statue was dedicated in Washington in 1853. The New Orleans statue was put up in 1856 and the Nashville replica in 1880. It is very similar to one of Czar Peter the Great in St. Petersburg, Russia.

2. *Webster's New Geographical Dictionary* (Springfield, Mass., 1984), lists fifty-five place-names for Washington, forty-nine for Jackson or Jacksonville (including one mountain in Antarctica).

3. There are several biographies of Jackson, most of which are multivolume. James Parton, who relied on the recollections of many of Jackson's contemporaries, published his three-volume *Life of Andrew Jackson* (New York: Mason Brothers, 1861); John Spencer Bassett published his two-volume *Life of Andrew Jackson* (Garden City, N.Y.: Doubleday, Page, 1911); Marquis James wrote *Andrew Jackson: The Border Captain* (Indianapolis: Bobbs-Merrill, 1933) and *Andrew Jackson: Portrait of a President* (Indianapolis: Bobbs-Merrill, 1937). The most thorough is Robert V. Remini's rousing three-volume opus, *Andrew Jackson and the Course of American Empire, 1767–1821* (New York: Harper & Row, 1977), hereafter cited as *Jackson and Empire*; *Andrew Jackson and the Course of American Freedom, 1822–1832* (New York: Harper & Row, 1981), hereafter cited as *Jackson and Freedom*; and *Andrew Jackson and the Course of*

American Democracy, 1833–1845 (New York: Harper & Row, 1984), hereafter cited as *Jackson and Democracy*. See also H. W. Brands, *Andrew Jackson, His Life and Times* (New York: Doubleday, 2005); Henrick Booraem, *Young Hickory* (Dallas: Taylor Trade, 2001). More recently, Sean Wilentz's *Andrew Jackson* (New York: Times Books, 2005) and Jon Meacham's *American Lion: Andrew Jackson in the White House* (New York: Random House, 2008) deal mostly with Jackson's presidency.

4. Arthur Schlesinger Jr. and Fred L. Israel, eds., *History of American Presidential Elections*, 4 vols. (New York: Chelsea House, 1971), 1:362; Henry A. Wise, *Seven Decades of the Union* (Philadelphia: J. B. Lippincott, 1881), 151–52.

5. Arthur M. Schlesinger Jr., "Rating the Presidents: Washington to Clinton," *Political Science Quarterly* 11 (Summer 1997): 179–90. Jackson usually comes in around sixth or seventh, behind Jefferson and Theodore Roosevelt and ahead of Harry Truman, although a C-SPAN poll of historians conducted in 1999 dropped him to thirteenth place. A *Wall Street Journal* poll conducted of "conservative" historians in 2000 still ranked Jackson sixth. See also Robert K. Murray and Tim H. Blessing, "The Presidential Performance Study: A Progress Report," *Journal of American History* 70 (December 1983): 535–55.

6. John William Ward, *Andrew Jackson: Symbol for an Age* (New York: Oxford University Press, 1955).

7. Quoted in Charles Grier Sellers Jr., "Andrew Jackson versus the Historians," *Mississippi Valley Historical Review* 44 (March 1958): 615. See also Alfred A. Cave, *Jacksonian Democracy and the Historians* (Gainesville: University of Florida Press, 1964); Douglas R. Egerton, "An Update on Jacksonian Historiography," *Tennessee Historical Quarterly* 34 (1987): 79–85.

8. Frederick Jackson Turner, *The Frontier in American History* (New York: H. Holt, 1920), 268.

9. Two recent comprehensive studies of the Jackson era are examples of the divergence in interpreting both the man and the age. Sean Wilentz's *The Rise of American Democracy: Jefferson to Lincoln* (New York: W. W. Norton, 2005) is the best example of analysis from an essentially pro-Jackson perspective. It may be contrasted with Daniel Walker Howe's *What Hath God Wrought* (New York: Oxford University Press, 2007), which is dedicated to the memory of John Quincy Adams. Both Howe's book and Edward Pessen's earlier *Jacksonian America: Society, Personality, and Politics* (Homewood, Ill.: Dorsey Press, 1978) frequently cast doubt on much of the conventional wisdom regarding the Age of Jackson, going so far

as to question the usefulness of the term itself. Lee Benson, in *The Concept of Jacksonian Democracy: New York as a Test Case* (Princeton, N.J.: Princeton University Press, 1961), titled his concluding chapter "Jacksonian Democracy—Concept or Fiction?" 329–39.

10. Michael Paul Rogin, *Fathers and Children: Andrew Jackson and the Subjugation of the American Indian* (New York: Knopf, 1975); James C. Curtis, *Andrew Jackson and the Search for Vindication* (Boston: Little, Brown, 1976); Andrew Burstein, *The Passions of Andrew Jackson* (New York: Knopf, 2003).

11. Ronald P. Formisano, *The Transformation of Political Culture: Massachusetts Parties, 1790s–1840s* (New York: Oxford University Press, 1983), 18.

12. See, e.g., the works of Remini, Brands, and Wilentz, cited above.

13. Richard J. Moss, "Jacksonian Democracy: The Origins and Growth of the Term," *Tennessee Historical Quarterly* 34 (1975): 145–53.

14. Joseph Ellis's *Founding Brothers* (New York: Knopf, 2000) and David McCullough's *John Adams* (New York: Simon & Schuster, 2001) helped to regenerate interest in the Founders. Each was subsequently made into a television series. Earlier, Anthony Hopkins was nominated for an Academy Award for his portrayal of John Quincy Adams in the film *Amistad* (1997).

15. David Hackett Fischer, *Albion's Seed: Four British Folkways in America* (New York: Oxford University Press, 1989), 651; Booraem, *Young Hickory*, 13–26; Robert Kelley, "Ideology and Political Culture, from Jefferson to Nixon," *American Historical Review* 82 (June 1977): 535.

16. Remini, *Jackson and Empire*, 1–5.

17. For many years the Adams papers were closed to the public, handicapping would-be biographers. The first modern biographer to have access to them was Samuel Flagg Bemis, whose *John Quincy Adams and the Foundations of American Foreign Policy* (New York: Knopf, 1949), followed by his *John Quincy Adams and the Union* (New York: Knopf, 1956), still set the pace. Since then there have been Marie Hecht's *John Quincy Adams: A Personal History of an Independent Man* (New York: Macmillan, 1972); Paul Nagel, *John Quincy Adams: A Public Life, a Private Life* (New York: Knopf, 1997); and Lynn Hudson Parsons, *John Quincy Adams* (Madison, Wisc.: Madison House, 1998).

18. Fischer, *Albion's Seed*, 183.

19. Booraem, *Young Hickory*, 45–52; Remini, *Jackson and Empire*, 12–14; James, *Andrew Jackson: The Border Captain*, 8–25.

20. Remini, *Jackson and Empire*, 21; Brands, *Andrew Jackson*, 24–28; James, *Andrew Jackson: The Border Captain*, 26.

21. Parton, *Jackson*, 1:85–96; James, *Andrew Jackson: The Border Captain*, 18–36.
22. Bemis, *Adams and Foreign Policy*, 9–21; Parsons, *John Quincy Adams,* 13–35.
23. Remini, *Jackson and Empire*, 26.
24. Ibid., 29–33; James, *Andrew Jackson: The Border Captain*, 36–38.
25. John Quincy Adams to John Adams, June 2, 1777, in *Adams Family Correspondence,* 6 vols., ed. Lyman Butterfield, Wendell Garrett, Richard Alan Ryerson, Celeste Walker, and Gregg Lint (Cambridge, Mass.: Harvard University Press, 1963–), 2:254.
26. Jackson to Avery, August 12, 1788, cited in Remini, *Jackson and Empire*, 38–39.
27. Burstein, *Passions of Andrew Jackson*, 17–19; Bertram Wyatt-Brown, "Andrew Jackson's Honor," *Journal of the Early Republic* 17 (Spring 1997): 1–36.
28. Fischer, *Albion's Seed*, 669–71.
29. Harriet C. Owsley, in "The Marriages of Rachel Donelson," *Tennessee Historical Quarterly* 36 (1978): 479–92, argues for both a first and second Jackson marriage, but the evidence is unclear. The record for a first marriage, if any, has yet to be found. See Remini, *Jackson and Empire*, 64–65; Burstein, *Passions of Andrew Jackson*, 241–48.
30. Mary French Caldwell, *Andrew Jackson's Hermitage* (Nashville: Ladies' Hermitage Association, 1933), 15; Remini, *Jackson and Empire*, 56.
31. Jackson to John McKee, May 16, 1794, Jackson, *Correspondence*, 1:12–13.
32. Jackson to McKee, May 16, 1794, Jackson, *Correspondence*, 1:12–13. For more on Spanish activity on the frontier during this period, see Arthur P. Whitaker, "Spanish Intrigue in the Old Southwest," *Mississippi Valley Historical Review* 12 (September 1925): 162, 172.
33. Remini, *Jackson and Empire*, 76–77.
34. Ibid., 83–84, 102–3.
35. The most readable and engaging account of this period is Joseph Ellis's *Founding Brothers*, but it should be supplemented by Stanley Elkins and Eric McKitrick, *The Age of Federalism* (New York: Oxford University Press, 1993).
36. The literature on the subject is immense. Bernard Bailyn's *The Ideological Origins of the American Revolution* (Cambridge, Mass.: Harvard University Press, 1967) initiated a significant overhaul in the interpretation of postrevolutionary America. It is summed up in Robert E. Shallhope, "Toward a Republican Synthesis: The Emergence of an Understanding of Republicanism in American

Historiography," *William and Mary Quarterly* 29 (January 1972): 49–80, and the same author's "Republicanism and Early American Historiography," *William and Mary Quarterly* 39 (April 1982): 334–56. To avoid or at least minimize confusion, the word "republican," uncapitalized, refers to underlying principles; "Republican," capitalized, refers to the political party.

37. John Quincy Adams to Abigail Adams, December 30, 1786, in John Quincy Adams, *Writings of John Quincy Adams,* 7 vols., ed. W. C. Ford (New York: Macmillan, 1913–17), 1:29.

38. See, e.g., Bernard Bailyn, *Pamphlets of the American Revolution, 1750–1776* (Cambridge, Mass.: Harvard University Press, 1965): 38–39; Elkins and McKitrick, *Age of Federalism,* 4–7. Harry L. Watson's, *Liberty and Power: The Politics of Jacksonian America* (New York: Hill and Wang, 1990) applies the concept to the entire Jackson era.

39. Quoted in Marc W. Kruman, "The Second American Party System and the Transformation of Revolutionary Republicanism," *Journal of the Early Republic* 12 (Winter 1992): 511. See also Ralph Ketcham, *Presidents above Party* (Chapel Hill: University of North Carolina Press, 1984), 3–5, 89–99.

40. Kruman, "Second American Party System," 519; Adams to Jonathan Jackson, October 2, 1780, in John Adams, *Works,* 10 vols., ed. C. F. Adams (Boston: Little, Brown, 1850–56), 9:511; "Farewell Address," in *A Compilation of Messages and Papers of the Presidents, 1789–1897,* 10 vols., ed. James D. Richardson (Washington, D.C., 1896), 1:231; Richard Hofstadter, *The Idea of a Party System: The Rise of Legitimate Opposition in the United States, 1789–1840* (Berkeley: University of California Press, 1969), 53; Madison, *The Federalist,* Essay No. 10 (New York, 1945), 54–62.

41. Elkins and McKitrick, *Age of Federalism,* especially chapters 7 and 8.

42. Thomas Jefferson to John Rutledge, June 24, 1797, quoted in Ellis, *Founding Brothers,* 86.

43. Marshall Smelser, "The Federalist Period as an Age of Passion," *American Quarterly* 10 (Winter 1958): 391–419; John R. Howe Jr., "Republican Thought and the Political Violence of the 1790's," *American Quarterly* 19 (Summer 1967): 147–65. Ellis's *Founding Brothers* offers a more benign view of the period.

44. David Hackett Fischer, *The Revolution of American Conservatism* (New York: Harper & Row, 1965), xix.

45. Jackson to Nathaniel Macon, October 4, 1797, quoted in Remini, *Jackson and Empire,* 79, 93.

46. Andrew Jackson to John Donelson, January 18, 1798, in Andrew Jackson, *The Papers of Andrew Jackson,* 6 vols., ed. Sam B. Smith and

Harriet Chappell Owsley (Knoxville: University of Tennessee Press, 1980–), 1:168.

47. Parton, *Jackson* 1:203–26; Remini, *Jackson and Empire*, 109–12.

48. Parton, *Jackson*, 1:219–20.

49. Jackson to Cocke, June 25, 1798, quoted in Remini, *Jackson and Empire*, 108.

50. Jackson, *Papers*, 1:486.

51. John Quincy Adams, "Publicola Letters," in *Writings*, 1:65–110; Bemis, *Adams and Foreign Policy*, 26–110; Parsons, *John Quincy Adams*, 42–64.

52. Elkins and McKitrick, *Age of Federalism*, 691–754.

53. Remini, *Jackson and Empire*, 114, quoting Parton, *Jackson*, 1:227.

54. Remini, *Jackson and Empire*, 100–102.

55. Wyatt-Brown, "Andrew Jackson's Honor," 8.

56. Remini, *Jackson and Empire*, 140–46; Burstein, *Passions of Andrew Jackson*, 51–57.

57. See Joanne B. Freeman, *Affairs of Honor: National Politics in the New Republic* (New Haven, Conn.: Yale University Press, 2001), 178–79.

58. Brands, *Andrew Jackson,* 136–41; Remini, *Jackson and Empire*, 142–43; Burstein, *Passions of Andrew Jackson*, 142.

59. See, e.g., Adams's manuscript diary, September 2, 1802, Adams Papers Microfilms, Massachusetts Historical Society, Boston, reel 27. For more on the differences between northern and southern honor, see Bertram Wyatt-Brown, *Honor and Violence in the Old South* (New York: Oxford University Press, 1986), 19–22, 42–43.

60. Adams to Abigail Adams, April 14, 1801, in Adams, *Writings*, 2:528–29; to Thomas Boylston Adams, September 27, 1801, Adams Papers Microfilms, reel 401; Adams, *Memoirs*, 1:249 (January 28, 1802).

61. Adams to Abigail Adams, December 22, 1803, Adams Papers Microfilms, reel 402.

62. John Quincy Adams, *An Oration Delivered at Plymouth, December 22, 1802....* (Boston: Russell and Cutler, 1802).

63. Jackson to Jefferson, August 7, 1804, in Andrew Jackson, *The Correspondence of Andrew Jackson,* 7 vols., ed John S. Bassett (Washington, D.C.: Carnegie Institution, 1926–35), 1:68.

64. Quoted in Bemis, *Adams and Foreign Policy*, 123.

65. Bemis, *Adams and Foreign Policy*, 135–49; Adams, *Memoirs*, 5:136 (May 31, 1820).

66. Parsons, *John Quincy Adams*, 86; Bemis, *Adams and Foreign Policy*, 135–49.

67. Remini, *Jackson and Empire*, 148; Jackson to the Tennessee Militia, October 4, 1806, in Bassett, *Correspondence*, 1:150.

68. For Jackson's role in the Burr conspiracy, see Nancy Isenberg, *Fallen Founder* (New York: Viking, 2007), 294–96, 300–310, 351, and Walter McCaleb's older but thorough *The Aaron Burr Conspiracy* (New York: Wilson-Erickson, 1936), 218–19.

69. Remini, *Jackson and Empire*, 149.

70. Burstein, *Passions of Andrew Jackson*, 79, citing Parton, *Jackson*, 1:333–34.

71. Excellent studies on the background to the war are Bradford Perkins, *Prologue to War: England and the United States, 1805–1812* (Berkeley: University of California Press, 1961); Roger Brown, *The Republic in Peril* (New York: Columbia University Press, 1964); J. C. A. Stagg, *Mr. Madison's War: Politics, Diplomacy, and Warfare in the Early American Republic, 1783–1830* (Princeton, N.J.: Princeton University Press, 1983).

72. Quoted in Remini, *Jackson and Empire*, 168–69.

73. Jackson to Madison, March 15, 1813, quoted in Remini, *Jackson and Empire*, 176.

74. Remini, *Jackson and Empire*, 180; Parton, *Jackson*, 1:384, 486.

75. Remini, *Jackson and Empire*, 181.

76. Ibid., 181–85; Burstein, *Passions of Andrew Jackson*, 93–97.

77. Jackson to John Coffee, September 29, 1813, quoted in Remini, *Jackson and Empire*, 190–91.

78. Davy Crockett, *Life of Davy Crockett* (New York, 1854), 75; Jackson to Rachel Jackson, November 4, 1813, quoted in Remini, *Jackson and Empire*, 193.

79. Burstein, *Passions of Andrew Jackson*, 97–106; Remini, *Jackson and Empire*, 197–201, 211–12.

80. Jackson to Pinckney, March 28, 1814, in Jackson, *Papers*, 3:52.

81. Remini, *Jackson and Empire*, 232.

82. Rogin, *Fathers and Children*; Remini, *Jackson and Empire*, 194.

83. Quoted in Remini, *Jackson and Empire*, 209.

84. A. W. Crosby, *America, Russia, Hemp, and Napoleon* (Columbus: Ohio State University Press, 1965); Norman Saul, *Distant Friends: The United States and Russia, 1763–1867* (Lawrence: University Press of Kansas, 1991).

85. Adams to Thomas Boylston Adams, May 1/13, 1811, in Adams, *Writings*, 4:69, to William Plumer, August 13, 1813, 505.

86. Adams to Abigail Adams, June 30, 1811, in Adams, *Writings*, 4:128.

87. Quoted in George Dangerfield, *The Era of Good Feelings* (London, 1953), 7.

88. Adams to Louisa Catherine Johnson, February 7, 1797, in Adams, *Writings*, 2:109n.

89. Jackson to Rachel Jackson, August 5, 1814, quoted in Remini, *Jackson and Empire*, 232–33.

90. Remini, *Jackson and Empire*, 247.

91. Adams to Louisa Catherine Adams, August 9, 1814, in Adams, *Writings*, 5:74.

92. Adams, *Memoirs*, 3:27–29 (September 1, 1814).

93. Adams to Louisa Catherine Adams, November 29, 1814, in Adams, *Writings*, 5:220.

94. There are several descriptions of the Battle of New Orleans, besides those to be found in Remini and Parton. A contemporary account, based on interviews with participants on both sides, is Alexander Walker, *Jackson and New Orleans: An Authentic Narrative of the Memorable Achievements of the American Army, under Andrew Jackson, before New Orleans, in the Winter of 1814, '15* (New York: Derby, 1856). See also Robin Reilly, *The British at the Gates* (New York: Putnam, 1974); Robert Remini, "Andrew Jackson's Account of the Battle of New Orleans," *Tennessee Historical Quarterly* 26 (Spring 1967): 26–31.

95. Jackson to Governor Claiborne, September 21, 1814, quoted in Remini, *Jackson and Empire*, 253–54.

96. Jackson's address to the troops, in Jackson, *Correspondence*, 2:118–19. According to Parton, *Jackson*, 2:63, this is in Livingston's handwriting.

97. Examples found in John William Ward, *Andrew Jackson: Symbol for an Age* (New York: Oxford University Press, 1955), 216.

98. Adams, *Memoirs*, 3:126 (December 24, 1814); Bradford Perkins, *Castlereagh and Adams* (Berkeley: University of California Press, 1964); Fred L. Engelman, *The Peace of Christmas Eve* (New York: Harcourt, Brace, and World, 1962).

99. Charlton Heston played the role of Andrew Jackson in *The Buccaneer,* a film made in 1958, which probably inspired Jimmy Driftwood's song "The Battle of New Orleans" (1959), which later was voted one of the ten most popular American songs of all time.

100. Justice Joseph Story, quoted in Robert H. Wiebe, *The Opening of American Society from the Adoption of the Constitution to the Eve of Disunion* (New York: Vintage, 1985), 190.

101. Ward, *Andrew Jackson*, 7–10.

102. Quoted in Remini, *Jackson and Empire*, 295.

103. Jackson to Colonel Matthew Arbuckle, March 5, 1815, quoted in Remini, *Jackson and Empire*, 310.

104. Alexander Dallas to Jackson, April 12, 1815, quoted in Remini, *Jackson and Empire*, 315.

105. John Reid and John H. Eaton, *The Life of Andrew Jackson* (Philadelphia: M. Carey & Son, 1817).

106. Andrew Hynes to Jackson, October 24, 1815, and William Carroll to Jackson, October 4, 1815, quoted in Remini, *Jackson and Empire*, 320; Burstein, *Passions of Andrew Jackson*, 124.

107. Cited in Parton, *Life of Jackson,* 2:351-52.

108. John Quincy Adams to John Adams, January 1, 1817, in Adams, *Writings*, 6:131-32.

109. Monroe to Jefferson, February 23, 1817, quoted in Adams, *Writings*, 6:166n.

110. Jackson to Monroe, March 18, 1817, in Jackson, *Papers*, 4:102.

Chapter Two

1. Harry Ammon, *James Monroe: The Quest for National Identity* (New York: McGraw-Hill, 1971); Arthur Styron, *The Last of the Cocked Hats: James Monroe and the Virginia Dynasty* (Norman: University of Oklahoma Press, 1945).

2. Quoted in Robin Reilly, *The British at the Gates: The New Orleans Campaign in the War of 1812* (New York: Putnam, 1974), 326.

3. John Spear Smith to Senator Samuel Smith, June 9, 1810, quoted in Norman E. Saul, *Distant Friends: The United States and Russia, 1763–1867* (Lawrence: University Press of Kansas, 1991), 61; Adams, *Memoirs*, 4:388 (June 4, 1819).

4. Morris Birkbeck, quoted in George Dangerfield, *The Era of Good Feelings* (London, 1953), 116.

5. Still the best on this subject is George Rogers Taylor, *The Transportation Revolution, 1815–1860* (New York: Rinehart, 1951), now supplemented by Carol Sheriff, *The Artificial River: The Erie Canal and the Paradox of Progress, 1817–1862* (New York: Hill and Wang, 1996).

6. William G. Shade, "Political Pluralism and Party Development: The Creation of a Modern Party System," in *The Evolution of American Electoral Systems,* ed. Paul Kleppner (Westport, Conn.: Greenwood, 1981), 105.

7. Phyllis Lee Levin, *Abigail Adams: A Biography* (New York: St. Martin's, 1987), 484; *Columbian Centinel*, July 12, 1817, quoted in Dangerfield, *Era of Good Feelings*, 95.

8. Edward C. Carter II, "Mathew Carey and 'The Olive Branch,' 1814–1818," *Pennsylvania Magazine of History and Biography* 79 (October 1965): 399, 409.

9. Stanley Elkins and Eric McKitrick, *The Age of Federalism* (New York: Oxford University Press, 1993), 501–3; Joanne B. Freeman, *Affairs of Honor: National Politics in the New Republic* (New Haven, Conn.: Yale University Press, 2001), xxii–xxiii, 174–76.

10. Quoted in Richard Hofstadter, *The Idea of a Party System: The Rise of Legitimate Opposition in the United States, 1789–1840* (Berkeley: University of California Press, 1969), 196–97.

11. Jackson to Monroe, November 12, 1816, in Jackson, *Correspondence*, 2:265; Adams to William Eustis, July 25, 1815, in Adams, *Writings*, 4:329.

12. James M. Banner Jr., *To the Hartford Convention* (New York: Knopf, 1970), 335; Linda K. Kerber, *Federalists in Dissent: Imagery and Ideology in Jeffersonian America* (Ithaca, N.Y.: Cornell University Press, 1970); Shaw Livermore Jr., *The Twilight of Federalism: The Disintegration of the Federalist Party, 1815–1830* (Princeton, N.J.: Princeton University Press, 1962).

13. Adams to Eustis, July 25, 1815, in Adams, *Writings*, 4:329; Jackson to Monroe, January 6, 1817, in Jackson, *Correspondence*, 2:272–73.

14. This is the argument laid out in Sean Wilentz's *The Rise of American Democracy: Jefferson to Lincoln* (New York: W. W. Norton, 2005), 13–71. See also Gordon Wood, *The Radicalism of the American Revolution* (New York: Knopf, 1992), 271–369.

15. John Adams to James Sullivan, 1776, in John Adams, *Works,* 10 vols., ed. Charles Francis Adams (Boston: Little, Brown, 1850–56), 9:377–78, quoted in Alexander Keyssar, *The Right to Vote: The Contested History of Democracy in the United States* (New York: Basic Books, 2000), 1. See also Chilton Williamson, *American Suffrage: From Property to Democracy, 1760–1860* (Princeton, N.J.: Princeton University Press, 1960).

16. M. J. Heale, *The Presidential Quest: Candidates and Images in American Political Culture, 1787–1852* (London: Longman, 1982), 20; Keyssar, *Right to Vote,* 5–10; Ronald P. Formisano, "Deferential-Participant Politics: The Early Republic's Political Culture, 1789–1840," *American Political Science Review* 68 (June 1974): 473–87; J. R. Pole, "Historians and the Problem of Early American Democracy," *American Historical Review* 67 (December 1962): 635–36.

17. Merrill Peterson, ed., *Democracy, Liberty and Property: The State Constitutional Conventions of the 1820's* (Indianapolis: Bobbs-Merrill, 1966).

18. Fischer, *Revolution of American Conservatism*, 187–92. See also Jeffrey L. Pasley, "The Cheese and the Words: Popular Political Culture and Participatory Democracy in the Early American Republic," 31–56, and Andrew W. Robertson, "Voting Rites and Voting Acts: Electioneering Ritual, 1790–1820," 57–78, both in David Waldstreicher, Jeffrey L. Pasley, and Andrew W. Robertson, *Beyond the Founders: New Approaches to the Political History of the Early American Republic* (Chapel Hill: University of North Carolina Press, 2004).

19. Richard P. McCormick, "New Perspectives on Jacksonian Politics," *American Historical Review* 65 (January 1960): 288–301, especially table 1, 292; Mary W. M. Hargreaves, *The Presidency of John Quincy Adams* (Lawrence: University Press of Kansas, 1985), 18.

20. Adams, *Memoirs*, 4:193 (December 17, 1818).

21. Adams to Abigail Adams, June 30, 1811, in Adams, *Writings*, 4:128.

22. John Quincy Adams, *An Oration Delivered at Plymouth, December 22, 1802....* (Boston: Russell and Cutler, 1802), 8–9.

23. Adams, *Writings*, 5:98–99. Lynn Hudson Parsons, "'A Perpetual Harrow upon My Feelings': John Quincy Adams and the American Indian," *New England Quarterly* 47 (September 1973): 339–79.

24. Robert Remini, *Andrew Jackson and the Course of American Empire, 1767–1821* (New York: Harper & Row, 1977), 303–5, 321–25, hereafter cited as *Jackson and Empire;* Kenneth Wiggins Porter, "Negroes in the Seminole War, 1817–1818," *Journal of Negro History* 36 (July 1951): 249–80.

25. Remini, *Jackson and Empire,* 345.

26. Cited in Remini, *Jackson and Empire*, 347. See also Dangerfield, *Era of Good Feelings*, 124–36; Daniel Walker Howe, *What Hath God Wrought* (New York: Oxford University Press, 2007), 98–99.

27. Jackson to Monroe, January 6, 1818, in Jackson, *Correspondence*, 2:345–46.

28. Jackson to Rachel Jackson, April 10, 1818, quoted in Remini, *Jackson and Empire*, 356.

29. Jackson to John C. Calhoun, April 26, 1818, in Jackson, *Correspondence*, 2:363; Howe, *What Hath God Wrought*, 102; Frank Owsley Jr., "Arbuthnot and Ambrister," *Journal of the Early Republic* 5 (Autumn 1985): 289–308.

30. Quoted in Remini, *Jackson and Empire*, 364.

31. Ibid., 470n; Dangerfield, *Era of Good Feelings*, 138–39; R. R. Stenberg, "Jackson's Rhea Letter Hoax," *Journal of Southern History* 2 (1936): 480–96.

32. Adams, *Memoirs*, 4:107–14 (July 15–21, 1818).

33. Ibid., 4:87 (May 4, 1818), 4:102 (June 18, 1818).

34. Adams to Don Luis de Onis, July 23, 1818, and to George William Erving, November 28, 1818, in Adams, *Writings*, 6:386–94, 498–99. For the long-range diplomatic implications of Adams's letter, see William Earl Weeks, *John Quincy Adams and American Global Empire* (Lexington: University of Kentucky Press, 1992), 21–36; David S. Heidler and Jeanne Heidler, *Old Hickory's War: Andrew Jackson and the Quest for Empire* (Mechanicsburg, Penn.: Stackpole, 1996), 94–108; David S. Heidler, "The Politics of National Aggression: Congress and the First Seminole War," *Journal of the Early Republic* 13 (Winter 1993): 501–30.

35. Lynn Hudson Parsons, *John Quincy Adams* (Madison, Wisc.: Madison House, 1998), 143; Dangerfield, *Era of Good Feelings*, 149.

36. Charles Francis Adams, *The Diary of Charles Francis Adams*, ed. David Donald and Aida Donald, 2 vols. (Cambridge, Mass.: Harvard University Press, 1964), 2:296–97 (October 19, 1828).

37. Remini, *Jackson and Empire*, 371, quoting James Parton, *Life of Andrew Jackson* (New York: Mason Brothers, 1861), 2:533; Adams, *Memoirs*, 4:214 (January 23, 1819).

38. Henry Clay, "Speech on the Seminole War" (January 20, 1819), in *The Papers of Henry Clay*, ed. James Hopkins and Mary W. M. Hargreaves (Lexington: University of Kentucky Press, 1961), 2:636–62; Remini, *Jackson and Empire*, 372–73.

39. Quoted in Howe, *What Hath God Wrought*, 106.

40. Jackson to W. B. Lewis, January 25, 30, 1819, quoted in Remini, *Jackson and Empire*, 373.

41. Ibid., 373–74; Dangerfield, *Era of Good Feelings*, 151; *Annals of Congress*, 15th Congress, 2nd Session, 1136–38, 515–530, 583–1138; Howe, *What Hath God Wrought*, 106.

42. Adams, *Memoirs*, 4:243, 247–48, 282, 287 (February 3 and 9, March 4 and 8, 1819).

43. Quoted in Remini, *Jackson and Empire*, 376.

44. Louisa Catherine Adams diary, March 4, 1819, Adams Papers Microfilms, reel 264.

45. Remini, *Jackson and Empire*, 376; *Annals of Congress*, 15th Congress, 2nd Session, appendix, 2350–78; Adams, *Memoirs*, 4:294–95, 433–34 (March 12 and November 5, 1819).

46. Samuel Flagg Bemis, *John Quincy Adams and the Foundations of American Foreign Policy* (New York: Knopf, 1949), chapter 16; James Chace and Caleb Carr, "The Odd Couple Who Won Florida and Half the West," *Smithsonian* 19 (April 1988): 134–40; Philip C. Brooks, *Diplomacy and the Borderlands: The Adams-Onís Treaty of 1819* (Berkeley: University of California Press, 1939).

47. Adams, *Memoirs*, 4:239 (February 3, 1819).
48. Ibid., 5:321–22 (March 8, 1821).
49. Jackson to Dr. James Bronaugh, February 11, 1821, quoted in Remini, *Jackson and Empire*, 400.
50. Remini, *Jackson and Empire*, 409–14.
51. Jackson to Adams, August 26, 1821, quoted ibid., 414.
52. Wirt to Monroe, October 11, 1821, quoted in Jackson, *Papers*, 5:119n.
53. Adams, *Memoirs*, 5:366–67 (October 23, 1821).
54. Quoted in Remini, *Jackson and Empire*, 416.
55. Jackson to James Gadsden, December 6, 1821, in Jackson, *Papers*, 5:121; Adams, *Memoirs*, 5:473 (January 2, 1822).
56. *Historical Statistics of the United States* (New York, 1976), 1018; George Dangerfield, *The Awakening of American Nationalism, 1815–1828* (New York: Harper & Row, 1965), 73–74, 87; Murray Rothbard, *The Panic of 1819* (New York: Columbia University Press, 1962), 11–27.
57. See Norman K. Risjord, *The Old Republicans: Southern Conservatism in the Age of Jefferson* (New York: Columbia University Press, 1965).
58. Dangerfield, *Awakening of American Nationalism*, 11–15.
59. Maurice G. Baxter, *Henry Clay and the American System* (Lexington: University Press of Kentucky, 1995); Robert V. Remini, *Henry Clay, Statesman for the Union* (New York: W. W. Norton, 1991), 225–33; Howe, *What Hath God Wrought*, 270–71.
60. Hargreaves, *Presidency of John Quincy Adams*, 4–12.
61. Dangerfield, *Era of Good Feelings*, 166–74; Howe, *What Hath God Wrought*, 144–47.
62. Dangerfield, *Era of Good Feelings*, 187.
63. Quoted in Charles G. Sellers Jr., "Banking and Politics in Jackson's Tennessee," *Mississippi Valley Historical Review* 41(June 1954): 70.
64. Remini, *Jackson and Empire*, 381; Sellers, "Banking and Politics," 76.
65. The standard defense of the Bank for many years has been Bray Hammond, *Banks and Politics in America: From the Revolution to the Civil War* (Princeton, N.J.: Princeton University Press, 1957). A more critical stance may be found in Charles G. Sellers Jr., *The Market Revolution: Jacksonian America, 1815–1846* (New York: Oxford University Press, 1991).
66. Adams, *Memoirs*, 4:325, 375, 395–96, 499 (April 5, May 27, June 24, 1819, January 8, 1820).
67. Glover Moore, *The Missouri Controversy, 1819–1821* (Lexington: University Press of Kentucky, 1953); Dangerfield, *Era of Good Feelings*, 217–45.

68. Quoted in Howe, *What Hath God Wrought*, 148. See also Robert Pierce Forbes, *The Missouri Compromise and Its Aftermath: Slavery and the Meaning of America* (Chapel Hill: University of North Carolina Press, 2007).

69. Jackson to Donelson, April 1, 1822, in Jackson, *Correspondence*, 3:137; Jackson to Donelson, no date, quoted in Remini, *Jackson and Empire*, 391. Wilentz, *Rise of American Democracy*, 224–40.

70. Parsons, *John Quincy Adams*, 77.

71. Adams, *Memoirs*, 4:492 (December 27, 1819), 5:210 (November 29, 1820); Parsons, *John Quincy Adams*, 160–62.

72. Quoted in Burstein, *Passions of Andrew Jackson*, 72, 89.

73. Adams, *Memoirs*, 4:349 (April 24, 1819).

74. John Quincy Adams, *Report of the Secretary of State upon Weights and Measures* (Washington, D.C., 1821; reprint, New York, 1980). For an analysis of the report, see Donald M. Goodfellow, "A Neglected American Classic," *Carnegie Technical* 9 (April 1945): 16–50.

75. John Quincy Adams, *An Address Delivered at the Request of a Committee of the Citizens of Washington; On the Occasion of Reading the Declaration of Independence, on the Fourth of July, 1821* (Washington, D.C., 1821), quoted in Parsons, *John Quincy Adams*, 149–50; Walter LaFeber, ed., *John Quincy Adams and American Continental Empire* (Chicago: Quadrangle, 1965), 42–46.

76. Adams, *Memoirs*, 4:438–39 (November 16, 1819), 5:253 (February 26, 1821).

77. Bemis, *Adams and Foreign Policy*, 382–408; Adams, *Memoirs*, 6:177–79 (November 7, 1823).

78. Edward P. Crapol, "John Quincy Adams and the Monroe Doctrine," *Pacific Historical Review* 48 (August 1979): 413–19; Harold E. Bergquist Jr., "John Quincy Adams and the Promulgation of the Monroe Doctrine," *Essex Institute Historical Collections* 111 (January 1975): 37–52.

79. Jackson to W. B. Lewis, December 7, 1823, quoted in Robert Remini, *Andrew Jackson and the Course of American Freedom, 1822–1832* (New York: Harper & Row, 1981), 67, hereafter cited as *Jackson and Freedom*.

80. Adams to Louisa Catherine Adams, October 7, 1822, in Adams, *Writings*, 7:316; John Adams to John Quincy Adams, April 23, 1794, Adams Papers Microfilms, reel 377.

81. See, e.g., W. J. Spooner, *Review of the Address Delivered by the Hon. John Quincy Adams* (Boston, 1821), and a defense by J. B. Moore, *A Vindication of Mr. Adams's Oration* (Concord, N.H., 1821).

82. Ernest R. May, *The Making of the Monroe Doctrine* (Cambridge, Mass.: Harvard University Press, 1975).

83. Lynn W. Turner, "The Electoral Vote against Monroe in 1820—An American Legend," *Mississippi Valley Historical Review* 42 (September 1955): 250–73.

Chapter Three

1. The American Antiquarian Society in Worcester, Massachusetts, under the direction of Philip Lampi and with support from Tufts University and the National Endowment for the Humanities is in the process of compiling state and local election returns from every state in the Union through 1825. The project, entitled "A New Nation Votes," may be accessed through the society's Web site. For presidential results, see note 99 below.

2. James F. Hopkins, "The Presidential Election of 1824," in *History of American Presidential Elections*, 4 vols., ed. Arthur M. Schlesinger Jr. and Fred L. Israel (New York: Chelsea House, 1971), 1:346–409; Lynn Hudson Parsons, "The Election of 1824," in *American Presidential Campaigns and Elections,* 3 vols., ed. William G. Shade and Ballard C. Campbell (Armonk, N.Y.: Sharpe, 2003), 1:214–24.

3. M. J. Heale, *The Presidential Quest: Candidates and Images in American Culture, 1787–1852* (London: Longman, 1982), 38.

4. Richard P. McCormick, *The Second American Party System: Party Formation in the Jackson Era* (Chapel Hill: University of North Carolina Press, 1966), 4; Everett S. Brown, "The Presidential Election of 1824–1825," *Political Science Quarterly* 40 (September 1925): 384–403; Paul C. Nagel, "The Election of 1824: A Reconsideration Based on Newspaper Sources," *Journal of Southern History* 26 (August 1960): 325–29; Donald B. Cole, *Jacksonian Democracy in New Hampshire, 1800–1851* (Cambridge, Mass.: Harvard University Press, 1970), 16–18; Robert P. Hay, "The Presidential Question: Letters to Southern Editors, 1823–24," *Tennessee Historical Quarterly* 31 (Winter–Spring 1972): 170–86; William E. Ames and S. Dean Olsen, "Washington's Political Press in the Election of 1824," *Journalism Quarterly* 40 (Summer 1963): 343–50.

5. Adams, *Memoirs*, 4:497 (January 8, 1820). See Charles S. Sydnor, "The One-Party Period in American History," *American Historical Review* 51 (April 1946): 439–51.

6. Jackson to James Gadsden, December 6, 1821, in Jackson, *Papers,* 5:121.

7. Ibid.; Robert V. Remini, *Andrew Jackson and the Course of American Empire, 1767–1821* (New York: Harper & Row, 1977), 324, 341, 370–71, hereafter cited as *Jackson and Empire*.

8. Quoted in Everett S. Brown, ed., *The Missouri Compromises and Presidential Politics, 1820–1825* (St. Louis: Missouri Historical Society, 1926), 52n.

9. Joseph Story to Ezekiel Bacon, March 12, 1818, quoted in Adams, *Writings*, 6:301n.

10. Dr. James Bronaugh to Jackson, December 30, 1821, in Jackson, *Papers*, 5:125; "Friend" to Jackson, October 29, 1821, in Jackson, *Papers*, 5:113. Kim T. Phillips, "The Pennsylvania Origins of the Jackson Movement," *Political Science Quarterly* 91 (Fall 1976): 496.

11. Less is known about Crawford than any of the other players in the 1824 election, owing to the destruction of most of his letters by fire in 1867. See Chase Mooney, *William Harris Crawford, 1772–1834* (Lexington: University Press of Kentucky, 1974).

12. Adams, *Memoirs*, 5:315 (March 3, 1821), 5:326 (March 9, 1821).

13. Samuel Flagg Bemis, *John Quincy Adams and the Union* (New York: Knopf, 1956), 25; Adams, *Memoirs*, 1:460 (February 3, 1807), 8:444 (December 27, 1831).

14. John Niven, *John C. Calhoun and the Price of Union* (Baton Rouge: Louisiana State University Press, 1988); Gerald M. Capers, *John C. Calhoun: Opportunist* (Gainesville: University of Florida Press, 1960); Charles M. Wiltse, *John C. Calhoun, Nationalist* (Indianapolis: Bobbs-Merrill, 1944).

15. Quoted in Jeffrey L. Pasley, *The Tyranny of Printers* (Charlottesville: University Press of Virginia, 2001), 364–68.

16. See Evan Cornog, *The Birth of Empire: DeWitt Clinton and the American Experience, 1769–1828* (New York: Oxford University Press, 1998); Craig Hanyan with Mary L. Hanyan, *DeWitt Clinton and the Rise of the People's Men* (Montreal: McGill-Queen's University Press, 1996).

17. Michael Wallace, "Changing Concepts of Party in the United States: New York, 1815–1828," *American Historical Review* 74 (December 1968): 456.

18. Quoted in Robert V. Remini, *Martin Van Buren and the Making of the Democratic Party* (New York: Columbia University Press, 1959), 11.

19. Ibid., 8.

20. Van Buren's *Autobiography*, quoted in Mark W. Kruman, "The Second American Party System," 521.

21. Quoted in Remini, *Martin Van Buren*, 15.

22. Van Buren to Charles Dudley, January 10, 1822, quoted in Remini, *Martin Van Buren*, 23.

23. J. R. Pole, "Historians and the Problem of Early American Democracy," *American Historical Review* 67 (December 1962): 626–46; R. R. Palmer, "Notes on the Use of the Word 'Democracy,'" *Political Science Quarterly* 68 (June 1953): 23–26.

24. Jefferson to Gallatin, October 29, 1822, quoted in Harry Ammon, *James Monroe: The Quest for National Identity* (New York, 1971), 508.

25. Norman K. Risjord, *The Old Republicans* (New York: Columbia University Press, 1965), 204–30.

26. Remini, *Martin Van Buren*, 36–39.

27. Charles G. Sellers Jr., "Jackson Men with Feet of Clay," *American Historical Review* 62 (April 1957): 537–51.

28. Robert V. Remini, *Andrew Jackson and the Course of American Freedom, 1822–1832* (New York: Harper & Row, 1981), 49, hereafter cited as *Jackson and Freedom*; Jackson to J. C. Bronaugh, July 18, 1822, quoted in Remini, *Jackson and Freedom*, 37.

29. Adams, *Memoirs* 5:242, 298–99 (January 22, 25, 1821).

30. Joseph Hopkinson to Louisa Catherine Adams, January, 1823, in Adams, *Memoirs*, 6:130.

31. Adams, *Writings*, 7:361; Adams, *Memoirs*, 5:242 (January 22, 1821).

32. The concept is discussed in Heale, *Presidential Quest*, 4.

33. M. Ostrogorski, "The Rise and Fall of the Nominating Caucus, Legislative and Congressional," *American Historical Review* 5 (December 1899): 259–77; William G. Morgan, "The Decline of the Congressional Nominating Caucus," *Tennessee Historical Quarterly* 24 (Winter–Spring 1965): 244–55.

34. Both quoted in Morgan, "Decline of the Congressional Nominating Caucus," 247–50.

35. Adams, *Memoirs*, 6:237 (January 25, 1824).

36. *Address to Our Democratic Representatives of Congress and of our State Legislature, and to the Democratic Republicans of Pennsylvania* (Pittsburgh, 1824), 1–5.

37. Quoted in Morgan, "Decline," 252.

38. Quoted in Schlesinger and Israel, *History of American Presidential Elections,* 1:392–93.

39. Ibid., 1:394–95.

40. Kim T. Phillips, "The Pennsylvania Origins of the Jackson Movement," *Political Science Quarterly* 91 (Fall 1976): 489–508.

41. Remini, *Jackson and Freedom*, 51–52.

42. Bemis, *Adams and the Union*, 20–21; Adams, *Memoirs*, 5:323 (March 9, 1821), 6:26 (June 20, 1822), 5:496 (April 22, 1822).

43. Adams to Jackson, February 19, 1823, Jackson to Monroe, February 19, 1823, Jackson to Adams, March 15, 1823, in Jackson, *Correspondence,* 3:187–89, 192–93; Adams, *Memoirs*, 6:127–29 (November 12, 1823).

44. Samuel Flagg Bemis, *John Quincy Adams and the Foundations of American Foreign Policy* (New York: Knopf, 1949), 502; John Quincy Adams, *The Duplicate Letters, the Fisheries, and the Mississippi* (Washington, D.C., 1822).

45. Jackson to Donelson, June 28, Jackson to Richard Keith Call, June 29, 1822, in Jackson, *Papers*, 5:196, 198.

46. Adams to Louisa Catherine Adams, August 23, 1822, in Adams, *Writings*, 7:296.

47. *Letters of the Hon. John Quincy Adams in Reply to . . . a Letter of the Hon. Alexander Smyth* (Washington, D.C., 1823).

48. Eaton to Jackson, January 11, 1823, in Jackson, *Papers*, 5:236.

49. Eaton to Jackson, February 23, 1823, in Jackson, *Papers*, 5:255.

50. Heale, *Presidential Quest*, 60; Phillips, "Pennsylvania Origins," 495; Jackson to John Coffee, March 10, 1823, in Jackson, *Papers*, 5:258.

51. Jackson to John Donelson, February 9, 1824, in Jackson, *Correspondence*, 3:227.

52. Jackson to Rachel Jackson, December 7, 1823, in Jackson, *Correspondence*, 3:216.

53. Adams, *Memoirs,* 6:234–35 (January 20, 1824), 242 (January 30, 1824), 269 (March 27, 1824); McCormick, *Second American Party System*, 51, 81.

54. Jackson to Rachel Jackson, December 21, 1823, in Jackson, *Correspondence*, 3:220.

55. Catherine Allgor, in *Parlor Politics: In Which the Ladies of Washington Help Build a City and a Government* (Charlottesville: University Press of Virginia, 2000), describes the ball in detail, 175–82. *Harper's Bazaar* wrote about it in 1871: "Mrs. John Quincy Adams' Ball, 1824" (March 18, 1871), 116–18. See also Adams, *Memoirs*, 6:229 (January 8, 1824); Paul C. Nagel, *The Adams Women: Abigail and Louisa Adams, Their Sisters and Daughters* (New York: Oxford University Press, 1987), 209.

56. Jackson to John Coffee, December 31, 1823, in Jackson, *Correspondence*, 3:220.

57. Quoted in Heale, *Presidential Quest*, 60. For the Jackson movements in the various states at this time, see, in addition to the Phillips essay cited above, Harry Stevens, *The Early Jackson Party in Ohio*

(Durham, N.C.: Duke University Press, 1957); Logan Esarey, "The Organization of the Early Jacksonian Party in Indiana," *Proceedings of the Mississippi Valley Historical Association for the Year 1913–1914,* 7:22043 (Cedar Rapids, Iowa: Torch Press); Cole, *Jacksonian Democracy*; Herbert Ershkowitz, "The Election of 1824 in New Jersey," *New Jersey Historical Society Proceedings* 84 (April 1966): 113–32; Mark H. Haller, "The Rise of the Jackson Party in Maryland, 1820–1829," *Journal of Southern History* 28 (August 1962): 307–26; Edwin A. Miles, *Jacksonian Democracy in Mississippi* (Chapel Hill: University of North Carolina Press, 1960); A. R. Newsome, *The Presidential Election of 1824 in North Carolina* (Chapel Hill: University of North Carolina Press, 1939); Richard Arden Wire, "John M. Clayton and the Rise of the Anti-Jackson Party in Delaware," *Delaware History* 15 (1973): 256–68.

58. Plumer Jr., to Plumer, December 3, 1823, quoted in Brown, *Missouri Compromises*, 85.

59. J. P. Mower to Thurlow Weed, March 4, 1824, quoted in Remini, *Jackson and Freedom*, 78.

60. Quoted in Brown, *Missouri Compromises,* 86n.

61. Jackson to George W. Martin, January 2, 1824, Eaton to Rachel Jackson, December 18, 1823, in Jackson, *Correspondence*, 3:222, 217; Jackson to Donelson, March 19, 1824, quoted in Remini, *Jackson and Freedom,* 59; Adams, *Memoirs,* 6:258 (March 15, 1824).

62. Remini, *Jackson and Freedom*, 67; Jackson to James W. Lanier, May 15, 1824, in Jackson, *Correspondence*, 3:253–54.

63. Jackson to L. H. Coleman, April 24, 1824, in Jackson, *Correspondence*, 3:249–50.

64. Parsons, *John Quincy Adams*, 162–63; Bemis, *Adams and Foreign Policy*, 432–35.

65. Adams, *Memoirs*, 6:332–33 (May 15, 1824).

66. Tallmadge to Jackson, March 6, 1824, Jackson to Tallmadge, March 12, 1824, in Jackson, *Papers*, 5:373–75.

67. Adams, *Memoirs*, 6:333–34 (May 8, 1824).

68. Niven, *Calhoun and the Price of Union*, 106.

69. Schlesinger and Israel, *History of Presidential Elections*, 1:392–93.

70. Both quoted in ibid., 1:321, 324, 325.

71. Ibid., 1:322–23.

72. Richard H. Brown, "The Missouri Crisis, Slavery, and the Politics of Jacksonianism," *South Atlantic Quarterly* 65 (Winter 1966): 66, Schlesinger and Israel, *History of Presidential Elections*, 1:317.

73. Schlesinger and Israel, *History of Presidential Elections,* 1:392–93.

74. *Address of the State Convention, held at Trenton, New-Jersey, on the Nomination of Presidential Electors for This State* (n.p., 1824), 3, copy in the Massachusetts Historical Society, Boston.
75. *Principles and Men, Considered with Reference to the Approaching Election of President, by a Citizen of Rhode Island* (Providence, 1823). Copy in the Massachusetts Historical Society, Boston.
76. Ibid., 19.
77. *New Jersey Address*, 3.
78. Quoted in Heale, *Presidential Quest*, 30.
79. Jesse Benton, *Address to the People of the United States, on the Presidential Election* (Nashville, 1824), copy in the New-York Historical Society, quoted in Burstein, *Passions of Andrew Jackson*, 155.
80. Quoted in Hay, "*Wyoming* Letters," 139n.
81. Heale, *Presidential Quest*, 38.
82. See "An Esteemed Friend Touches Hearts," chapter 1 of Andrew Burstein, *America's Jubilee, July 4, 1826: A Generation Remembers the American Revolution after Fifty Years of Independence* (New York: Knopf, 2001), 8–33; Robert P. Hay, "The American Revolution Twice Recalled: Lafayette's Visit and the Election of 1824," *Indiana Magazine of History* 69 (March 1973): 43–62.
83. Hay, "*Wyoming* Letters," 170–86.
84. *The Letters of "Wyoming" to the People of the United States on the Presidential Election and in Favour of Andrew Jackson* (Philadelphia, 1824), 12, copy in the Boston Public Library.
85. Ibid., 21, 23.
86. Ibid., 3, 15, 28; *New Jersey Address*, 5.
87. *Letters of "Wyoming,"* 36, 46–47.
88. Ibid., 54–55, 62–67.
89. Ibid., 59, 88, 69.
90. *New Jersey Address*, 4.
91. *Letters of "Wyoming,"* 10; Hay, "*Wyoming* Letters," 149–50.
92. Jackson to Andrew Jackson Donelson, April 4, 1824, in Jackson, *Correspondence*, 1:243–44.
93. Adams, *Memoirs*, 6:416 (September 9, 1824).
94. McCormick, *Second American Party System*, 151–53.
95. Ibid., 313–14.
96. Dangerfield, *Era of Good Feelings*, 332–35; Dixon Ryan Fox, *Decline of the Aristocracy in the Politics of New York, 1801–1840* (New York: Harper & Row, 1965), 299–301; McCormick, *Second American Party System*, 116.

97. Donald J. Ratcliffe, "The Role of Voters and Issues in Party Formation: Ohio, 1824," *Journal of American History* 59 (March 1973): 848–63.

98. McCormick, *Second American Party System*, 129, 141–45.

99. Schlesinger and Israel, *History of American Presidential Elections*, 1:409. Because in 1824 (and again in 1828) there was no "official" tally of results, historians have depended on newspaper sources, which are not always consistent.

100. Richard P. McCormick, "New Perspectives on Jacksonian Politics," *American Historical Review* 65 (January 1960): 292; McCormick, *Second American Party System*, 88, 215, 261. McCormick assumed that by the 1820s nearly all adult white males could vote, and so based his percentages on the appropriate census figures.

101. McCormick, *Second American Party System*, 332.

102. Jackson to W. S. Fulton, July 4, Jackson to Samuel Swartwout, September 27, 1824, in Jackson, *Papers*, 5:428, 445.

103. Adams, *Memoirs*, 6:417 (September 19, 1824); Plumer to Plumer, December 9, 1824, quoted in Brown, *Missouri Compromises*, 120–21.

104. Adams, *Memoirs* 6:438–66 (December–January 1824–25).

105. Bemis, *Adams and the Union*, 42–43; Robert V. Remini, *Henry Clay, Statesman for the Union* (New York: W. W. Norton, 1991), 271.

106. Parsons, *John Quincy Adams*, 173.

107. Henry Clay to Francis P. Blair, January 8, 1825, in *Papers of Henry Clay*, 4:9–10.

108. Clay to Blair, January 29, 1825, in *Papers of Henry Clay*, 4:46–48.

109. Jackson to Lewis, December 27, 1824, Jackson to Coffee, January 10, 1825, quoted in Remini, *Jackson and Freedom*, 85, 86.

110. Adams, *Memoirs*, 6:465 (January 9, 1825).

111. Ibid., 465n.

112. Jackson to William B. Lewis, January 29, 1825, quoted in Remini, *Jackson and Freedom*, 87; Adams, *Memoirs*, 6:491 (February 2, 1825).

113. Dangerfield, *Era of Good Feelings*, 342.

114. Jackson to Overton, February 10, 1825, quoted in Remini, *Jackson and Freedom*, 96.

115. John Pemberton to Jackson, February 15, 1825, in Jackson, *Papers*, 6:30.

116. Andrew Jackson Donelson to John Coffee, February 19, 1825, quoted in Remini, *Jackson and Freedom*, 95.

117. Quoted in Robert V. Remini, *The Election of Andrew Jackson* (Philadelphia: Lippincott, 1963), 25; Adams, *Memoirs*, 6:502 (February 9, 1825).

118. Adams, *Memoirs,* 7:98 (December 31, 1825).

119. Barnes F. Lathrop, "Monroe on the Adams-Clay 'Bargain,'"
     American Historical Review 42 (January 1937): 273–76.

120. Quoted in Dangerfield, *Era of Good Feelings*, 345.

121. Jackson to Lewis, February 14 1825, Jackson to Squire Grant,
     February 18, 1825, in Jackson, *Correspondence*, 3:276.

122. Adams, *Memoirs*, 6:474 (January 17, 1825).

123. Plumer to Plumer, March 4, 1825, quoted in Brown, *Missouri
     Compromises*, 144.

124. Quoted in Mary W. M. Hargreaves, *The Presidency of John Quincy
     Adams* (Lawrence: University Press of Kansas, 1985), 48, 255.

125. *A Compilation of Messages and Papers of the Presidents, 1789–1897*,
     10 vols., ed. James D. Richardson (Washington, D.C., 1896),
     2:292–99.

126. Bemis, *Adams and the Union*, 53; Dangerfield, *Era of Good Feelings*,
     343.

Chapter Four

1. *Niles' Register*, July 5, 1828.

2. Martin Van Buren, *Autobiography*, 2 vols., ed. John C. Fitzpatrick
   (Washington, D.C.: Government Printing Office, 1920), 1:192, 2:268;
   Thomas Hart Benton, *Thirty Years' View*, 2 vols. (New York: D.
   Appleton, 1854), 1:48; William G. Morgan, "John Quincy Adams
   versus Andrew Jackson: Their Biographers and the 'Corrupt
   Bargain' Charge," *Tennessee Historical Quarterly* 26 (Spring 1967):
   43–58; R. R. Stenberg, "Jackson, Buchanan, and the 'Corrupt
   Bargain' Calumny," *Pennsylvania Magazine of History and Biography*
   58 (1934): 61–85.

3. Robert V. Remini, *Henry Clay, Statesman for the Union* (New
   York: W. W. Norton, 1991), 272; Dangerfield, *Era of Good Feelings*
   (London, 1953), 344–45.

4. Quoted in John Niven, *John C. Calhoun and the Price of Union* (Baton
   Rouge: Louisiana State University Press, 1988), 109; Adams, *Memoirs*,
   6:506–7 (February 11, 1825); Mary W. M. Hargreaves, *The Presidency
   of John Quincy Adams* (Lawrence: University Press of Kansas, 1985),
   249.

5. Jackson to Swartwout, February 22, March 5, 1825, in Jackson,
   Correspondence, 3:279–81.

6. Jackson to Henry Lee, October 7, 1825, in Jackson, *Correspondence*,
   3:291–92.

7. Robert V. Remini, *Andrew Jackson and the Course of American
   Freedom, 1822–1832* (New York: Harper & Row, 1981), 106–7,

hereafter cited as *Jackson and Freedom*; Jackson, *Correspondence*, 3:293–96.

8. Adams, quoted in William H. Seward, *Life and Public Services of John Quincy Adams* (Auburn, N.Y.: Derby, Miller, 1849), 142–43; Adams to John Adams, August 1, 1816, Adams to James Lloyd, October 1, 1822, in Adams, *Writings*, 6:60, 7:312.

9. Dangerfield, *Era of Good Feelings*, 348–49; Lynn Hudson Parsons, *John Quincy Adams* (Madison, Wisc.: Madison House, 1998), 179–81.

10. See Ralph Ketcham, *Presidents above Party* (Chapel Hill: University of North Carolina Press, 1984), 130–40; *A Compilation of Messages and Papers of the Presidents, 1789–1897*, 10 vols., ed. James D. Richardson (Washington, D.C., 1896), 2:315–16.

11. Robert V. Remini, *Martin Van Buren and the Making of the Democratic Party* (New York: Columbia University Press, 1959), 101; Niven, *Calhoun and the Price of Union*, 113.

12. Dangerfield, *Era of Good Feelings*, 349; Adams, *Memoirs*, 7:105–6 (January 17, 1826); Jefferson to William B. Giles, December 26, 1825, in *The Writings of Thomas Jefferson,* ed. Andrew A. Lipscomb and Avery Ellery Bergh, 20 vols. (Washington, D.C., 1905), 16:146; Madison to Thomas Ritchie, December 18, 1826, in *Letters and Other Writings of James Madison*, 4 vols. (Philadelphia: Lippincott, 1865), 1:502; William Ernest Smith, *The Francis Preston Blair Family in Politics,* 2 vols. (New York: Macmillan, 1933), 1:38; Charles H. Ambler, *Thomas Ritchie: A Study in Virginia Politics* (Richmond, Va.: Bell, Book & Stationery, 1913), 109.

13. Quoted in Remini, *Martin Van Buren*, 101.

14. Jackson to John Branch, March 3, 1826, Jackson to Richard Keith Call, March 9, 1826, in Jackson, *Papers,* 6:143,150–51.

15. Remini, *Henry Clay*, 284. See also Daniel Walker Howe, *What Hath God Wrought* (New York: Oxford University Press, 2007), 252–54.

16. Quoted in E. Malcolm Carroll, *Origins of the Whig Party* (New York: Da Capo, 1970), 13–14.

17. Adams, *Memoirs,* 6:520–21 (March 5, 1825), 6:546–47 (May 13, 1825), 7:425 (February 7, 1828); Hargreaves, *Presidency of John Quincy Adams*, 65.

18. Quoted in Dangerfield, *Era of Good Feelings*, 361–62.

19. Andrew Burstein, *America's Jubilee, July 4, 1826: A Generation Remembers the American Revolution after Fifty Years of Independence* (New York: Knopf, 2001) 159–60.

20. Ibid., 166–67.

21. Jackson to John Coffee, October 12, 1825, Jackson to the Tennessee Legislature, October 12, 1825, in Jackson, *Correspondence*, 3:292–96.

22. Burstein, *America's Jubilee*, 167–69.

23. Hargreaves, *Presidency of John Quincy Adams*, 150–52; Charles Wilson Hackett, "The Development of John Quincy Adams's Policy with Respect to an American Confederation and the Panama Congress, 1822–1825," *Hispanic American Historical Review* 9 (November 1928): 496–526.

24. Quoted in Samuel Flagg Bemis, *John Quincy Adams and the Union* (New York: Knopf, 1956), 76–77; L. H. Butterfield, "The Jubilee of Independence, July 4, 1826," *Virginia Magazine of History and Biography* 61 (April 1953): 132; Howe, *What Hath God Wrought*, 257.

25. Jackson to John Branch, March 3, 1826, Jackson to Richard Keith Call, March 9, 1826, Jackson to Hugh Lawson White, March 16, 1826, in Jackson, *Papers*, 6:140; 151, 153.

26. Adams, *Memoirs*, 7:111 (January 31, 1826).

27. Hargreaves, *Presidency of John Quincy Adams*, 158.

28. Dangerfield, *Era of Good Feelings*, 358; Benton, *Thirty Years' View*, 1:71–77.

29. Eaton to Jackson, May 5, 1826, in Jackson, *Papers*, 6:168.

30. Jackson to Houston, April 15, 1826, Charles P. Tutt to Jackson, April 2, 1826, in Jackson *Papers*, 6:164, 159–60; Robert V. Remini, *The Election of Andrew Jackson* (Philadelphia: Lippincott, 1963), 46.

31. Calhoun to Jackson, June 4, 1826, in Jackson, *Papers,* 6:177.

32. Calhoun's odyssey from economic and constitutional nationalist to strict constructionist and states' righter may be followed in Niven, *Calhoun and the Price of Union,* 127–64; Irving Bartlett, *John C. Calhoun: A Biography* (New York: W. W. Norton, 1993), 139–52; Gerald M. Capers, *John C. Calhoun: Opportunist* (Gainesville: University of Florida Press, 1960), 104–9.

33. Jackson to Calhoun, July 18, 1826, in Jackson, *Papers*, 6:187–88.

34. Burstein, *America's Jubilee*, chapter 10.

35. Ibid., 247–53; Butterfield, "The Jubilee of Independence," 122; Adams, *Memoirs*, 7:121 (July 5, 1826).

36. Adams, *Memoirs*, 7:122, 125 (July 6 and 9, 1826); Jackson, *Papers*, 6:574n. See Nashville *Republican*, July 29, 1826.

37. Jackson to Richard Keith Call, July 26, 1826, in Jackson *Papers*, 6:191; Adams, *Memoirs*, 7:150 (October 6, 1826).

38. Clay to James Brown, May 22, 1826, Clay to Webster, June 14, 1826, in Clay, *Papers*, 5:388, 434.

39. Warfield to Clay, July 5, 1826, January 5, 1827, in Clay, *Papers*, 5:524, 6:17–20.
40. Joseph Bellinger to Clay, July 29, 1826, in Clay, *Papers*, 5:576–77. Also John Geddes to Clay, September 7, 1826, Thomas R. Mitchell to Clay, November 11, 1826, in Clay, *Papers*, 5:673, 891.
41. Remini, *Henry Clay*, 289.
42. Culver H. Smith, "Propaganda Technique in the Jackson Campaign of 1828," *East Tennessee Historical Society Publications* 6 (1934): 54–55.
43. Adams, *Memoirs,* 7:544, 8:25 (May, 17, June 3, 1828).
44. Richard R. John, *Spreading the News: The American Postal System from Franklin to Morse* (Cambridge, Mass.: Harvard University Press, 1995), 69–83.
45. Clay to Adams, July 25, 1826, Clay to J. S. Johnston, August 2, 1826, in Clay, *Papers*, 5:568, 585–86.
46. Untitled circular in the New-York Historical Society.
47. Ninian Edwards to Clay, September 21, 1826, in Clay, *Papers*, 5:700.
48. Hargreaves, *Presidency of John Quincy Adams*, 271–73.
49. To Benjamin F. Butler, December 25, 1825, quoted in Florence Weston, *The Presidential Election of 1828* (Washington, D.C.: Ruddick, 1938), 84.
50. Quoted in Remini, *Election of Andrew Jackson*, 48.
51. Remini, *Martin Van Buren*, 120, 53–54.
52. Van Buren, *Autobiography*, 514.
53. Van Buren to Ritchie, January 13, 1827. Quoted in Remini, *Election of Jackson,* 57.
54. Remini, *Election of Andrew Jackson*, 55–57; Remini, *Martin Van Buren*, 130–32. See also Richard H. Brown, "The Missouri Crisis, Slavery, and the Politics of Jacksonianism," *South Atlantic Quarterly* 65 (Winter 1966): 55–72.
55. Remini, *Election of Andrew Jackson*, 59.
56. Albert Castel, "The Founding Fathers and the Vision of a National University," *History of Education Quarterly* 4 (December 1964): 280–302; Hargreaves, *Presidency of John Quincy Adams*, 167–72.
57. Hargreaves, *Presidency of John Quincy Adams*, 167, 180–81, 222–23.
58. Weston, *Presidential Election of 1828*, 25; Curtis Nettels, "The Mississippi Valley and the Constitution, 1815–1829," *Mississippi Valley Historical Review* 11 (1924–25): 338–39.
59. Hargreaves, *Presidency of John Quincy Adams*, 5.
60. Remini, *Martin Van Buren*, 138–46; Dangerfield, *Era of Good Feelings,* 402.
61. Quoted in Remini, *Martin Van Buren*, 140.

62. James Hamilton Jr. to Jackson, February 16, 1827, in Jackson, *Correspondence*, 3:344.

63. Adams, *Memoirs*, 7:272–73 (May 12 and 13, 1827); Dangerfield, *Era of Good Feelings*, 402.

64. Van Buren to Harmanus Bleecker, February 25, 1827, quoted in Remini, *Election of Andrew Jackson*, 125.

Chapter Five

1. Allan Campbell to Jackson, February 4, 1827, in Jackson, *Correspondence*, 3:333.

2. Quoted in Robert V. Remini, *The Election of Andrew Jackson* (Philadelphia: Lippincott, 1963), 94.

3. Culver Smith, "Propaganda Technique in the Jackson Campaign of 1828," *East Tennessee Historical Society Publications* 6 (1934): 46.

4. Charles H. Levermore, "The Rise of Metropolitan Journalism," *American Historical Review* 6 (April 1901): 446–52; Andrew W. Robertson, *The Language of Democracy: Political Rhetoric in the United States and Britain, 1790–1900* (Charlottesville: University of Virginia Press, 2005), 38; *Niles' Weekly Register*, June 21, 1828.

5. Smith, "Propaganda Technique," 44–66; Ronald P. Formisano, "Deferential-Participant Politics: The Early Republic's Political Culture, 1789–1840," *American Political Science Review* 68 (June 1974): 483–87.

6. Smith, "Propaganda Technique," 63.

7. Remini, *Election of Andrew Jackson*, 76–77.

8. Jeffrey L. Pasley, *The Tyranny of Printers* (Charlottesville: University Press of Virginia, 2001), 356, 392.

9. Quoted in Mary W. M. Hargreaves, *The Presidency of John Quincy Adams* (Lawrence: University Press of Kansas, 1985), 270.

10. Smith, "Propaganda Technique," 65.

11. Remini, *Election of Andrew Jackson*, 86–89; Florence Weston, *The Presidential Election of 1828* (Washington, D.C.: Ruddick, 1938), 99–100.

12. Remini, *Election of Andrew Jackson*, 89.

13. Quoted in Erik Eriksson, "Official Newspaper Organs and the Campaign of 1828," *Tennessee Historical Magazine* 8 (January 1925): 236.

14. Hargreaves, *Presidency of John Quincy Adams*, 298.

15. Remini, *Election of Andrew Jackson*, 132; *Telegraph* quoted in Eriksson, "Official Newspaper Organs," 240.

16. Remini, *Election of Andrew Jackson*, 81.

17. Ibid., 85–86.

18. Sean Wilentz, *The Rise of American Democracy: Jefferson to Lincoln* (New York: W. W. Norton, 2005), 301.

19. Van Buren to Jackson, September 14, 1827, in Jackson, *Papers,* 6:392–93.

20. Adams, *Memoirs*, 7:390 (December 28, 1827).

21. Quoted in E. Malcolm Carroll, *Origins of the Whig Party* (New York: Da Capo, 1970), 18–19.

22. Quoted in Robert V. Remini, *Andrew Jackson and the Course of American Freedom, 1822–1832* (New York: Harper & Row, 1981), 119, hereafter cited as *Jackson and Freedom.*

23. Bertram Wyatt-Brown, "Andrew Jackson's Honor," *Journal of the Early Republic* 17 (Spring 1997): 1–36.

24. Lynn Hudson Parsons, *John Quincy Adams* (Madison, Wisc.: Madison House, 1998), 80. Also see *Address of the Republican General Committee of Young Men of the City and County of New York*, 45, cited in John William Ward, *Andrew Jackson: Symbol for an Age* (New York: Oxford University Press, 1955), 65; Isaac Hill, *Brief Sketch of the Life, Character, and Services of Major General Andrew Jackson* (Concord, N.H., 1828), 48, copy in the American Antiquarian Society, Worcester, Massachusetts.

25. M. J. Heale, *The Presidential Quest: Candidates and Images in American Political Culture, 1787–1852* (London: Longman, 1982), 70; Eaton to Jackson, January 27, February 8, 1827, in Jackson, *Papers*, 6:268, 287.

26. See the Owsley essay, cited in chapter 1, note 29, Robert Remini's comment in *Jackson and Freedom,* 411n., and John Buchanan, *Jackson's Way: Andrew Jackson and the People of the Western Waters* (New York: Wiley, 2001), 117–19.

27. Remini, *Jackson and Freedom,* 119; Remini, *Election of Andrew Jackson*, 152.

28. Remini, *Jackson and Freedom*, 119; Steubenville, Ohio, *Ledger* (May 17, 1827), quoted in Schlesinger and Israel, *History of Presidential Elections*, 2:454; Norma Basch, "Marriage, Morals, and Politics in the Election of 1828," *Journal of American History* 80 (December 1993): 908.

29. Remini, *Election of Andrew Jackson*, 153; Remini, *Jackson and Freedom*, 119; H. W. Brands, *Andrew Jackson: His Life and Times* (New York: Doubleday, 2005), 401.

30. Jackson to Houston, December 15, 1826, quoted in Remini, *Jackson and Freedom*, 120; Jackson to Richard Keith Call, May 3, 1827, in Jackson, *Correspondence*, 3:354.

31. *United States Telegraph,* June 16 and 18, 1827; Duff Green to Jackson, July 8, 1827, in Jackson, *Papers,* 5:355; Jackson to Green, August 13, 1827, quoted in Remini, *Jackson and Freedom,* 126; Hill, *Brief Sketch,* 49.

32. Jackson to Houston, October 23, 1826, in Jackson, *Papers,* 6:229.

33. Southard to Jackson, February 9, 1827, in Jackson, *Correspondence,* 3:342–43; Jackson to Southard, March 6, 1827, in Jackson, *Papers,* 6:299; Michael Birkner, "The General, the Secretary, and the President," *Tennessee Historical Quarterly* 42 (1983): 243–53.

34. Jackson to Carter Beverly, June 5, 1827, in Jackson, *Correspondence,* 3:331.

35. Jackson, "To the Public," July 18, 1827, in Jackson, *Correspondence,* 3:361–66.

36. Jackson to Buchanan, July 15, 1827, in Jackson, *Correspondence,* 6:359–60; Buchanan quoted in Hargreaves, *Presidency of John Quincy Adams,* 286; R. R. Stenberg, "Jackson, Buchanan, and the 'Corrupt Bargain' Calumny," *Pennsylvania Magazine of History and Biography* 58 (1934): 61–85.

37. Hargreaves, *Presidency of John Quincy Adams,* 286; Robert V. Remini, *Henry Clay, Statesman for the Union* (New York: W. W. Norton, 1991), 320–21; *Niles' Weekly Register,* January 5, 12, 1828.

38. Adams, *Memoirs,* 7:367 (December 3, 1827).

39. Ibid., 7:383 (December 17, 1827).

40. Joseph G. Tragle, Jr., "Andrew Jackson and the Continuing Battle of New Orleans," *Journal of the Early Republic* (Winter 1981): 384–85.

41. James A. Hamilton, *Reminiscences of James A. Hamilton* (New York: C. Scribner, 1869), 70.

42. Remini, *Jackson and Freedom,* 131–33.

43. Tragle, "Jackson and New Orleans," 386.

44. Ibid., 384–86; *Niles' Weekly Register,* February 9, 1828; *Running for President,* ed. Arthur M. Schlesinger, Jr., 2 vols. (New York: Simon & Schuster, 1994), 1:105. Jackson to Livingston, February 21, 1828, quoted in Remini, *Jackson and Freedom,* 133.

45. Hargreaves, *Presidency of John Quincy Adams,* 283; *Niles' Weekly Register,* August 18, 1828.

46. Adams, *Memoirs,* 7:479 (March 20, 1828); Tragle, "Jackson and New Orleans," 387n.

47. Nathaniel Greene, *An Address Delivered at Faneuil Hall, Boston, January 8, 1828* (Boston, 1828), copy in the American Antiquarian Society, Worcester, Massachusetts.

48. Donald B. Cole, *Jacksonian Democracy in New Hampshire, 1800–1851* (Cambridge, Mass.: Harvard University Press, 1970), 69–70.

49. Francis V. Yvonnet, *An Oration Delivered at the Baptist Church in the City of Troy on the Eighth Day of January, 1828 in Commemoration of the Victory Obtained at New-Orleans...by Andrew Jackson and the Forces Under His Command* (Troy, N.Y., 1828), copy in the American Antiquarian Society, Worcester, Massachusetts.

50. *United States Telegraph*, January 8, 1828, and for the next three weeks.

51. Sean Wilentz, *The Rise of American Democracy: Jefferson to Lincoln* (New York: W. W. Norton, 2005), 294.

52. Edwin A. Miles, "President Adams' Billiard Table," *New England Quarterly* 45 (March 1972): 31–43.

53. Ibid., 37.

54. Adams, *Memoirs*, 7:13 (May 24, 1825).

55. Parsons, *John Quincy Adams*, 185; Adams to Louisa Catherine Adams, July 11, 1827, Adams to George Sullivan, July 24, 1827, Adams to Robert Walsh, July 27, 1827, Adams Papers Microfilm, reel 148, Massachusetts Historical Society, Boston.

56. Adams, *Memoirs*, 7:42–43 (August 9, 1825).

57. Ibid., 7:329–32 (October 12–13, 1827), 8:76–77 (August 6, 1828); Parsons, *John Quincy Adams*, 185, 196.

58. Adams, *Memoirs*, 7: 346–47, 412–413, 469–70 (October 29, 1827, January 25, March 3, 1828).

59. Samuel Flagg Bemis, *John Quincy Adams and the Union* (New York: Knopf, 1956), 118–19; Hargreaves, *Presidency of John Quincy Adams*, 252–53; George Dangerfield, *The Awakening of American Nationalism, 1815–1828* (New York: Harper & Row, 1965), 238–39; Paul Nagel, *Descent from Glory: Four Generations of the John Adams Family* (New York: Oxford University Press, 1983), 144–45; Adams, *Memoirs*, 7:311 (July 31, 1827).

60. Quoted in Heale, *Presidential Quest*, 79.

61. Remini, *Election of Andrew Jackson*, 124–25; Dangerfield, *Era of Good Feelings*, 370–81; Hargreaves, *Presidency of John Quincy Adams*, 91–112.

62. Lynn Hudson Parsons, "'A Perpetual Harrow upon My Feelings': John Quincy Adams and the American Indian," *New England Quarterly* 46 (September 1973): 351–59; Hargreaves, *Presidency of John Quincy Adams*, 202–7; Daniel Walker Howe, *What Hath God Wrought* (New York: Oxford University Press, 2007), 255–56.

63. Jackson to Wilson Lumpkin, February 15, 1828, in Jackson, *Papers*, 6:418.

64. Remini, *Election of Andrew Jackson,* 74.

65. Wilentz, *Rise of American Democracy*, 298–300; Charles G. Sellers Jr., *The Market Revolution: Jacksonian America, 1815–1846* (New York, 1991), 296–97.

66. Wilentz, *Rise of American Democracy*, 298–99; Howe, *What Hath God Wrought*, 274–75.

67. Remini, *Election of Andrew Jackson*, 146; Hargreaves, *Presidency of John Quincy Adams*, 193–97, 275; Weston, *Presidential Election of 1828*, 36–38; Adams, *Memoirs*, 7:365 (December 1, 1827).

68. Hargreaves, *Presidency of John Quincy Adams*, 283–84; Adams, *Memoirs*, 7:400–401 (January 9, 1828).

69. Hargreaves, *Presidency of John Quincy Adams*, 194–97; Robert V. Remini, *Martin Van Buren and the Making of the Democratic Party* (New York: Columbia University Press, 1959), 170–85; Wilentz, *Rise of American Democracy*, 299–300.

70. Quoted in Remini, *Election of Andrew Jackson*, 178–79.

71. Dangerfield, *Era of Good Feelings*, 410–12; Wilentz, *Rise of American Democracy*, 300.

Chapter Six

1. The background of the song is described in John William Ward, *Andrew Jackson: Symbol for an Age* (New York: Oxford University Press, 1955), 13–15, and in Robert V. Remini, *Andrew Jackson and the Course of American Freedom, 1822–1832* (New York: Harper & Row, 1981), 134, hereafter cited as *Jackson and Freedom*.

2. Donald B. Cole, *A Jackson Man: Amos Kendall and the Rise of American Democracy* (Baton Rouge: Louisiana State University Press, 2004), 84; Andrew W. Robertson, *The Language of Democracy: Political Rhetoric in the United States and Britain, 1790–1900* (Charlottesville: University of Virginia Press, 2005), 14, 36–37, 68–81.

3. Mary W. M. Hargreaves, *The Presidency of John Quincy Adams* (Lawrence: University Press of Kansas, 1985), 268; Florence Weston, *The Presidential Election of 1828* (Washington, D.C.: Ruddick, 1938), 114, 175; David Trimble to Clay, October 20, 1828, quoted in Weston, 177; *Running for President* 2 vols. ed. Arthur M. Schlesinger, Jr. (New York: Simon & Schuster, 1994), 1:105.

4. Culver Smith, "Propaganda Technique in the Jackson Campaign of 1828," *East Tennessee Historical Society Publications* 6 (1934): 62; Weston, *Presidential Election of 1828*, 143–47; Thurlow Weed, *Life of Thurlow Weed*, ed. Harriet Weed (Boston: Houghton Mifflin, 1883), 308–9.

5. Abner Greenleaf, "Address Delivered at Jefferson-Hall, Portsmouth, N.H., Jan 8, 1828, Being the Thirteenth Anniversary of Jackson's Victory at New-Orleans," Portsmouth, N.H., 1828; "Republican Sentiments in New Hampshire, July 4, 1828," 30; *The Political Character of John Quincy Adams Delineated Being a Reply to Certain*

Observations in the Address of Gen. Peter Porter and Others (Albany, 1828), 7. Copies of each in the library of the New-York Historical Society.

6. Norma Basch, "Marriage, Morals, and Politics in the Election of 1828," *Journal of American History* 80 (December 1993): 904–9.

7. Sean Wilentz, *The Rise of American Democracy: Jefferson to Lincoln* (New York: W. W. Norton, 2005), 302–3.

8. M. J. Heale, *The Presidential Quest: Candidates and Images in American Political Culture, 1787–1852* (London: Longman, 1982), 58–59; Daniel Walker Howe, *What Hath God Wrought* (New York: Oxford University Press, 2007), 259; Wilentz, *Rise of American Democracy*, 303.

9. "Mirror for Politicians"; *Address of the Central Committee Appointed by a Convention of both branches of the Legislature friendly to the election of John Q. Adams as president and Richard Rush as vice-president of the U. States, held at the State-House in Boston, June 10, 1828* (Boston, 1828), 24. Copies of each in the library of the Massachusetts Historical Society.

10. "Address to the People of Virginia," quoted in Arthur Schlesinger Jr. and Fred L. Israel, eds., *History of American Presidential Elections*, 4 vols. (New York: Chelsea House, 1971), 2:469–70; *Substance of Mr. Storrs's Remarks, at the Meeting of the Friends of the Administration, Held at Whitesboro, July Fourth, 1828* (Utica, N.Y. 1828), 23. Copy in the library of the New-York Historical Society.

11. "Address to the People of Virginia," quoted in Schlesinger and Israel, *History of Presidential Elections*, 2:471; "Proceedings of the Delegates of the Friends of the Administration of John Quincy Adams, Assembled at Baton Rouge," New Orleans, 1827, 21; "A Defence of the National Administration in an Address to the People of New Hampshire, By Cato [Ezekiel Webster]," Concord, N.H., 1828, 17; *Substance of Mr. Storrs's Remarks*, 27–28. Copies of the last three in the library of the New-York Historical Society.

12. "Address…at Concord," 11; "Address to the People of Maryland, November 6, 1828," quoted in Schlesinger and Israel, *History of Presidential Elections*, 2:480–81; "Report of the State Convention Held in the City of Albany to Select Suitable Candidates for President and Vice President," New York, 1828, 25, 33. Copy in the library of the New-York Historical Society.

13. Anonymous, *An Impartial and True History of the Life and Services of Major General Andrew Jackson* (n.p., n.d.), 40, quoted in Ward, *Andrew Jackson*, 64.

14. *United States Telegraph*, April 7, 1828, quoted in Erik Eriksson, "Official Newspaper Organs and the Campaign of 1828," *Tennessee Historical Magazine* 8 (January 1925): 242–43; *Niles Register*, April 8, 1828. See also Gerard H. Clarfield, *Timothy Pickering and the American Republic* (Pittsburgh: University of Pittsburgh Press, 1980).

15. *The Principles and Acts of Mr. Adams' Administration Vindicated against the Aspersions Contained in the Address of the Jackson Convention, Assembled at Concord, on the 11th and 12th of June, 1828,* By a Freeman (Concord, N.H., 1828), 30. Copy in the library of the Massachusetts Historical Society, Boston.

16. Quoted in Eriksson, "Official Newspaper Organs," 245; "Address to the People of New York," cited in Schlesinger and Israel, *History of Presidential Elections*, 2:475–76.

17. Ward, *Andrew Jackson*, 71; Francis Baylies, *The Contrast; or Military Chieftains and Political Chieftains* (Albany, N.Y., 1828), 20, copy in the library of the American Antiquarian Society, Worcester, Massachusetts.

18. Francis Yvonnet, "An Oration…January 8, 1828," 12; *Address of the Republican General Committee of Young Men of the City and County of New York*, quoted in Ward, *Andrew Jackson*, 65.

19. Quoted in Hargreaves, *Presidency of John Quincy Adams*, 287.

20. Robert V. Remini, *The Election of Andrew Jackson* (Philadelphia: Lippincott, 1963), 122–23.

21. Samuel D. Ingham, *An Exposition of the Political Character and Principles of John Quincy Adams* (Philadelphia, 1827), 12–13; *The Principles and Acts of Mr. Adams' Administration Vindicated,* 30; Hargreaves, *Presidency of John Quincy Adams*, 287; Schlesinger and Israel, *History of Presidential Elections*, 2:484.

22. Quoted in James S. Chase, *The Emergence of the Presidential Nominating Convention, 1789–1832* (Urbana: University of Illinois Press, 1973), 108.

23. Ibid., 109.

24. *Substance of Mr. Storrs's Remarks*, 26.

25. *Proceedings and Address of the Republican Young Men of the State of New-York, Assembled at Utica, on the 12th Day of August, 1828* (Utica, N.Y., 1828), 18. Copy in the library of the New-York Historical Society.

26. Missouri *Intelligencer*, April 25, 1828, quoted in Hattie M. Anderson, "The Jackson Men in Missouri," *Missouri Historical Review* 34 (April 1940): 329; Virginia Anti-Jackson Convention,

December 12, 1827 (Richmond, 1828), copy in the New-York Historical Society; quoted in Schlesinger and Israel, *History of Presidential Elections*, 2:464–75.

27. Quoted in Hargreaves, *Presidency of John Quincy Adams*, 301; Samuel Flagg Bemis, *John Quincy Adams and the Union* (New York: Knopf, 1956), 140, quoting James Parton, *Life of Andrew Jackson* (New York: Mason Brothers, 1861), 3:166.

28. The controversy can be followed in *Niles' Register*, September 8, 15, 1827, January 19, 1828; Bemis, *Adams and the Union*, 163–65.

29. Ingham, *Exposition*, title page.

30. *United States Telegraph,* August 2, 1828, quoted in Hargreaves, *Presidency of John Quincy Adams*, 287; David Henshaw, *A Voice from the Interior: Who Shall Be President? The Hero of New-Orleans or John the Second, of the House of Braintree?* (Boston: True and Greene, 1828).

31. Weston, *Presidential Election of 1828*, 11.

32. Jefferson to John Taylor, no date, quoted in Frederick Jackson Turner, *Frontier and Section*, ed. Ray Allen Billington (Englewood Cliffs, N.J.: Prentice Hall, 1961), 130; Everett S. Brown, ed., *The Missouri Compromises and Presidential Politics, 1820–1825* (St. Louis: Missouri Historical Society, 1926), 66; Robert V. Remini, *Martin Van Buren and the Making of the Democratic Party* (New York: Columbia University Press, 1959), 42.

33. Kentucky circular: *To the People of the First Congressional District in the Sate of Kentucky. April 21, 1828*, 21–22, copy in the library of the American Antiquarian Society, Worcester, Massachusetts; Richard H. Brown, "The Missouri Crisis, Slavery, and the Politics of Jacksonianism," *South Atlantic Quarterly* 65 (Winter 1966): 66; Weston, *Presidential Election of 1828*, 46.

34. *Address of the Central Committee, Appointed by a Convention of both branches of the Legislature friendly to the election of John Q. Adams as president and Richard Rush as vice-president of the U. States, held at the State-House in Boston, June 10, 1828*, 4, 7, copy in the library of the Massachusetts Historical Society, Boston.

35. *Address of the Great Convention of Friends of the Administration, Assembled at the Capitol in Concord, June 12, 1828*, 21–22, copy in the library of the Massachusetts Historical Society, Boston.

36. *The Principles and Acts of Mr. Adams' Administration Vindicated against the Aspersions Contained in the Address of the Jackson Convention Assembled at Concord On the 11th and 12th of June, 1828* (Concord, N.H., 1828), 31; Weston, *Presidential Election of 1828*, 31.

37. Richard H. Brown, "The Missouri Crisis, Slavery, and the Politics of Jacksonianism," *South Atlantic Quarterly* 65 (Winter 1966): 69–70;

Leonard L. Richards, "The Jacksonians and Slavery," in *Antislavery Reconsidered: New Perspectives on the Abolitionists*, ed. Lewis Perry and Michael Fellman (Baton Rouge: Louisiana State University Press, 1979), 99–118.

38. Quoted in Richard R. John, "Affairs of Office: The Executive Departments, the Election of 1828, and the Making of the Democratic Party," in *The Democratic Experiment*, ed. Meg Jacobs, William J. Novak, and Julian E. Zelizer (Princeton, N.J.: Princeton University Press, 2003), 70.

39. *A Plain Account of the Lives of the Candidates Andrew Jackson and John Quincy Adams* (n.p., 1828), 9, copy in the library of the New-York Historical Society.

40. Circular, "Jackson and Negroes," 3; Alvan Stewart, "Common Sense," 3. Copies of each in the library of the New-York Historical Society. Weston, *Presidential Election of 1828*, 92.

41. Kentucky circular, 21–22, copy in the library of the American Antiquarian Society, Worcester, Massachusetts; *Proceedings and Address of the Republican Young Men*, 17.

42. John Ferling, *Adams vs. Jefferson: The Tumultuous Election of 1800* (New York: Oxford University Press, 2004), 153–54.

43. Ely, *The Duty of Christian Freemen to Elect Christian Rulers, A Discourse Delivered on the Fourth of July, 1827, in the Seventh Presbyterian Church in Philadelphia* (Philadelphia, 1828), 6; *United States Telegraph*, January 18, 1828.

44. James A. Hamilton, *Reminiscences of James A. Hamilton* (New York: C. Scribner, 1869), 79.

45. Jackson, *Papers*, 6:358–59 (July 12, 1827). Parts of this letter were published in the *Nashville Republican*, April 1, 1828.

46. Weston, *Presidential Election of 1828*, 168.

47. "Fenelon," *Aux Catholics des Etat-Unis* (New Orleans, 1828), 9–13, copy in the library of the Massachusetts Historical Society, Boston.

48. Remini, *Election of Andrew Jackson*, 105.

49. Ibid., 104–5; Yvonnet, *An Oration . . .*,18–19; Weston, *Presidential Election of 1828*, 187–88.

50. Weston, *Presidential Election of 1828*, 164; Lee Benson, *The Concept of Jacksonian Democracy* (Princeton, N.J.: Princeton University Press, 1961), 321–22.

51. *A History of the Life and Public Services of Major General Andrew Jackson, Compiled from the Most Authentic Sources* (n.p., 1828), 2, 19; *An Impartial and True History of the Life and Services of Major General Andrew Jackson* (n.p., n.d), 2, 16. Copies of each in the library of the New-York Historical Society.

52. *Address of the Central Committee Appointed by a Convention of both branches of the Legislature friendly to the election of John Q. Adams as president and Richard Rush as vice-president of the U. States, held at the State-House in Boston, June 10, 1828* (Boston, 1828), 19, copy in the library of the Massachusetts Historical Society, Boston.

53. *Niles' Register*, April 26, 1828; Hargreaves, *Presidency of John Quincy Adams*, 211; Samuel Flagg Bemis, "The Scuffle in the Rotunda: A Footnote to the Presidency of John Quincy Adams and to the History of Dueling," *Massachusetts Historical Society Proceedings* 71 (October 1953–May 1957): 156–66; Adams, *Memoirs*, 7:509 (April 15, 1828).

54. Cole, *Jackson Man*, 98–100.

55. Weston, 51, quoting the Albany *Argus*, August 5, 1828.

56. "Republican Sentiments in New Hampshire, July 4, 1828," copy in the New-York Historical Society.

57. Quoted in Hargreaves, *Presidency of John Quincy Adams,* 179; Bemis, *Adams and the Union*, 102.

58. Adams, *Memoirs*, 8:76 (August 5, 1828).

59. Ronald P. Formisano and Kathleen S. Kutolowski, "Antimasonry and Masonry: The Genesis of Protest, 1826–1827," *American Quarterly* 39 (Summer 1977): 139–65; Kathleen Smith Kutolowski, "Antimasonry Reexamined: Social Bases of the Grass-Roots Party," *Journal of American History* 71 (September 1984): 269–93.

60. Remini, *Martin Van Buren*, 189.

61. Weston, *Presidential Election of 1828*, 162; Hargreaves, *Presidency of John Quincy Adams*, 284.

62. Weston, *Presidential Election of 1828*, 108–9, 162.

63. Cole, *Jackson Man*, 98–100.

64. Quoted in Culver Smith, "Propaganda Technique in the Jackson Campaign of 1828," *East Tennessee Historical Society Publications* 6 (1934): 64–65.

65. Leonard F. Curry, "Election Year—Kentucky, 1828," *Register of the Kentucky Historical Society* 55 (July 1957): 203; Richard P. McCormick, *The Second American Party System: Party Formation in the Jackson Era* (Chapel Hill: University of North Carolina Press, 1966), 315.

66. Donald J. Ratcliffe, "Voter Turnout in Early Ohio," *Journal of the Early Republic* 7 (Autumn 1987): 248–51; *Niles' Register*, October 25, 1828.

67. *U.S. Telegraph*, October 20, 1828, quoted in Remini, *Election of Andrew Jackson*, 181; *National Intelligencer*; quoted in Schlesinger and Israel, *History of Presidential Elections*, 2:480–81; *An Address to*

the Electors of the Ninth Ward, copy in the library of the New-York Historical Society.

68. Curry, "Election Year," 207–8.

69. Herbert J. Ershkowitz, *The Origins of the Whig and Democratic Parties in New Jersey, 1820–1837* (Washington, D.C.: University Press of America, 1982), 80–81.

70. Schlesinger and Israel, *History of American Presidential Elections,* 1:492. Other sources give slightly different figures, but with the same proportionate result.

71. Wilentz, *Rise of American Democracy,* 308–9.

72. Richards, "Jacksonians and Slavery," 101.

73. Hargreaves, *Presidency of John Quincy Adams,* 298.

74. Heale, *Presidential Quest,* 240n; Samuel Kernell, "Life before Polls: Ohio Politicians Predict the 1828 Presidential Vote," *Political Science and Politics* 33 (September 2000): 569–74; Weston, *Presidential Election of 1828,* 115; Howe, *What Hath God Wrought,* 283; Wilentz, *Rise of American Democracy,* 310.

75. Edward Channing, quoted in Edward Pessen, *Jacksonian America: Society, Personality, and Politics* (Homewood, Ill.: Dorsey Press, 1978), 165.

76. Quoted in Wilentz, *Rise of American Democracy,* 305.

77. McCormick, "New Perspectives," 294.

78. In many cases, the exact figures on participation can only be inferred, especially in the 1820s and 1830s. Ben J. Wattenberg, ed., *The Statistical History of the United States* (New York, 1976), 1071–72, has somewhat higher percentages than does McCormick, "New Perspectives," 294. In most cases McCormick's more conservative numbers have been used.

79. Andrew Burstein, *The Passions of Andrew Jackson* (New York: Knopf, 2003), 225; David Hackett Fischer, *The Revolution of American Conservatism* (New York: Harper & Row, 1965), 49; Pessen, *Jacksonian America,* 97–99.

80. Wilentz, *Rise of American Democracy,* 306–7; Remini, *Jackson and Freedom,* 148; Howe, *What Hath God Wrought,* 282–83.

81. Remini, *Election of Andrew Jackson,* 203; Weston, *Presidential Election of 1828,* 191.

82. Wilentz, *Rise of American Democracy,* 307.

83. Howe, *What Hath God Wrought,* 279, 282.

84. Pessen, *Jacksonian America,* 167; H. W. Brands, *Andrew Jackson, His Life and Times* (New York: Doubleday, 2005), chapter 30.

85. "Fellow Citizens of Queens County," copy in the New-York Historical Society; Weston, *Presidential Election of 1828,* 167.

86. Charles G. Sellers Jr., *The Market Revolution: Jacksonian America, 1815–1846* (New York, 1991), 299–300; Robert Kelley, "Ideology and Political Culture from Jefferson to Nixon," *American Historical Review* 82 (June 1977): 531–62. Richard L. McCormick, "Ethno-Cultural Interpretations of Nineteenth-Century Voting Behavior," *Political Science Quarterly* 89 (June 1974): 351–77, deals mostly with the post-Jackson era but explores some of the issues involved. See also Lee Benson, *Toward the Scientific Study of History* (Philadelphia: Lippincott, 1972), 47–48.

87. Wilentz, *Rise of American Democracy*, 310; Howe, *What Hath God Wrought*, 282; Sellers, *Market Revolution*, 299–300. In later years historians would try to make sense of the election by referring to the Jacksonians as "Democratic" Republicans and the Adams men as "National" Republicans, the difference supposedly being in the adjective. Although there is some validity to this, in reality both sides in 1828 described themselves as "democratic" and "national." The terms would have more relevance in the future. When Henry Clay unsuccessfully challenged Jackson in his campaign for reelection in 1832 he was nominated by a national convention of National Republicans. By that time the Jacksonians were simply calling themselves Democrats.

88. Donald B. Cole, *Jacksonian Democracy in New Hampshire, 1800–1851* (Cambridge, Mass.: Harvard University Press, 1970), 78; Tragle, "Jackson and New Orleans," 388; Weston, *Presidential Election of 1828*, 52.

89. Both quoted in Hargreaves, *Presidency of John Quincy Adams*, 292.

90. Ronald P. Formisano, "Federalists and Republicans: Parties, Yes—Systems, No," in *The Evolution of American Electoral Systems*, ed. Paul Kleppner (Westport, Conn.: Greenwood, 1981), 60.

91. George Dangerfield, *Era of Good Feelings* (London, 1953), 424–25.

Epilogue

1. Rachel Jackson to Elizabeth Watson, July 18, 1827, in Jackson, *Papers*, 6:367; Robert V. Remini, *Andrew Jackson and the Course of American Freedom, 1822–1832* (New York: Harper & Row, 1981), 173, hereafter cited as *Jackson and Freedom*; Bertram Wyatt-Brown, "Andrew Jackson's Honor," *Journal of the Early Republic* 17 (Spring 1997): 32.

2. Quoted in Robin Reilly, *The British at the Gates: The New Orleans Campaign in the War of 1812* (New York: Putnam, 1974), 326.

3. Quoted in H. W. Brands, *Andrew Jackson, His Life and Times* (New York: Doubleday, 2005), 403.

4. Rachel Jackson to Mrs. L. A. W. Douglas, December 3, 1828, in Jackson, *Papers*, 6:537.

5. Adams, *Memoirs*, 8:104 (March 3, 1829).

6. Studies of Jackson's presidency include Sean Wilentz, *Andrew Jackson* (New York: Times Books, 2005); Donald B. Cole, *The Presidency of Andrew Jackson* (Lawrence: University Press of Kansas, 1993); Richard B. Latner, *The Presidency of Andrew Jackson: White House Politics, 1829–1837* (Athens: University of Georgia Press, 1979).

7. Quoted in Daniel Walker Howe, *What Hath God Wrought* (New York: Oxford University Press, 2007), 331.

8. Richard R. John, *Spreading the News: The American Postal System from Franklin to Morse* (Cambridge, Mass.: Harvard University Press, 1995), 210, citing the *Telegraph*, November 3, 11, and 18, 1828.

9. Howe, *What Hath God Wrought*, 333–34. The phrase came from a declaration by William Marcy, a Van Burenite: "To the victor belong the spoils." Remini, *Jackson and Freedom*, 347.

10. Andrew Burstein, *The Passions of Andrew Jackson* (New York: Knopf, 2003), 173–80. See also John F. Marszalek, *The Petticoat Affair: Manners, Mutiny, and Sex in Andrew Jackson's White House* (New York: Free Press, 1997); Kirstin E. Wood, "'One Woman So Dangerous to Public Morals': Gender and Power in the Eaton Affair," *Journal of the Early Republic* 17 (Summer 1997): 237–75.

11. Jackson to William J. Duane, quoted in Howe, *What Hath God Wrought*, 387–88.

12. Remini, *Jackson and Freedom*, 234–37, 326–27.

13. Richard E. Ellis, *The Union at Risk: Jacksonian Democracy, States' Rights, and the Nullification Crisis* (New York: Oxford University Press, 1987), 170–77.

14. Howe, *What Hath God Wrought*, 356–57.

15. For differing perspectives on Jackson's Indian policies, see Ronald N. Satz, *American Indian Policy in the Jacksonian Era* (Lincoln: University of Nebraska Press, 1975); Francis Paul Prucha, *The Great Father: The United States and the American Indians*, 2 vols. (Lincoln: University of Nebraska Press, 1984), 1:214–42.

16. Wilentz, *Rise of American Democracy*, 392–401, and Howe, *What Hath God Wrought*, 373–83, offer differing perspectives on the Bank war.

17. Robert V. Remini, "Election of 1832," quoted in Schlesinger and Israel, *History of Presidential Elections*, 1:495–516.

18. William Nisbet Chambers, "Election of 1840," quoted in Schlesinger and Israel, *History of Presidential Elections*, 1:643–84. See also chapter 5, "The Whigs Take to the Woods," in John William Ward, *Andrew*

Jackson: Symbol for an Age (New York: Oxford University Press, 1955), 79–97.

19. Leonard Richards, *The Life and Times of Congressman John Quincy Adams* (New York: Oxford University Press, 1986); Lynn Hudson Parsons, "In Which the Political Becomes the Personal, and *Vice Versa*: The Last Ten Years of John Quincy Adams and Andrew Jackson," *Journal of the Early Republic* 23 (Fall 2003): 421–43.

20. Goodlett to Jackson, March 7, 1844, Andrew Jackson Papers (Microform), Library of Congress, Washington, D.C.; Jackson to Goodlett, March 12, 1844, in Jackson, *Correspondence*, 6:273–75.

21. Quoted in Robert V. Remini, *Andrew Jackson and the Course of American Democracy, 1833–1845* (New York: Harper & Row, 1984), 527.

22. Adams diary, June 18, 1845, Adams Papers Microfilm, reel 48, Massachusetts Historical Society, Boston.

23. Samuel Flagg Bemis, *John Quincy Adams and the Union* (New York: Knopf, 1956), 538.

Index